D1569295

The Case for Workers' Co-ops

The Case for Workers' Co-ops

Robert Oakeshott

Routledge & Kegan Paul
London, Henley and Boston

First published in 1978
by Routledge & Kegan Paul Ltd
39 Store Street,
London WC1E 7DD,
Broadway House,
Newtown Road,
Henley-on-Thames,
Oxon RG9 1EN and
9 Park Street,
Boston, Mass. 02108, USA
Set in 10 on 12 pt Times by
Computacomp (UK) Ltd. Fort William, Scotland
and printed in Great Britain by
Redwood Burn Ltd
Trowbridge and Esher

British Library Cataloguing in Publication Data

Oakeshott, Robert
The case for workers' co-ops.
1 Works councils   2 Co-operative societies
I Title
334'.6   HD5650   78–40732

ISBN 0 7100 0041 3

For my father and in memory of my mother, and for Kate

Contents

Acknowledgments

Formal copyright acknowledgments apart, there are two main and partly overlapping groups of people whom it is my pleasure and agreeable duty to thank. There are first those more or less directly involved in the theory or practice of democratically structured enterprises. By their actions and in discussion they have helped to shape my ideas and interpretation of workers' control and worker ownership. Second, there are those who have lent invaluable helping hands with the labours of actual book-writing and checking. In the last chapter I express the hope that what appears in the following pages is roughly 90 per cent right. Apart from other services, without the help of those in the second group that percentage figure – to be realistic – would have had to be sharply scaled down.

Mick Pearce must be the person I thank most warmly and first of all. For nearly five years, up to March 1978, he carried the enormous burden of keeping Sunderlandia afloat. It is easy to be critical of the Sunderlandia experience. I am not uncritical myself, and I am sharply critical of myself. On the other hand, the evidence was just beginning to come in as I finished this book that, by comparison with rather similar Manpower Services Commission enterprises elsewhere in the UK, Sunderlandia's results may have been surprisingly good: 'What, your losses were as low as that' – was the reaction of someone who knew results from elsewhere when he was shown the Sunderlandia figures.

I would also like to thank Michael Pattison who, in the face of innumerable batterings and set-backs, has retained his loyalty to Sunderlandia since he came forward – the first in Sunderland to do so – applying to join in the spring of 1973. The large number of others who have worked for the company over the last five years also deserve my thanks. There are far too many of them to mention by name. Equally deserving of my thanks are two institutions, the Scott-Bader Commonwealth and the East Midlands Housing Association, who lent money to the enterprise when it started. And so is that larger group, relations and friends of Mick Pearce and myself, who generously subscribed to Sunderlandia's loan stock. In the latter group I would like

ix

x Acknowledgments

to thank Eric de Rothschild by name. His involvement has gone much
further than subscription to loan stock; his help and support have been
invaluable. Among the same group of loan stock holders Willie and
Anne Charlton deserve my special thanks – apart from anything else for
their unfailing interest and hospitality over five years.

In the wider, though still small world of democratic enterprises in the
UK, I would like to thank the following either for help and advice with
particular sections of the book, or on more general grounds: John
Leyland of Scott-Bader, David Speckley of Landsman's, Margaret Elliott
and Marie Smith of 'Little Women', Mike Angerson of Trylon, Victor
Bewley of Bewley's Cafés, Michael Jones of Michael Jones Jewellers, Bun
Burnett, lately of the late Rowen Onllwyn, Connor Wilson of Airflow
Developments, Dick Jenkins of Kirkby Manufacturing and Engineering,
and Felix Keen of Meriden Motor Cycles Ltd. Finally in this same world
I would like to thank Roger Sawtell, the founder of Trylon and the
Chairman of Industrial Common Ownership Finance (ICOF).

My main debt in France is to François Espagne, the Assistant General
Secretary of the French confederation of industrial co-ops. I have the
most delightful memories of Paris evenings in the joint company of
François Espagne and Eric de Rothschild. More seriously, François
Espagne seems to me to be the best informed, and at the same time both
the most sympathetic and realistic, judge of workers' co-operative
experience in Western Europe. In France, too, I would like to thank
Gerard Denjean of that magnificent enterprise: La Verrerie Ouvrière
d'Albi and Hellen Barreux of the sadly short-lived Co-op Sport-
Vacances.

In Italy my chief debt is to Fabio Carpanelli, President of the industrial
co-ops' section of the Italian Lega co-operative grouping. He has
confirmed, what I always suspected, that it is possible to have a splendid
evening with an unrepentant and leading member of a communist party.
I should also like to thank Bruno Catalano, Carpanelli's opposite number
at the Confederation grouping of Italian co-ops; and Renato Ragliani,
President of the country's third co-operative grouping: the Association. I
should also like to thank Raffaello Petracchi of the Co-op Lavoratori
Fonderia Officina Cure, outside Florence. Finally, in Italy, I would like to
thank my old friend Marina Orloff-Davidoff whose hospitality, buoyant
company and fluent Italian made my researches in that country not only
possible but agreeable.

In the Basque provinces of Spain my greatest debt is to Inaki Gorrono
of the Caja Laboral Popular in Mondragon. Others who have helped me
on various visits to Mondragon are too numerous to mention by name; I
hope they will forgive the omission. Someone whom I must thank

personally and by name is Charles Nicholson of the British Consulate in Bilbao.

In relation to Mondragon I should also thank the growing number of people with whom I have visited those remarkable enterprises and whose reactions have encouraged me to believe that these co-ops must be of interest to the non-specialist audience of all reasonable people. In particular I would like to thank Charles Keen, Geraldine Norman and Alastair Campbell, co-authors with me of a report* on the Mondragon experience. I would also like to take this opportunity to thank the Anglo German Foundation for financing that study.

In the composite chapter on experience elsewhere I acknowledge my debt to Paul Derrick and to Alastair Campbell. But I should do so here as well. In Holland I would like to thank particularly Ir C. L. Provily, President of the Dutch workers' co-ops Federation and Ir van der Graaf of Ko-op bouwbedrijf Moes v.a. Henk Thomas and Chris Logan, of the Institute of Social Studies in the Hague, deserve my thanks for helping me to understand the position in Holland and for a most valuable discussion of Mondragon. I await their joint book on Mondragon with the greatest interest. Finally, in the US, I have to thank my friend Jancis Long who, apart from her sturdy subscription to Sunderlandia's loan stock, has invariably been encouraging and supportive when I have crossed the Atlantic. And I also have to thank Alvin Warner, the owner of an unusually cheery bowling alley in Lowell, Vermont – and a man of many other parts besides.

Among scholars and academics easily my greatest debt is to Derek Jones. As well as for my reliance on his work, I have to thank him for going through most of my book in draft and for many valuable suggestions. I should also like to express my thanks to Jaroslav Vanek. More than anyone else he has been responsible for the re-awakening of interest in democratically structured enterprises, and for making that interest respectable. Apart from my general debt I would like to thank him for invaluable discussions.

On this side of the Atlantic the academic to whom my main thanks are due is Alan Fox. As I explain in the Introduction, I was not aware of his most important work in this field – and particularly of his *Beyond Contract: Work Power and Trust Relations* (Faber & Faber, 1974) – when I was writing the relevant parts of *The Case for Workers' Co-ops*. My early discussion of the necessary conditions which any successful enterprise must satisfy would otherwise have been much clearer and

---

* *Worker Ownership: The Mondragon Achievement*, Anglo German Foundation for the Study of Industrial Society, 1977.

tighter. I would commend his work most strongly. I would also like to thank him for reading the first and last sections of this book in draft and for some most helpful criticisms.

As I also explain in the Introduction, when I wrote most of this book, I was equally unaware of the important and highly relevant work on property rights, worker motivation and related topics by Joe Stiglitz, Felix Fitzroy and others. I was introduced to some of it, and by Felix to Alan Fox's work, at a splendid seminar, mainly organized by Edward Goodman and the Acton Society, outside Siena, in the autumn of 1977. I have particular and general debts to acknowledge to Edward and to the Society. One of Edward's main interests which I share is in the reform of the enterprise – so as to make it less inhuman, less conflict-ridden and less absurd than it often is today. And it was he, well before Schumacher, who drew public attention to the key importance of enterprise scale in his pamphlet, *The Impact of Size* (Acton Society, 1969). I would like to thank him for numerous most valuable insights and for most generous hospitality and support over a number of years.

I also have to thank Edward Goodman as a Trustee of the Joseph Rowntree Social Service Trust: had it not been for the generous awards made to me by the Trustees in 1976 and 1977, I would never have been able to muster the time and other resources needed to write this book. Among the other Trustees, my special thanks are due to Pratap Chitnis and Jo Grimond. My debt to Jo is, in fact, much wider and of much longer duration – for his early moral support for Sunderlandia and for his readiness to be stirred by Mondragon and its implications; as well as for stimulus, cheeriness and an evergreen supply of good jokes over a number of years.

My thanks for a rather different kind of help – over removing some of the warts in a recurringly ill-spelt, ill-written and disorganized draft – are due chiefly to two people: my father, and my old friend, John Cavill. My debt to both is immense and it is the more strongly felt because that was the stage of 'book production' that I always dreaded most. I have also greatly valued their support and encouragement – as I did at an earlier juncture that of another old friend, Peter Mackay. Peter undertook the cheerless task of reading through most of the book in its earliest version. The fact that he is now in far away Africa does not make me any less in his debt. I am also greatly indebted to another old friend, Anthony Sheil who found me a publisher when it looked as if all was lost, and to Gwen Margrie who did a tremendous re-typing job under extreme pressure of time.

Finally, before coming on to the formal acknowledgments I would like to thank the *Financial Times, The Economist* and *Lloyds Bank*

Review for giving an airing to some of my views and researches on this subject. In particular I would like to thank John Elliott, Freddy Fisher and Christopher Lorenz of the *Financial Times*, Andrew Knight, Norman Macrae and John Grimond of *The Economist* and Christopher Johnson and Geoff Lipscombe of the *Lloyds Bank Review*.

I need hardly say that none of the people I have mentioned bears any responsibility either for the views expressed or for the mistakes which remain in this book.

I am grateful to the following authors and publishers for permission to quote from published or duplicated work: Dame Margaret Cole and William Heinemann Ltd for passages from *The Story of Fabian Socialism*; Inaki Gorrono, especially for extensive use of statistical material from his *Experiencia Co-operativa en el Pais Vasco*, Bilbao, 1975; Walter Kendall for extracts from various of his pamphlets and lectures; Mavis Kirkham for extensive use of her MA thesis 'Industrial Producer Co-operation in Great Britain: Three Case Studies' (Sheffield University unpublished thesis, 1971); Quintin Garcia Munoz and Editions Ouvrières for references to *Les Co-operatives industrielles de Mondragon*, Paris, 1970; Andrew McGregor for permission to quote his description of the experience of the Rochdale textile co-op from his thesis 'Capital, Rent Extraction and the Survival of the Producer Co-operative' (Cornell University, duplicated thesis 1974); and Claude Vienney for statistical and other material which I have taken from his *L'Economie du Secteur Co-operatif Français*, Editions Cujas, Paris, 1966. I have already acknowledged my general and great debt to Derek Jones. Here I would acknowledge my gratitude to him and to Paul Lambert, Editor of the *Annals of Public and Co-operative Economy*, for permission to quote from his 'British Economic Thought on Associations of Labourers 1848–1974', (*APCE*, 1976, no. 11); to him and to Branko Horvat, Editor of *Economic Analysis and Workers' Management*, in respect of his 'The Economics and Industrial Relations of American Producer Co-operatives 1791–1939' (*E A & W M*, 1977, vol. XI, pp. 3–4); and lastly I would like to thank Professor Jones for permission to quote from his 'British Producer Co-operatives' in Ken Coates (ed.), *The New Worker Co-operatives*, Spokesman Books for the Institute for Workers' Control, Nottingham, 1976.

Introduction

The main aim of this book is to provide a rough and ready but reasonably up-to-date account of independent workers' co-operatives and their history in the UK and other selected European countries – and, more sketchily, world wide. It has been written with the general reader chiefly in mind. On the other hand there is not, to my knowledge, any existing academic study which is remotely comprehensive; the partial and particular work which has been published has frequently taken the form of articles in obscure journals, or even less accessible university theses. It may be, therefore, that students and other specialists will find *The Case for Workers' Co-ops* of some value, at least until the academics have come up with a new comprehensive study.

I do not make a claim of anything like total detachment; quite apart from connections with Sunderlandia, I see myself unashamedly as a participant in, as well as an observer of, the current debate about 'industrial democracy' and the reform of enterprise structures more generally. Thus, I make no apology for the fact that my account of the actual experience of workers' co-ops is preceded by a look, deliberately controversial, at the state of the current debate. In a subsequent early section I have also, on similar grounds, thought it right to trace the attitudes of the main political forces in Britain to enterprises of this kind. For one factor which may help to explain the rather unexciting record in Britain is that the characteristic attitudes both on the Right and the Left have been hostile, or dismissive, for most of the last century.

There are two main omissions in the account of the experience. I do not deal either with Yugoslavia or with the industrial Kibbutzim in Israel. Yugoslavia has already a vast literature. In any case, whatever the similarity between a typical Yugoslav enterprise and a typical workers' co-op, there is the vital difference of relevant environment. Democratically structured enterprises are the conventional (and almost the only) ones in Yugoslavia. Elsewhere they are invariably in a tiny minority. I have neglected the Israeli Kibbutzim because the social and other values underlying them seem to me to be so unusual that their experience is unlikely to be widely replicated.

More serious in the way of omissions is the fact that I have not included any real discussion of the theoretical economics of these enterprises or of what one might call their group psychology. Apart from the innovatory work on their economics by Jaroslav Vanek, there are highly relevant contemporary re-examinations going on of, for example, property rights and enterprise organization. Professor Stiglitz in Oxford and Felix Fitzroy in Berlin are among the people working in these and related directions. I must confess that I was simply unaware of this work before the autumn of 1977, when most of this book was already in draft. It was too late to undertake the major re-write job which would have been needed if their work was to be more than referred to. In any case I am far from sure that I would have been competent to get it right. However, so far as I can judge, the implications of the work of Stiglitz, Fitzroy and others seem to be more positive than negative for workers' co-ops of the right kind.

I was also ignorant, up to the autumn of 1977, of the important work which Alan Fox has been doing in areas which come very close to a number of points touched upon in the first part of this book. In particular his *Beyond Contract: Work Power and Trust Relations* seems to me to be a most valuable contribution to the current debate and essential reading for anyone who is seriously involved. Had I been familiar with his parallel and linked distinctions between high- and low-trust relationships, and high and low discretion roles inside the enterprise, I should almost certainly have written my opening section rather differently – and quite possibly better. However, apart from other considerations, I became aware of his work at too late a date.

The other part of my excuse for neglecting the 'group dynamics' aspect of the subject is the common-sense view that we do not need elaborate or theoretical studies to tell us that there is too much conflict and antagonism in conventional enterprises, particularly in the UK. Common sense also makes clear that the alternative models which I and others commend would certainly not be conflict-free; but they just might be less conflict-ridden if the right structures were chosen. The proviso is important. For my experience in Sunderlandia and my observation elsewhere tell me that if workers' co-ops are incorrectly structured they may even generate more conflict than conventional enterprises.

There is one other 'psychological' point to which I would like to refer. Is it plausible to suppose that energetic and talented young men and women would choose to join workers' co-ops if the credibility of these enterprises and the opportunities within them could be substantially increased and improved? Or is there some fatal contradiction between the personal goals of the energetic and the constraints imposed by working within democratic structures? My short answer is that any such contradiction is more apparent than real. My evidence is the apparently growing hostility of the younger generation to conventional enterprises and their increasing interest in co-operative type ventures. I would, of course, concede that unless workers' co-ops can attract men and women of ability and talent, their future is unlikely ever to be more than marginal.

I should emphasize that though I am undeniably partisan, I have not painted a particularly rosy picture of the general record of workers' co-ops. The reason is simple. Aside from the group centred on Mondragon in the Basque provinces of Spain and a handful of isolated cases elsewhere, the record has been at best only modestly positive. Essentially what I have tried to do is to explain why it has not been better; and to suggest what would have to be done if there was the political will to make workers' co-ops an important sector in the economies of the future. The case for trying to galvanize such a political will rests chiefly, in my opinion, in the manifest demoralization which is now so widespread throughout conventional enterprise. For a whole host of reasons a growing number of people in conventional enterprises (so I suspect) prefer days in which they have found excuses for not working, to days at the end of which they can feel satisfied by a good job done – that cannot be a satisfactory state of affairs. Workers' co-ops, if correctly structured, could provide a way out.

Outside the world of instant publishing, all books with a contemporary dimension are liable to be overtaken by events. The period between the final hand over of my typescript (mid-March 1978) and the correction of page proofs (mid-July) has not been totally motionless for workers' co-ops. In France the Left was, of course, defeated in the National Assembly elections, thus eliminating the threat of state take-over which had been hanging over at least one of the French co-ops: La Verrerie Ouvrière d'Albi. In France, too, the new 'workers' co-op' law, foreshadowed almost two years before by Giscard d'Estaing, finally jumped the last of its parliamentary hurdles on 1 July, 1978. It will do something to improve the structures of the enterprises and will boost workers' membership. On balance it may also slightly strengthen their financial position and may encourage the 'conversion' of larger numbers of conventional enterprises into co-operative forms. Nor has the position been static in the UK. A Co-operative Development Agency Bill moved with all-party support and unusual rapidity through both Houses of Parliament in the early summer – in time to be enacted at the beginning of July and for the appointment of Lord Oram, as its first Chairman, to be announced on 12 July. There was also a surprising measure of all-party support for a set of new clauses to the 1978 Finance Bill which would, if passed, have introduced significant tax concessions for *bona fide* workers' co-ops. As it turned out these new clauses were never 'called', but they could prove to be some sort of portent for the future. Meanwhile, at the enterprise level, the Meriden Motorcycle Co-op published its third set of accounts. These showed that its operations over its latest accounting period had still not been profitable, but they appeared to be reconcilable with the view that the business had just started to break even. Informal reports from the other surviving 'Wedgwood Benn' co-op, Kirkby Manufacturing and Engineering (KME) were more pessimistic. Finally, from the remote mining village of Lowell in upper state Vermont, *The Economist* reported on 22 April that the workforce had sold out to a group of capitalists.

1
The current debate

All sensible people must welcome the fact that the reports of the Bullock Committee on Industrial Democracy have opened up the possibility of serious and long-overdue debate about British industrial arrangements. It has been clear for a long time (at least since the early 1950s, if not since the 1870s) that British industry has been consistently outperformed by most of its competitors in the economically advanced countries of the mixed economy world – in the US, Japan, Canada and by most West European industry.

Yet up to this point the debate begun by Bullock seems, if anything, to have fogged rather than clarified the issues. For one thing the whole concept of industrial democracy is far from straightforward. The Webbs used it eighty years ago as the title of a book the aim of which, in their words, was to offer a 'scientific analysis of trade unionism'.* It was not clear then that trade unionism, democratic or otherwise, had much to do with industrial democracy. Indeed, it is far from clear now whether an arrangement, as proposed in Bullock's majority report, which would give parity of seats to employees' representatives (chosen by trade unions) and to shareholders' representatives on the boards of large public companies, should count as an advance towards industrial democracy. At face value it looks much more like just another step towards formalized dual (trade union and capitalist) control than like a step in an essentially democratic direction. However, the main point here is that the public should not be asked to accept Lord Bullock's recommendations as constituting industrial democracy at all until the whole concept, and its various possible forms, have been much more thoroughly discussed.

There is, however, a more important criticism of the debate so far than this failure to deal adequately with the notion of a democracy at the place of work. It is that so far neither supporters (mainly the trade union establishment), nor opponents (led by the Confederation of British Industry) of the Bullock majority proposals, have really come to grips

---
* Sidney and Beatrice Webb, *Industrial Democracy*, 2 vols, Longmans Green, London, 1897.

with the main shortcomings of our industrial set-up as it is. It is extraordinary, given the volume of contributions to the debate, that the 'British Disease' has scarcely been mentioned. Instead, by arguing for preservation of the *status quo* with only minor qualifications, the opponents of the Bullock majority are either ignoring the very bad shape of industry – or suggesting, quite implausibly, that their own minor modifications will transform the scene. As for the advocates of the Bullock majority proposals, they are simply inviting the rest of us to make an act of faith. They seem to say: 'Allow the trade unions to choose employee representatives to sit in equal numbers with the representatives of capital on company boards and all will be well; that is the way to release new energies and that, hey presto, will prove to be just what the doctor should have ordered as a cure for the "British Disease".' Or, at a slightly more sophisticated level, they argue that the introduction of union-selected employee representatives on to company boards will put the relationship between capital and labour on a new basis. We are invited to believe that if only that is done then in due course a new era of harmony, co-operation, improved management and positive shop-floor attitudes to production will sweep in through the factory gates; that the social relations in our industries will come to resemble those of a Sweden or a West Germany. More fundamentally, we are invited to believe that if this alone is done, the ancient, structural division of interest between capital and labour will be largely transcended.

Few, I think, would seriously want to argue that the modest proposals for change reluctantly recommended in their minority report by the 'business' members of the Bullock Committee would affect the performance of British industry very much one way or the other. Their position in any case has much more to do with fears about the adverse consequences of implementing the majority proposals than with any very enthusiastic belief in the positive effects of their own. So we can reasonably leave them on one side. But what of the majority proposals? No one is entitled to be sure, before they are introduced, what the results would be. On the other hand, I feel bound to make clear at the outset that I am profoundly sceptical about the suggested beneficial effects. My scepticism is based on a combination of educated intuition, my reading of history and broad analysis.

Intuitive or gut feeling can be very easily expressed. Particularly after four years of living with and working alongside ordinary people in the old industrial North of England, I do not believe that shop-floor attitudes to production and profits will be changed in the slightest degree by the introduction of trade union chosen employee representatives to sit opposite shareholders' representatives on company boards. It is deeply naive, in my opinion, to think otherwise. A parallel from earlier industrial history reinforces this gut feeling. Did not an earlier generation of industrial reformers – the Webbs, Herbert Morrison – invite their contemporaries to believe that more positive shop-floor attitudes would flow from nationalization? And are not the two cases more like than unlike? For the expectation of benefits rests in both cases on the belief that formal changes of structure, without any corresponding shift in the economic interests of the workers, will improve shop-floor attitudes to work. I see no good reason to believe that the expectations of the majority of the Bullock Committee in this respect will prove any more well-founded than those of the Webbs.

Moreover, and despite what is said about a new relationship between labour and capital by the Bullock majority, I see no reason to believe that the heart of the labour and trade union movements in Britain – still less their more vocal and zealous elements – have suddenly abandoned their traditional hostility to the mixed economy or to a market system more generally. It would be very odd if positions fiercely held over generations – and most forcefully expressed in debates and battles over public ownership – had been suddenly abandoned during the eighteen months or so between the setting up of the Bullock Committee and publication of its report. Given that those positions are strongly held, it would also be very strange if employee representation on management boards was a sufficient *quid pro quo* for their surrender.

And yet implicit in the positive references to the German experience in the majority Bullock report, is the suggestion that we have only to introduce a very much more radical version of German co-determination, and the British working-class movement will drop its insistence on extending public ownership. It is surely most improbable that anything of the kind will happen. History and intuition are supported in this doubt by broad analysis.

This can be most easily understood if we ask briefly what are the social and economic requirements which enterprises, groups or teams of producers, need to satisfy if they are to perform with success. Or, to put it in a slightly different way and leaving aside questions of skill and technology, what conditions will optimize the motivation of those in an enterprise to work well and ensure the best possible team-work.

If we take the question of team-work, the need plainly is for a set of arrangements which will give all members of the team the same objectives. At the very least we must avoid any pattern which gives quite different objectives to different sub-groups within the production team. For that is to choose a system with a built-in source of conflict.

Of course, the arrangements which exist in both private and state capitalism are precisely of the second kind. Under both systems net business income, the net product of the enterprise after payment of all expenses, including financial charges, is divided into two quite separate parts: one part, called wages and salaries (normally in some sense fixed), goes to labour; the rest – and this may, of course, be a profit or loss – goes to capital. If we add that for more or less formal reasons one group of workers in a production team traditionally links its main interests with those of capital while the other, the shop floor, having no very direct interest in doing so, rarely does, it is easy to see why existing structures simply divide the enterprise into the two separate (and normally hostile) camps of management and labour. It is surely impossible to believe that rational and intelligent people, starting from scratch, would choose such a structure when organizing activities which depend on team-work for their success. Today's generation, however, has had no choice; they have had to accept the structures handed down from the past.

Once we have perceived that this 'conflict structure' is the key feature of the enterprise organization we have inherited, then much that is often puzzling, at least to middle-class intellectuals, is more or less explained. It becomes clear, for example, why profit-sharing schemes introduced within existing structures seem invariably to have zero or even negative impact. Of course, there are problems of designing schemes which clearly link any incentives to the efforts and commitment of shop-floor workers. But the key reason is different. Seen from the shop floor, such schemes are introduced to increase the final (post wages and profit share) surplus in which labour will have no part. It is thus easy to understand negative or hostile attitudes on the part of the shop floor when good profits are announced. For given the way that the shop floor's interests are structured, an increase in profits is correctly seen as an increase in the degree to which its labour has been exploited.

It is true, perhaps particularly in Britain, that the conflict between management and shop floor – the absence of what might be called vertical team-work between the two – also has cultural and historical roots. All the same, if the success of an enterprise depends as much on team-work and enterprise solidarity as it does on individual skills and technology, then it is surely absurd that this key source of conflict in our organizational arrangements should continue unquestioned.

Common sense and simple analysis tell us, therefore, that the interests of all members of an enterprise should be put on the same footing as a first step towards optimum team-work. What does common sense tell us next about the best way to maximize motivation among team members as individuals?

I used to think that the view of Tawney (and the Webbs) was correct on this second point: that once a set-up basically acceptable to them and in line with their interests was achieved, working people would not be especially concerned with getting something 'extra' – with taking a share in 'profit'. In those circumstances my feeling was that they – and everyone else – would be satisfied, in Tawney's phrase, with the equivalent of the 'clergyman's stipend'; now I am not so sure. Four years in England's old industrial North inclines me to think that there is at least as much of a little capitalist (or canny peasant) underneath the blue overalls of a working man as there is of the little socialist. Certainly, the enthusiam with which he will discuss the profitable sale of his own back-garden leeks or onions – or the successful disposal of some piece of old scrap – is in most marked contrast to his attitude when enterprise profits are being discussed. Of course, the position is not clear cut. If working people had the choice of the relative security (but normally lower incomes) of a state-planned system or the relative insecurity (with higher incomes plus a share of any profits) of a mixed but mainly market system, I am still not sure how many would choose the first, how many the second. It is particularly difficult to make a sensible guess because at least in Britain (and in France) it is often possible to choose employment (as with the local authorities or Civil Service, for example) which combines both higher earnings and greater security than are available in the private sector.

What I am clear about, on the other hand, is that few working people would have an ideological objection to getting something extra – their share of profits – once their interests in the overall enterprise results had been put on the same footing as those of management. More than that; quite apart from arguments about spreading wealth (which we shall consider later) it seems to me that the motivation to work will unquestionably be improved in a system, under which ordinary people become the owners of profits as well as of wages.

So far I have offered two answers to the question of how to optimize work motivation and team-work. I have suggested that we eliminate the source of conflict between capital (and indirectly, management) and labour which is rooted in the way that net business income is divided between wages and profits. I have suggested too that if the workforce becomes the owner of profits as well as of wages that can hardly have other than a positive effect on work motivation.

However, there are two other conditions which common sense and simple analysis tell us must be satisfied to achieve an optimal set of arrangements for industry. If we are to secure optimum team-work then, I suggest we must also attempt to align the interests of all members of the enterprise in other respects as well the division of business income. The functional distinction between management and shop floor will, as I shall argue most strongly later on, have to be maintained. Nevertheless there is no reason why, accepting that distinction, all enterprise workers should not be on the same footing in ultimate responsibility and control. More than that. Unless all established enterprise workers *are* so involved (presumably through a one man one vote system in an enterprise general assembly), then I suggest that the division into two 'sides' will continue to prejudice team-work and a rational deployment of resources.

It is not only that the ultimate control and responsibility arrangements inside the enterprise must be acceptable to the entire workforce – and thus ultimately democratic; there is one further need. The overall economic and social environment within which enterprises work needs to be as acceptable as possible to as many people as possible.

It should be obvious that quite apart from counterproductive features within enterprise, one of the main reasons for the wretched performance of British industry is that this last condition does not begin to be met. It is probably true that a much smaller percentage of ordinary working people in Britain than, say, in Germany or Sweden (the two Bullock models) or in the US or Japan, accept the overall economic and social arrangements in which they live and in which enterprises operate as being fair and reasonable. Moreover, it is no good claiming, as do defenders of the *status quo*, that this is simply a matter of cussedness or of an absurd 'class consciousness' among ordinary working people. For the fact is that, much more so than in the countries I have just mentioned, the reality of class divisions in Britain (and I suspect, in France and Italy) has survived. Leaving industry aside, class division is still the dominant characteristic in at least three key areas of British life; housing, education and health.

I suspect too that there are other objective factors which explain why a rejection of the present overall set-up tends to be that much stronger among British working people. The experience of 'industrial wage-packet life' is two or more generations longer in Britain than elsewhere. So today's working people in Britain might well be cumulatively more demoralized by it than their counterparts on the continent of Europe or in the US. Then again the small farm holding – and the links with 'sturdy yeoman values' which it provided – had been virtually eliminated in Britain (except possibly in Scotland's handful of crofting counties) by the time of the Napoleonic wars; whereas in France and Germany and Italy these small farm holdings are still a significant feature today (with which a back-yard tomato patch in Sunderland cannot seriously be compared). Third, and with the possible exception of Lille, I doubt if Europe has any social and physical environments which compare with the old industrial cities of nothern England, in Lancashire, Yorkshire, on the North East coast and on Clydeside.

Whatever the causes, there can be little doubt about the reality of this widespread 'rejection'. Certainly there is no doubt whatsoever that many of the working-class movement's most vocal representatives in the trade unions and in the Labour Party, have translated this grass-roots dissatisfaction into a determination to change the set-up; and what they are most committed to changing is the private enterprise sector of the present mixed economy.

It is easy to see that this final requirement for optimizing enterprise performance – that the social and economic totality should be broadly accepted – will be particularly hard to satisfy in Britain. In the trade union movement, on the shop floor, the supporters of extended public ownership are strong. There can be no real doubt that their aim is the more or less unlimited extension of the state sector, whether in the name of 'workers' control' or of the 'leadership role' of the working class. The emotive appeal of such rhetoric makes it difficult to believe that the private sector as we know it can long survive. And it is most improbable, in my opinion, that some British version of Giscard d'Estaign's 'advanced liberal society' will do the trick. In my experience concepts of that kind do not cut much ice with ordinary working people, even supposing they are properly understood.

The hope, therefore, must be that by transforming enterprise systems in the way I have suggested, we will also take the other trick at the same time. In other words, by changing the enterprise we will at least be changing peoples' negative feelings about the system as a whole. By making the workforce the owners of profits as well as of wages, and by assigning to it ultimate responsibility and control, we will induce positive feelings about at least a partial and modified market system among much larger numbers of working people – that at any rate must be the hope.

What would be the implications of such change for the present role of private capital in enterprises? The single most dramatic implication is clear: the outside private share and the outside private shareholder would simply fall away. Finance from outside the enterprise, like any other external service, would be supplied on a market price basis. Of course, the need for internally owned enterprise capital would not be eliminated, but the main point is that private capital, in the sense of outside shareholders, would disappear. The enterprise would become a unity; the whole thorny problem of the 'relationship' between capital and labour inside the enterprise would pass into history. So, I suspect in due course, would the trade unions as we know them today. But that, whether an alluring prospect or otherwise, is another matter.

Apart from the brief digression of the last paragraph, I have attempted to analyse the conditions that need to be met if an industrial or other enterprise is to work well. Leaving on one side skill, technology and indeed the availability of capital, I have suggested that there are four:

1 Management and labour must be enabled to achieve the greatest possible degree of team-work through the elimination of structural sources of conflict.

2 The motivation of the workforce to achieve the goals of the enterprise must be as strong as possible.

3 The internal arrangements which govern final control and responsibility inside the enterprise must be acceptable to the workforce.

4 The general set-up outside the enterprise – the macro-economic arrangements – must be acceptable to as many people as possible.

In terms of this analysis is it correct to be sceptical about the likely outcome if the proposals recommended by the majority of the Bullock Committee are put into effect? Remembering the main recommendation – that trade union chosen employee representatives should have an equality of seats with shareholders' representatives on the boards of large private companies – let us consider the Bullock majority ideas in terms of the four conditions suggested.

Whatever else is true, the recommendation of the Bullock majority certainly will not eliminate the structural source of conflict in private industry; its contribution to improved allround team-work, and in particular to that crucial requirement of vertical team-work between shop floor and management, will be at best very indirect. Opinions will differ about whether the amount of conflict would be greater or less if this Bullock recommendation was implemented than under present arrangements. Because of the obvious danger that the position of the two main groups on the reconstituted 'Bullock board' will tend to polarize, my feeling is that conflict would probably increase. Certainly, in my experience, it would be naive to expect more than the most modest reduction in conflict.

This Bullock recommendation would make no change in the financial motivation of the workforce. Would there be a change of motivation on non-material grounds? No one can be sure. But as I have said, my experience in the North of England makes me profoundly sceptical.

It is true that, on the face of it, the main Bullock recommendation should have beneficial results in making the 'arrangements which govern final control and responsibility inside the enterprise' much more acceptable to the workforce. After all, the trade union contingent on the Bullock Committee was the source of the recommendation, and its views must˙be presumed to bear some relationship to what the shop floor wants. Yet I am inclined to think that the ambiguities inherent in the arrangements proposed by the Bullock majority may make it harder, not easier, for ordinary working people to be confident about board-room leadership. There are all the potential contradictions associated with the juxtaposition of the trade union board-room presence, and the continuing trade union role in collective bargaining. In addition, at least some union nominees on boards will surely see the Bullock arrangements as basically a stepping stone towards state control. For this reason too the situation will be unstable and hard for ordinary shop-floor members to identify with.

Equally, because both the heart and the most vocal elements of the trade union movement will remain committed to overall state control, I am very doubtful whether the main Bullock recommendation would produce much benefit in relation to the last condition. In other words, I do not really believe that implementation of the Bullock majority report would have a significantly positive effect on the number of ordinary people who support British macro-economic and social arrangements.

Thus basic analysis, personal experience and historical precedent combine to make me sceptical about the reality of the benefits which the majority of the Bullock Committee foresee flowing from their recommendations. In fact there must be a serious risk that, if they were implemented, British industry would not only fail to get better – it would become worse. For, quite apart from the battles royal which its implementation could well unleash, I am most uneasy about the connection between power and responsibility on the reconstituted Bullock-style boards. It seems to me that, there is a real danger, that the employees' representatives on those boards would enjoy power without ultimate responsibility; conversely the shareholders' representatives, while still having ultimate responsibility (for the interlocked interests of their capital and the enterprise's success), would have inadequate power. Such a situation, in my own experience, contains the seeds of disaster.

So I conclude that the recommendations of the majority of the Bullock report are most unlikely to improve the performance of British industry – and might well make it worse. Since, however, I see the reluctant recommendations of Bullock's minority of business members as virtually certain not to affect anything one way or another, and since I am as acutely aware as anyone else of the need for action in relation to the 'British Disease', I propose to outline my own alternative approach.

Before that some brief account of the 'British Disease' is necessary.

Seen as a comparative failure of industrial and general economic performance, there is widespread agreement about the symptoms of the 'British Disease': we simply produce less in a given amount of working time than our main competitors. In a very relevant discussion of European holiday arrangements in the *New Statesman*, Professor Beckerman put the point more vividly.* It was true, he wrote, that British holidays were shorter than those elsewhere, but then we chose, he added, to take our holidays on the job.

Specific evidence for this account of the 'British Disease' has been coming in for some time. The best single piece is from the 1975 Central Policy Review Staff (Think Tank) Study on *The Future of the British Car Industry*. The report concluded quite flatly and without qualification: 'It takes almost twice as many man hours to assemble similar cars using the same or comparable plant and equipment in Britain as it does on the Continent.' Yet the evidence of what is happening on the large sites of the British civil engineering industry, contained in a report of the industry's Economic Development Committee (EDC) published in the autumn of 1976, is almost equally striking. The main relevant finding was that on many of the really large sites people were working for no more than 30 per cent of the paid working day. Third, there was that astonishing report about the comparative manning levels of British Railways carried in the Business News section of the *Sunday Times* in April 1976. The comparison was with the Illinois Gulf Central Railroad in the US which, the *Sunday Times* told its readers, 'has roughly the same freight loadings, track mileage and passenger figures as British Rail', Illinois Gulf Central required approximately one tenth of the manpower employed by British Rail.

This evidence, it may be objected, reflects the unsatisfactory state of particular sectors of British industry and cannot be taken to imply an indictment of the country's industrial performance as a whole. More comprehensive data are, however, available. There was the study published by the National Economic Development Office (NEDO) in 1976 which compared UK and West German manufacturing industry between the years 1954 and 1972. It showed that Britain was being outperformed by West Germany in virtually all sub-sectors of manufacturing. There is also the work of Mr C. F. Pratten which he admirably summarized in an article in the *Lloyds Bank Review*.† The

---

* W. Beckerman, *New Statesman*, 20 August 1976.

† C. F. Pratten, 'The Efficiency of British Industry', *Lloyds Bank Review*, January 1977.

focus of this work was differences in productivity in the subsidiaries of multi-national companies operating in different countries. Mr Pratten showed that US productivity, measured on the basis of this data, was 50 per cent ahead of that in the UK and that the corresponding advantage of West German and French industry was 35 per cent and 28 per cent respectively. Moreover, he argued that roughly half of the gap was accounted for in each case by differences in labour productivity, and not by other factors. In other words, we do not have to rely on anecdotal or single company evidence. What is more, we are entitled to conclude that a significant measure of the poor UK performance is due to the poor relative productivity of the country's workforce.

It is now clear that it is this very low labour productivity rather than a propensity to take what the Employment Ministry would classify as 'strike action' at the drop of a hat, which is the main manifestation of the 'British Disease'. But then, as the civil engineering EDC report makes clear, the distinction may be more a matter of classification than reality. If civil engineering workers effectively refuse to move out of their cabin for the first hour of the working day – insisting on drinking tea, gossiping and reading the *Sun* for this first hour (a situation described in some detail in the same report) – is that a 'strike' or just a manifestation of low productivity? The answer, of course, is that for the purposes of official statistics it does not constitute a strike. On the other hand, it is easy to see that the cumulative effect of this kind of behaviour over weeks, months, even years, may have a much more damaging effect on output and costs than a few short, sharp explosions which Employment Ministry officials would call strikes.

The EDC civil engineering report is relevant in another way. It describes a very generalized breakdown of relationships between line management and shop floor; from my own experience, that is the other main manifestation of the 'British Disease'. From the management side, if what I have seen myself is any guide, it is experienced as an almost unbearable atmosphere of conflict, suspicion and mistrust. It is as if the shop floor's objectives were not only structurally different from but in almost direct opposition to, those of management and of the long-term strength of the enterprise. Certainly I have found that the mistrust and suspicion across this 'interface' is at least as powerful as any between white and black in post-colonial Africa. I have also, incidentally, found that a significant number of building workers in the North of England seem to get more satisfaction from avoiding work on the job than from completing it successfully.

If I am right the 'British Disease', then, is characterized mainly by very low labour productivity and by very poor relationships between shop floor and management particularly at the 'interface' where these two groups are in direct contact. The experience of the second can be so disagreeable that I have sometimes found myself thinking that the poor line managers are in effect taking the whole pent-up resentment of the working class in their faces.

No doubt some who agree with this account of the 'British Disease' will argue that the present attitudes of British working people are, if not incorrigible, the result of either flabby management or socialism, and that what is needed is the smack of tough management and firm government. I would argue by contrast that it is basically the structure which is wrong; it is the structure which locks the two sides of industry in an absurd conflict and fails to provide anything like adequate work motivation – or enterprise solidarity motivation – for the majority of working people. However, I have already attempted to analyse the main defects of our present enterprise arrangements. Now I will move on to take a first glance at examples of undertakings which organize themselves in a rather different way.

2
A first look at alternative models

The formal and other arrangements which govern the enterprises which I will now outline, differ in a number of important respects. Some are or were formally co-operatives; some are or were formally private companies; at least one is formally both. We shall be looking at the various structural alternatives and their theoretical advantages and disadvantages when we try to unravel the whole concept of industrial democracy in the next chapter; here it is enough to say that all the enterprises have three main features in common:

1 Those who work for them are not, when their enterprise is profitable, making profits for anyone but themselves.
2 The workforce has no external masters (e.g. outside shareholders).
3 Within the enterprise a more-or-less democratic régime – one man one vote – prevails in the area of ultimate responsibility and control though management remains as strong and its functions remain as separate from production functions as in conventional enterprises.

There are two further introductory points. All the contemporary enterprises glanced at were alive early in 1977 and looked as if they were more likely than unlikely to survive at least until the 1980s. However, as we shall see in a moment, more than one had ceased to trade by early 1978. Their 1977–8 'death rate' thus vividly demonstrates one of the key lessons which their history will later suggest: by themselves individual enterprises of this kind are extraordinarily vulnerable. They can probably only succeed in substantial numbers and for long periods of time if they come together in groups.

The second introductory point explains a deliberate omission. Neither here nor later do I look at the experience of the industrial Kibbutzim in Israel. There is, it is true, a considerable body of evidence which indicates that they have been in many ways highly successful; but the special set of values and attitudes which lie behind them are not, in my opinion, widely replicable. And I choose, therefore, to overlook them.

Meriden Motorcycles Ltd is one of the three 'Wedgwood Benn' workers' co-ops. It is the co-op successor of the former Triumph division of Norton Villiers Triumph which the company decided to close down in September 1973. After eighteen months of part work-in part sit-in during which the workforce effectively refused to accept the close down, the co-op received a total of just less than £5m of taxpayers' money mainly in loan form and was thus enabled to start trading in March 1975. Two sets of audited accounts show that the co-op made substantial losses down to September 1977, but in early 1978 the co-op was claiming that its loss-making phase was over, that it was operating within its budgets and showing a modest profit. More solidly, it could point to quite sharp increases in productivity compared with the previous capitalist régime. Given negligible labour turnover at wage rates well below those prevailing in the neighbourhood, it could point to genuine shop-floor loyalty. Further, it could claim to have demonstrated its 'maturity' in having decided to appoint a fully professional management team of five at the end of 1977. And it could claim to have emerged with some credit from a period of collaboration with Sir Arnold Weinstock's General Electric Company which had been amicably brought to a close when its own professional management team had been appointed.

Bewley's Cafés is a very different enterprise. It has been in the café, tea and coffee, bakery and associated lines of business in Dublin since the middle of the last century and in 1977 it employed 400 people. For most of its history it could have been taken as an excellent model of the best kind of progressive but paternal family business with a reputation for being a very good employer. Then in the early 1970s the Bewley family, while retaining management control, handed over the ownership of all the company's assets to a new legal body – the Bewley Community Ltd – of which all the company's employees, after an initial qualifying period, could become members. In 1974, mainly because of price controls, the company's trading account moved temporarily into loss. It did so at a time when a general pay rise, under the Irish government's wages policy, was about to fall due. Overruling the company chairman, Victor Bewley, the elected community council decided that except in cases of personal need (and such cases would identify themselves) or where, as with Bewley's bakery workers, a union was involved, the wage increase would be foregone 'so that we can do something to help our company'. Unbeknown to their union, the majority of the bakery workers slipped the increase back to Bewleys.

La Verrerie Ouvrière d'Albi is different again from either Kirkby or Bewley's. Historically it belongs to the late nineteenth-century generation of working-class industrial co-ops. It was formed in 1896 after a prolonged and heroic struggle by the workers in a medium-sized, capitalist, glass-making enterprise some 10 miles north of Albi. Accounts of what the working people endured during that struggle read like Zola's famous imaginative reconstruction of a great French mining strike in *Germinal*; Jack Jones would have been proud to be associated with them. By the late 1970s, after a massive investment programme over the immediately preceding years, La Verrerie Ouvrière d'Albi had one of the most modern bottle-making plants in France. It was the country's fifth largest bottle producer and it employed over 500 people. A significant part of the cost of the new plant had come from the worker-owners at Albi. They had agreed to increase from 4 per cent to 10 per cent the capital deduction from their wage packets – and thus enabled the new investment to go ahead. In early 1977 they found themselves in the curious position, as a working-class enterprise, of having to anticipate a threat of nationalization if the French Left was to win the 1978 elections. However, despite their impeccable working-class history and credentials they talked in 1977 as if they would oppose any nationalization move in the name of freedom.

Co-op Sport-Vacances outside Angoulême in south west France, was a brave but short-lived workers' co-op which made canvas camping equipment and glass fibre boats for a period of about two years before it succumbed, in the face of difficult market conditions, in the autumn of 1977. Thus, like Kirkby, it belongs to the present late phase of multi-national capitalism and not to that much earlier tradition of workers' co-ops exemplified by La Verrerie Ouvrière d'Albi. Like Kirkby it was the child of a capitalist close down. The last capitalist owner of the antecedent enterprise was Beyer, of Munich. In 1974 Beyer decided to close down its operation in Angoulême on the grounds that it was insufficiently profitable. By late 1976 Co-op Sport-Vacances had managed to build itself up from the wreckage left by Beyer and had shown a modest profit in its first year's trading. Moreover, it had largely been financed not by government money, negotiated through the good offices of a French equivalent of Mr Wedgwood Benn, but by personal loans of £2,000 each from thirty of its seventy-five full-time workers. These loans for the most part had, in turn, been borrowed from French Credit Mutuel. And the people who borrowed and then lent were most of them sewing machine operators, mainly women. It succumbed after an all too short period of trading. We shall be looking at some of the lessons of its brief history later on.

An English enterprise which was made up entirely of women – for its first year at any rate – is a co-operative grocery store in Sunderland called 'Little Women'. It is much smaller than the others so far mentioned; for its first year, to the end of 1977, it involved only eight women and it involved them deliberately – because they were all young mothers – on a part-time basis. Most of the start-up capital came from private individuals and organizations, but the husbands of the women who started this fledgling co-op (in what before the absurd local government re-organization was called County Durham) guaranteed its overdraft. More important, the women agreed to limit their pay to 25p an hour until their enterprise was strong enough to afford an increase. It is hard to be sure whether, had he known about it, Lord Allen of the shop-workers union would have approved this starting wage rate.

Moving from one of the youngest to one of the oldest European co-operative enterprises it is appropriate that we should cross the Pennines from north east to north west England in the direction of Rochdale. But I am not concerned here with the famous store in Toad Lane set up by the Rochdale pioneers in the 1840s; that has come to stand for the historical starting point of co-operation among consumers – not producers. Yet it is insufficiently known that that was never the aim of the founders. On the contrary, in their initial vision consumer co-operation was secondary, and essentially a means by which co-operation in factory production could be financed. Soon after the inception of the store in Toad Lane, the pioneers started a co-operative textile factory. But they made an elementary blunder (which we shall examine in detail later) – they allowed outsiders to buy shares. Mainly, it seems, because of the fraternal cohesion among the factory's workers, and the consequently high productivity, the enterprise prospered. Indeed it prospered 'too well'. Within a few years a majority of its shares were bought up by outside financial interests and the whole enterprise was transformed.

So successful co-operatives, if they get their rules wrong, are all too likely to be transformed into capitalist undertakings. The Rochdale textile factory is by no means an isolated example. In the case of the next enterprise a structural transformation was also involved. This is the public passenger transport undertaking in Valencia, the third city of Spain. In the late 1950s and early 1960s its employees faced an uncertain future. The concession under which these urban transport services was operated by its capitalist owners was due to expire in 1964. Moreover the plant, tram lines and trams, was run-down, expensive to operate, and increasingly obsolete. It seemed altogether unlikely that the owners would seek to renew the concession. Sensing the palpable risk to their jobs, a group of the company's employees – three tram drivers, a maintenance mechanic and a young clerk – started talking among themselves. After lengthy discussions with the government in Madrid, the upshot was the setting up in 1964 of an entirely new kind of enterprise animal, a 'labour company' the Sociedad Anonima Laboral de

Transportes Urbanos de Valencia (SALTUV) (the literal English translation is the Labour Anonymous Society of Urban Transport in Valencia), the transfer to it of all urban passenger transport plant, and a once-and-for-all injection by the Spanish authorities of Pesetas 60m (£500,000) to provide a small capital base. This labour company has run Valencia's urban transport services ever since. The old system based on trams was transformed, via an intermediate trolley bus stage, into an exclusively single-man operated bus service. Moreover, Valencia's bus operation emerges creditably in an international comparative study of urban bus systems made in the early 1970s. It seemed clear in 1977 that at the very least SALTUV was performing no worse in those difficult days for urban bus operations than its more conventionally-structured counterparts in Spain and elsewhere. And there was some evidence that its performance was better than average. Certainly, I was impressed by the absence among Valencia's driver-conductors of that tiresome and officious tendency – which you meet so often when rash enough to try for a London bus – to stick rigidly to bureaucratically imposed occupancy rates. It is easy to see that the driver-conductors on Valencia's buses have an interest in insuring the long-term success of their enterprise.

Meriden Motorcycles Ltd, Bewley's Cafés, La Verrerie Ouvrière d'Albi, the short-lived Co-op Sport-Vacances, SALTUV, 'Little Women' all fall or fell during their lifetimes – below the threshold of 2,000 employees at which, under the proposals of the Bullock majority, companies will be obliged to introduce employee representatives on to their management boards. 'Little Women' had only eight part-time employees (more accurately members, but for convenience I shall continue to use the word employee in its non-technical sense) and at the other extreme SALTUV employed about 1,500 in 1977. Meriden, the Albi glassworks and Bewley's Cafés, were of 'good medium' enterprise size having roughly 750, 500 and 400 employees respectively in 1977. But there is another enterprise or group of enterprises which I want to include in these opening thumb-nail sketches. And one of the reasons for inclusion is that the provisions of Bullock's majority report would unquestionably apply to this last case. More exactly they would apply, if I have understood those provisions correctly, both to a single enterprise within the group and to the group as a whole.

This next example, like SALTUV, is taken from Spain. It consists of what have come to be known, from the small town in which it all began, as the Mondragon group of industrial co-operatives. In 1977 Mondragon had a population of roughly 40,000, having grown almost without interruption from 8,000 when the first industrial co-op was established in 1955. By the late 1970s it had unquestionably become one of the most prosperous towns in Guipuzcoa, itself the most economically advanced of Spain's four Basque provinces. Mondragon lies in mountainous country forty miles inland from the Bay of Biscay and slightly further from the two great Basque maritime centres of San Sebastian and Bilbao. It stands in relation to those two rather as Aberdare does to Cardiff and Swansea on the coast of South Wales.

We shall be looking at the phenomenon of the Mondragon co-operatives in detail later on. We shall see, for example, that this group not only includes industrial co-ops, but also agricultural co-ops, housing co-ops, schools and welfare organizations structured as co-ops, a consumer co-op, a co-operative bank, and sporting clubs formed as co-ops. But this initial sample is concerned exclusively with the sixty-two industrial co-ops in the Mondragon group. What I wish to establish at this stage is that, *prima facie* at any rate, they are working well; and that they would fall within the provisions of Bullock's majority report. On the second point it is enough to report that in 1976 the total number employed in the sixty-two interlinked industrial co-ops was over 14,000 and that 3,450 were employed in the largest single enterprise, ULGOR. To establish the first point, that they are working well, I hope it will suffice for now to point out that in only twenty-one years they had emerged as the leading producers of machine tools and domestic appliances in Spain; that by 1977 they had created roughly 20 per cent of the number of new jobs that had been created in the whole of Northern Ireland since the war; and that their performance in export markets was increasingly strong.

One further point about the Mondragon industrial co-ops needs to be introduced at this stage. It has been the rule almost from the beginning that all those who join must, subject to a short qualifying period, put up a substantial capital sum. The figures vary sharply depending on whether the enterprise being joined is a new one, being set up from scratch, or an already established co-op. In the former case the figure for 1977 was not much less than £2,000, but even in the latter it was nearly £1,000 – in other words, a significant sum. On the other hand the co-ops claim that because loan facilities are available no one has ever been prevented from joining by these provisions. For some old hands who joined the Mondragon co-ops in the early years, the initial capital contributions, increased by a share of annual ploughed-back profits, had become by 1977 considerable stores of wealth – worth as much as £15,000 or more on retirement. This capital contribution rule is clearly one of the key features of the whole Mondragon system and we shall have to look at it more closely later on.

Like Co-op Sport-Vacances, Rowen (after Robert Owen) Onllwyn was a casualty, at least in part, of the difficult economic conditions in 1977. But, relatively, it had a much longer life than that French co-op, having been established in the early 1960s. Its origin was basically charitable since the first objective of those who set it up was to provide some new productive employment for semi-disabled ex-miners who could no longer work in the pits. Starting capital was donated from various sources though a later capital injection took the form of a loan. It was never a large enterprise and at no time during its life was the workforce more than twenty: indeed at one stage, following the bankruptcy of one of its main customers, the workforce was reduced to two. Its career was also a chequered one in terms of products. In its early years it produced night storage heaters. However, by the 1970s it had switched to a combination of out-door furniture – mainly garden seats for local authority parks – and appliances for the disabled.

Yet the most interesting point about Rowen Onllwyn (Onllwyn is a small village alongside Seven Sisters in one of the South Wales valleys behind Neath) concerns its relationship with the local miners' union. Given that its initial object was to provide employment for ex-miners, the relationship with the union was at the beginning very close. Union officials were represented on a kind of 'consultative council'. More important, there was an understanding that the wages paid by Rowen should be linked to those paid to the corresponding grades of surface workers at the nearby pits. The enterprise's fluctuating fortunes were such, however, that on at least one occasion when the surface level mineworkers were awarded a wage increase, Rowen was unable to match it. There was, I understand, considerable 'unpleasantness' between the enterprise and the union, but the sovereign body of the Rowen workforce dug its toes in. It insisted in effect that as a democratically controlled and independent enterprise operating in the market, the final say on wage rates must come from itself and not from any outsiders – union officials or anyone else. Not surprisingly the union establishment in South Wales took rather less interest in Rowen after that.

I have introduced this brief catalogue of obscure – or anyway overlooked – enterprises at this early stage to show that my main concern is with the actual and practical rather than simply with the abstract and theoretical. In other words, my main interest is not to add to the volumes of academic literature on the subject, though some discussion of different theoretical types will be needed in the next chapter.

On the basis of the evidence adduced so far we can already go beyond the plain fact that there are real enterprises in the actual world which differ both from conventional ones (private or public) and from the kind of animal that might be expected to emerge from the proposals of the Bullock majority. For example, I think we are entitled to be sure, from the Mondragon experience, that these different structures can be applied successfully to fairly large-scale, medium technology and fairly capital-intensive enterprises, as well as to humbler operations like 'Little Women'. And we can be satisfied too that there is no reason to suppose, given the evidence of the Valencia buses, that they cannot be applied in the public (or local authority) sector as well.

More important, however, than this evidence of possible scope are the signs that they can result in very marked changes of attitude. The particular attitude changes may differ from one case to another; but all appear to demonstrate a much greater solidarity on the part of the workforce with the enterprise's longer-term goals: we have the shop floor at Meriden Motorcycles agreeing to work much more flexibly; we have the waitresses and others at Bewley's Cafés insisting that a wage increase should – at least temporarily – be foregone; we have the Albi glassworkers deciding to hoist from 4 per cent to 10 per cent the 'capital' deduction from their take-home pay; and we have the sovereign assembly of the Rowen Onllwyn shop floor effectively telling the local union officials to mind their own business.

We have some remarkable evidence too – from Albi and Angoulême, from Mondragon and to some extent from 'Little Women' – that the idea of working people making a capital commitment to the enterprise in which they work need not be dismissed as belonging to industrial science fiction. It is easy to see what an enormous difference in attitudes towards long-term enterprise success that sort of commitment can bring about. If the shop floor at Leylands had anything from £1,000 to £15,000 each invested in the company one cannot seriously believe that current levels of productivity would be tolerated by the workers themselves.

Of course, as we have seen already, there have been failures in the history of enterprises of this kind. However, this first glance has at least established that they are not necessarily doomed and that they can result in rather striking changes of attitude.

3
A typology of industrial democracy

In this chapter my main object is to distinguish between different forms of industrial democracy, or at any rate between various ways in which the concept is being or has been used. In effect what I shall attempt to present is a typology of the different kinds of arrangement which have been or may be presented as examples of 'industrial-democracy-in-action'. The main justification for including the section is the enormous confusion, the dense fog, which surrounds the whole concept. Moreover, it will be useful to be able to refer back to this typology when, in the main body of the book, the practical experience is reviewed in some detail. Those with no taste for theory may prefer to skip the whole section.

Perhaps the single most important confusion about the notion of industrial democracy derives from the fact that the enterprise as we know it is two-sided. If an enterprise consists of capital on one side and labour on the other – with management either attached to capital (as is normal in practice) or hovering between the two – how do you democratize such a structure? What would count as democratizing it?

A moment's reflection makes it fairly clear that unless you somehow eliminate the division between the two sides there is no way in which the enterprise can be democratized in any strict sense. For the essence of a democracy is precisely that all its members should be on the same footing in crucial matters such as the choice of leadership. If an enterprise is necessarily binary and two-sided that condition cannot strictly be met. Of course, you are at liberty to propose reforms to make the relative power positions of the two sides more equal or to install a regime of dual control on a formal basis. Still, and however desirable or undesirable, that is clearly something else.

However, my purpose is not to enlist the support of logic as an additional stick with which to beat the Bullock recommendations; it is to clarify the sources of confusion. Partly because these sources of confusion are so rarely uncovered the public has been offered, and is still being offered, some extraordinary models of what should count as industrial democracy.

Though at a different level it is obviously understandable, one of the oddest and blandest of these models is one put forward by Professor Hugh Clegg, widely regarded in the 1950s and 1960s as the leading British academic in the field of industrial relations. According to Professor Clegg the system which prevails in Britain at the moment, with strong trade unions acting out an opposition role against management, itself constitutes a version and indeed the most plausible version of industrial democracy in action – as opposed, say, to structured conflict. The core of Clegg's logical argument is that it is precisely the existence of two sides, a government and an Opposition, which is at the heart of a democracy.

The logic of Professor Clegg's argument has been convincingly dealt with by the American industrial sociologist Paul Blumberg.* There is no need for me to do the job again here. It is true that defenders of the Clegg position have other arguments on hand which help to explain it. Essentially, in this view the most important feature of present arrangements is the protective shield which the trade unions provide against the arbitrary exercise of power by management or capital. The argument then goes on to equate democracy with mechanisms which limit the use of power. Now there is clearly something in that, and it seems particularly helpful in a historical context because it enables us to see the struggles for recognition by the trade union movement as more like than unlike other struggles for protection against tyranny in the past. On the other hand, in the context of the present debate about industrial democracy turned out, *per impossibile*, to be the correct one, then there contemporary sense, Professor Clegg's conception of industrial democracy turned out, *per impossible*, to be the correct one, then there would have been no need for the Bullock report, still less for books like this one; only works on management–union relationships would be required.

It is easy to see that Professor Clegg's model deals with the tricky problem of how you democratize an essentially binary system, a system essentially two-sided, by treating the difficulty as if it did not exist. That basically is also the approach followed by the Bullock majority. The Bullock majority's version of industrial democracy is in effect a proposal to make more equal the position of the two sides and to formalize a structure of dual control in industry. The German word for this type of arrangement, *Mitbestimmung*, is normally translated not as 'industrial democracy' but 'co-determination'.

A quite separate, but still potent source of confusion can be traced to

---

* Paul Blumberg, *Industrial Democracy ; the Sociology of Participation*, Constable, London, 1968.

the Webbs, and may well have even earlier origins. I have already mentioned that the Webbs used *Industrial Democracy* as the title for a 'scientific study of trade unions'. The usage implies that the concept can be exclusively – or at least properly – applied to any institution or enterprise which is in some sense 'of the working class'. In an extreme form this usage is frequently adopted by militant public ownership zealots and the like in slogans calling for workers' industrial democracy or workers' industrial control. When used in this way such slogans should normally be regarded as synonymous with demands for a 'leadership role for the working class', the elimination of the private and market sectors of the economy and things of that sort.

There is a more specialized version of this usage. According to it, in a mixed economy any enterprise which is owned and controlled by a working-class institution may be described as an example of 'industrial democracy'. Thus the enterprises owned and controlled by the Israeli trade union movement (the Histadrut) are sometimes presented as 'industrial democracies'. So are the various 'commonweal' enterprises in West Germany, owned and controlled by the West German trade union movement or by its consumer co-ops or by a combination of the two. Examples of these enterprises include the highly successful West German 'Commonweal' bank (the Bank für Gemein Wirtschaft) and the so-called people's insurance company, the *Volksfürsorge*. Into this category too, in Britain, would fall productive enterprises owned by the Co-operative Wholesale Society; and indeed the brewery operation, Federation Ales, in the North East which is owned and controlled by the working men's clubs. Up to early 1977 there were also the various enterprises – a travel agency, some insurance brokers – owned and controlled by the National Union of Students.

However, we can get perhaps the most distinctive flavour of this usage if we glance briefly at a tremendous debate about possible structures which took place when the workers' glass-making enterprise in Albi was set up in 1896. The question was whether the new works should be set up as an enterprise belonging to and controlled by its own workers or whether it should be run by and for the working class as a whole. In favour of the first solution were those associated with the French co-operative and anarchist movements; in favour of the second were the French socialists and in particular a militant young socialist deputy for one of the neighbouring constituencies, a M. Jean Jaurès. Jaurès was in fact the main mobilizer of support, moral and financial, for the new works.

There were two specific matters of dispute. The first concerned control. Should there be a majority of its own workers on the governing body of the new enterprise – as the anarchists and men of the co-operative movement urged? Should representatives of the central French working-class institutions, the trade union federations in Paris, form the majority, as the socialists and Jaurès urged? There was a similar division of opinion about the name of the new enterprise. Should it be La Verrerie des Ouvriers d'Albi (the glassworks of the workers of Albi)? Or should it be called La Verrerie Ouvrière d'Albi (the working-class glassworks at Albi)?

It was Jaurès and the socialists who triumphed on both counts in 1896. On the other hand, as we shall see later, opposition to control by central institutions in far away Paris mounted steadily inside the new glassworks over the next thirty or forty years. In the 1930s, as a result of pressure from the works itself, the control arrangements – though not the name – were reformed. Since then there has always been a majority from inside the works on the governing body of the enterprise.

There are fascinating parallels, if you read today's Far Left writing on the 'Wedgwood Benn' co-ops, with the great debate in Albi in 1896. The real point, however, is that against the background of that debate it is easy to see how an identification has arisen in some quarters between the notion of industrial democracy and that of an enterprise controlled by the working class. A 'working-class enterprise' equals a 'people's enterprise' equals a 'democratic enterprise'. That is how the logic seems to operate, and it is by this sort of logical process that the strong public ownership zealots in Britain see all enterprises in the people's democracies as democratic enterprises; while those controlled by the state in a mixed economy are sometimes similarly characterized.

Once the equation of 'working-class controlled' with 'democratic' has been identified, the problem of this particular usage – and the position of these enterprises in any typology of industrial democracy – has been effectively cleared up. For there is no reason why enterprises owned and controlled by working-class institutions – still less enterprises operating in a political environment in which the working class enjoys a 'leadership role' – should be more or less democratic than any other. There are no correlations here.

There is, however, one further point to be made about the relationship between industrial democracy and workers' – or working-class institutional – control. Genuine industrial democrats will accept that 'workers', on almost any definition, form a majority in any enterprise of which we have experience. It follows that if genuinely democratic control structures were introduced throughout industry, and indeed the whole economy, then workers' control would have been achieved. On the other hand we must not overlook the crucial distinction between 'workers' and 'the working class' in this context – a distinction memorably symbolized by the argument over the words 'ouvriers' a¬d 'ouvrière' in the title of the Albi glassworks in 1896.

Two other very real sources of confusion need to be cleared up in any theoretical discussion of industrial democracy. The first concerns management and its relationship to ultimate responsibility and control. The second has to do with ownership in general and (internal) equity participation in particular.

The difficulty about management in any discussion about industrial democracy seems to be essentially twofold. There is the fact that the distinction between day-to-day management and ultimate responsibility and control, though perhaps logically clear and almost universally recognized, is sometimes hard to define in practice with sufficient precision. Branko Horvat the distinguished Yugoslav economist who has devoted a great deal of attention to these matters, suggests – some would argue too simplistically – that the distinction can best be understood as one between professional questions or functions and political questions or functions. But what of those essentially political questions with which an enterprise has to grapple – like wage rates – which have professional implications? However, it is probably acceptable to treat the dividing line between 'management' and 'final control and responsibility' as a practical issue and do no more at this stage than draw attention to it. We shall see, later on, how actual enterprises have dealt with the reality of the problem.

As well as this practical difficulty there is also the aspiration, or vague belief, that a fully democratic enterprise should eventually dispense with all (or almost all) the functions of management as we know them today and move on to a complete self-management or even a managementless régime. The first of these possibilities was given some encouragement in the late 1970s by an American fashion for using the term 'self-management'. Two or three International Self-management Conferences were held in the US between 1973 and 1977. Had they been convened in England, they would almost certainly have been called conferences about 'industrial democracy'.

Both my own experiences and those of the actual enterprises we have briefly glanced at make it quite clear that if self-management is equivalent to a régime which dispenses with separate management functions – to a managementless régime – then, at least in today's world, the notion is Utopian. More than that, a failure to perceive the importance of separate management functions in an enterprise has all too often proved disastrous. If anything, history shows that the management required in an enterprise ultimately controlled by its workforce must be particularly strong – if only to counteract anarchic and centrifugal tendencies – and certainly that it must be more like than unlike management in a conventional firm. Of course, where the workforce is ultimately sovereign, management may well need to adapt its style. There is also some, though rather mixed evidence that as such an enterprise gains experience and confidence the need for immediate work supervision may be reduced, as well as the need for enormous personnel departments. However, these are modest qualifications. An industrially democratic enterprise can no more dispense with professional management than it can dispense with ready money.

The main final source of confusion in theoretical discussions of industrial democracy concerns, as I have suggested, the question of ownership. Can an enterprise be democratically *owned*? If the essence of a democratic enterprise, or community, is that all its members should be on the same footing, can we devise arrangements to apply the principle to ownership?

An approach to these difficult questions, which has the great merit of limiting the extent to which we are liable to get bogged down, is to follow Professor Jaroslav Vanek, the leading theoretician in this whole field, and treat them as secondary. It was, I think, Vanek who first pointed out that perhaps the single most important distinction between different enterprises is between those in which control is based on work and those in which it is based on ownership.

Once this distinction is grasped it is easy to see that outside of Yugoslavia, and of a small minority of enterprises in the Atlantic world, virtually all businesses fall into the second category of control based on ownership rather than the first of control based on work. It is as much the case with the National Coal Board as it is with Imperial Chemical Industries; it is as much the case in the huge private capitalist enterprises in the US as it is in the huge state capitalist enterprises in the USSR. Up to now the link between ownership and control has been almost universal.

It is not, of course, impossible to devise arrangements where the control of an enterprise remains based on ownership, while that ownership is restricted to worker members in a way which ensures ultimate workforce control. But it is far simpler, following Vanek, to favour a system under which control is enjoyed by virtue of working in an enterprise rather than by owning it. This approach has the further merit of being able to cope with situations, as for example in Yugoslavia, in which 'ownership' in the conventional western capitalist sense has been at least partially eliminated.

Again, once it is agreed that control should be based on work, the secondary character of ownership questions – and alternatives – becomes apparent. An enterprise controlled by its workers may select from a whole range of alternatives so far as ownership is concerned. It can insist that all who join the enterprise have to 'buy themselves in' – but it need not. It may limit the share of profits which are distributed to working members as individuals – or it may not – or the law may lay down important conditions in this respect. Equally, either the law or the working members may restrict the ownership rights which will be enjoyed in the event of the voluntary liquidation of the enterprise. We shall be looking later at the very sophisticated and balanced arrangements in this area which have been devised by the Mondragon co-ops. But the point here is to emphasize the importance of linking control to work and thus avoid the many difficulties and confusions inherent in the opposite approach.

At this stage it may be helpful to summarize the main points so far in this theoretical discussion. I have tried to identify four main sources of confusion which have tended to fog discussion of industrial democracy:

1 The confusion which arises because it is logically difficult to devise a form of 'democracy' which fits an essentially binary organization which has two 'sides' – especially when the two sides are normally at odds.

2 The confusion which arises because enterprises owned or controlled by working-class organizations (like trade unions) or enterprises operating in countries where the working class has the 'leading role' are thought, for those reasons, to be examples of industrial democracy.

3 The confusion which arises because the distinction between management and ultimate control is often hard to draw in practice and because of Utopian dreams about the possibility of the 'managementless enterprise'. But the familiar management tasks are as vital in democratically controlled enterprises as in any other.

4 The confusion which arises because in most economies and legal systems which we know ownership and ultimate control go together. The best approach here is to favour an arrangement under which control is exercised by virtue of work – and to treat ownership as secondary.

Corresponding to the various confusions about industrial democracy which I have just identified, there are, of course, a set of models which have their different advocates. There is no particular point in attempting to restrict the use of the description or to ban its application so far as these models are concerned. We can simply think of them as 'different' models. All the same, there is one important logical or linguistic point worth making.

The vivid and easily comprehensible distinction between top-downwards and bottom-upwards power arrangements was introduced into discussion of this and similar topics especially by the Americans in the mid-1970s. When applied to political units it is easy to see that only bottom-upwards systems of power would normally qualify as being democratic. For in political discussion it is only when power flows genuinely upwards from the people at the bottom that we think it legitimate to talk of a democracy. By contrast, a traditional monarchy is a top-downwards political system; so is a traditional colony, like St Helena, Hong Kong or the Falkland Islands. Up to now nearly all enterprises − outside Yugoslavia since the 1950s, and the handful of enterprises in the West which we will be looking at in detail shortly − have been organized on a top-downwards basis.

When it comes to enterprises, as opposed to states, there seems to be much less diffidence about applying the description democratic to top-downwards systems of power. The Israeli Histadrut companies and the West German Commonweal enterprises fall obviously into this category. So do all the 'people's enterprises' in the democracies of Eastern Europe and elsewhere. In fact we can see that any enterprise owned and controlled by the working class or by a working-class institution is likely to be of this special type: a top-downwards enterprise described as democratic by virtue of its association with the working class.

We can adopt much the same approach in identifying the type or model of industrial democracy put forward by Professor Hugh Clegg. His suggestion was that any set-up in which − as in most of British industry today − a set of powerful trade unions opposed management in large private or public companies, was a version, indeed the only valid version, of industrial democracy. He does not propose any changes in the top-downwards character of the enterprises concerned. So we might consider this as a second special type of industrial democracy by virtue of the fact that its management faces a strong trade union opposition.

The common-sense notion of democracy is slightly less stretched when we come on to the next special type: the Bullock, diarchic or 'co-determination' model. In this case, if it is reckoned that the trade union chosen employee representatives on management boards will constitute a genuine upward flow of power from the bottom, then indeed the traditional top-downwards enterprise structure will have been to that extent modified. Perhaps it is most sensible to think of this model as being a diarchic or co-determinational type: a part top-downwards part bottom-upwards enterprise described as democratic by virtue of this special, co-determinational character.

There are finally Utopian models of industrial democracy. The special category of this type, to which I have already by implication drawn attention, is that based on the assumption that a democratic enterprise can afford to dispense with management. Enterprises of this sort are bottom-upwards; their essential problem is that the power which flows from the people at the bottom does not push upwards to a management structure of any kind. We shall find examples in the record of enterprises which have failed for very much these reasons.

Having disposed of the specialized models of industrial democracy we can consider the final and, some would argue, most important and only genuine variety: the non-Utopian bottom-upwards democratic industrial enterprise. The simpler issue of control can be dealt with first, the thornier one of capital second.

Ultimate control and responsibility will flow, by definition, from the bottom-upwards in this model. A general assembly of the workforce will be the ultimate sovereign body. On the other hand systematic arrangements for day-to-day management will be required, and in any enterprise with numbers in excess of about twenty, the assembly will have to delegate responsibilities to an elected committee or board.

So any enterprise of this type, whether in Yugoslavia or in the West, will normally have sovereign workforce assembly, a management team and an elected authority. Sometimes, as in most French industrial co-ops, the chairman of the elected authority, the President-Directeur-General, will be chosen from among those with relevant management experience and will, as his title implies, combine this role with that of chief executive in the management team. In other cases, in the Mondragon co-ops for example, the two posts of chairman and chief executive (respectively political and managerial), will be kept separate.

As we noticed earlier, it is rarely possible to draw an exact line between the competence of the management team and that of the elected authority. Depending on enterprise history and personalities the actual relationship between the two will vary. Nevertheless two general points can be made. First, the management team is always constitutionally subordinate to the elected body. Its job is to carry out the policies decided upon or approved by its elected masters. But second, if the enterprise is to compete successfully in the modern world, the management team will need as much freedom in the execution of agreed policy as is enjoyed by management in conventional business.

Apart from the unavoidable fuzziness in the relationship between elected authority and management team, the control system in the 'pure' model is clear enough. In practice, however, we find a number of deviations from this 'pure' type. In the first place such 'impurities' are often found in the control structures of enterprises which started out as conventional private capitalist firms and were converted along the road to a democratic constitution. Bewley's Cafés is an example, as is the Scott-Bader Commonwealth which manufactures chemicals outside Northampton and is probably, at least in commercial terms, the most successful democratic enterprise in this country. In neither (at least up to early 1978) was the management team fully subordinate either to a general assembly of the workforce or to its elected representatives. It was almost analogous to the situation when power is gradually transferred in a colonial territory. There were certain entrenched arrangements at Bewley's and at Scott-Bader, similar to the reserve powers of a colonial governor during the transition period of self-government, which the workforce cannot for the time being change. It is a fair bet, but no more, that these 'impurities' will eventually be purged; democratic pressures will eventually be too much for them.

Certain other cases produce a rather different impurity: weighted voting in the sovereign assembly of the workforce. Up until the early 1970s voting was weighted by wage levels in the general assemblies of the Mondragon industrial co-ops. There is still some element of weighting in the voting arrangements of the Valencia urban transport undertaking. Nearer home votes in Landsman's Co-ownership, which hires out industrial caravans near Huntingdon, are weighted in proportion to the number of voting shares held by workers. However, like the old workers' co-ops and industrial co-ops in France, Landsmans retains a system under which control is basically linked to *ownership* and not to work. Where there is weighted voting in an enterprise which links control to *work*, the probability must be that democratic pressures will force a change to one man one vote in due course. That has in fact happened in the Mondragon co-operatives.

There are two other more important, because they are more widely exemplified, deviations from the pure bottom-upwards system. They occur characteristically when control remains linked to capital (shares) and not to work. These are deviations essentially in the rights of membership to the sovereign workforce assembly and they can take one of two forms. Non-workers, for example pensioner ex-workers, friendly trade unionists or other supporters, may be admitted as members of the sovereign assembly. Or, in the opposite case, some workers may be excluded. Nor am I talking about the temporary exclusion of newcomers during a probationary period; I am talking about more or less permanent exclusion.

Now it is easy to see that unless there are specific rules to the contrary either one of these two situations, or both, are likely to occur when control remains linked to shares (capital) and not to work. Moreover this link has, of course, been maintained in the traditional structures of workers' co-operatives. For in those which derive from the Rochdale pioneers it is ownership of a share which gives the right to vote in the sovereign assembly. It is true that Rochdale pioneers insisted that no shareholder, however many shares he owned, should be entitled to more than one vote. On the other hand the Rochdale rules did not exclude non-workers from the body of shareholders and did not insist that all workers own shares.

As we shall see, the few surviving industrial workers' co-ops in this country – and the much larger number of industrial co-ops in France – operate in almost all cases on a version of the Rochdale rules. Control remains linked, notwithstanding the democratic principle, to shares not work. In most cases their sovereign bodies include some non-worker shareholders and exclude some worker non-shareholders. Only in a few of these enterprises, up to the late 1970s, had special supplementary rules been introduced which prevented either of these deviations from taking place.

Quite apart from the formal objection – that democracy is diluted – these structures derived from the Rochdale pioneers run the risk of either external or internal take-over. In the first case, if non-worker shareholders are permitted there is nothing in principle to prevent them forming a majority, taking the enterprise over, and converting it into a straightforward capitalist undertaking. As seen earlier, that is precisely what happened to the very successful textile co-operative launched by the Rochdale pioneers themselves. However, if, in the second case the co-op employs workers who are not enfranchised, then the initial membership group may take the enterprise over from the inside. There will be a group of privileged members, and there will be a more-or-less large group of second class non-members who may well come to do most of the actual work. A tendency in this direction can be observed in certain modern refuse collection co-ops in California, and there are fairly numerous examples in early British workers' co-op history.

Sidney and Beatrice Webb, who came to be implacably opposed to producer co-operatives, based an important part of their case on the tendency of enterprises of this type to succumb in one or other of the two ways I have just described. They talked, not altogether unreasonably, of built-in tendencies to 'degenerate'. Much less reasonably they argued that such degeneration was 'inevitable'. This particular argument, and indeed their whole position, has been

convincingly challenged in the recent past by Professor Derek Jones.*
What is odd, however, is that having correctly identified serious
structural weaknesses in the producer co-ops of their day, the Webbs did
not go on to point out that two fairly simple rule changes would be
sufficient to eliminate them.

There remains one main area for consideration: the alternative capital
and ownership arrangements open to a democratically controlled
enterprise. Given that an enterprise is controlled by its workforce, what
capital and ownership choices does it have? The constraints are, first,
that some internally owned capital will be needed and, second, that
while external capital may be used, it must not be permitted to control.

Essentially, the choices lie in a spectrum which runs from a
completely collective and indivisible capital core at one end to a fully
divided, and individually owned, capital – as in a partnership – at the
other. At the collective end and as a special case fall, among others, the
Yugoslav enterprises. They are a special case because, while there is no
individual ownership of capital in Yugoslavia's democratically
controlled enterprises, it is society, rather than the collective enterprise
itself, which is the legal owner. Slightly better examples of collectives are
provided in the British Isles by Bewley's Cafés and Scott-Bader. In both it
is the 'working community' as a whole, rather than individual workers,
which owns the capital. Except in a situation where a previously private
enterprise has been sold to its workforce, this sort of collective
ownership is fairly typical of companies which have a capitalist non-
democratic pre-history. Other British examples include Michael Jones,
the Northampton jewellers, and, at least in practise, the two surviving
'Wedgwood Benn' co-ops: Kirkby Manufacturing and Engineering and
Meriden Motorcycles, Ltd.

At the individuated ownership–partnership end of the spectrum
comes Landsman's Co-ownership. Landsman's, like Bewley's, Scott-Bader
and Michael Jones, has a capitalist pre-history; unlike them, Landsman's
was sold by its previous owners to the workforce. And at Landsman's
the capital is individually owned. This is perhaps the model to which the
phrase 'workers' capitalism' or 'granulated capitalism' can be most
appropriately applied. Such an arrangement, if it is to work, must
include rules which prevent the individual owners from suddenly
withdrawing their capital. There are also strong theoretical arguments
against a pure 'partnership' model, but for the moment these are matters
of detail.

---

* Derek Jones, 'British Producer Co-operatives' in Ken Coates (ed.), *The New
Worker Co-operatives*, published for the Institute for Workers' Control by
Spokesman Books, Nottingham, 1976.

Between these two extremes lie a whole range of part collective part individual capital ownership possibilities. Indeed in some countries, for example, France and Spain the relevant laws effectively impose some such combination. They do so by stipulating a minimum percentage of profits which must be 'indivisibly' ploughed back into the enterprise, thus ensuring that at least part of the capital comes to be collectively owned. There are strong theoretical arguments for this kind of ownership which is both collective and individual. It is notable too that the most successful of these enterprises, the Mondragon co-operatives, have chosen a parallel formula which will be examined later.

Three further points about ownership can be quickly dealt with. First there is the question of profit distribution. It is worth noticing that an arrangement of fully collective ownership, whether at Scott-Bader or in Yugoslavia, does not automatically mean that all (or indeed any) profits have to be assigned to the collectivity. In practice most companies so structured assign at least some profit percentage to individuals – at Scott-Bader a maximum of 20 per cent may be distributed to individual workforce members and must be shared equally. Alternatively, profit shares may vary with wage rates.

Second, there is the question – when all or part of the internal capital is collectively owned – of what happens in the event of voluntary liquidation. Should the individual worker members be entitled to benefit financially if the assets exceed the liabilities when liquidation takes place? In some countries the law steps in here. For example, in France the law does not permit a 'break-up dividend' to individual co-op members, and in a recent case, when a venerable tobacco pipe-making co-op was voluntarily liquidated, a considerable sum was transferred to central co-op funds. The recent common ownership law in Britain follows the French precedent in this case, while the Scott-Bader constitution, as well as those of similar enterprises, includes the same sort of provision.

Third, for all those enterprises in which the internal capital is wholly or partly owned by individual members, there are the intriguing and ideologically divisive questions of how these ownership stakes should be acquired, whether it is possible or sensible to impose more than a token entry fee, and the extent to which these individual holdings may be adjusted upwards or downwards in line with some percentage of retained profits or losses. The Mondragon co-operatives in particular have evolved a very sophisticated set of arrangements covering those various points.

There is one further point to make at this stage. It is that this discussion of alternative control and capital arrangements is only one part of any exhaustive 'typology' of democratic enterprises. There are other kinds of differences between enterprises – some more important, some less so – besides those I have outlined. For example, there can be major differences of character, flavour and ideology – depending on history; as between an enterprise started in its democratic form from scratch, say, and one with capitalist origins. A co-op started by artisans in the 1890s is likely to be rather different from one launched by middle-class professionals (or indeed anyone else) in the 1950s or 1960s. We shall get a picture of these other differences when we examine actual examples.

4
A cold climate in Britain

The funny thing is, I don't believe there's more than one or two
members of the present Labour Cabinet who really believe in the Co-
operative and want it to succeed. And it's the same with the great
majority of trade union officials whom I meet. Fundamentally they
are not on our side. In fact I sometimes ask myself whether we have
any friends, either on the left or the right.

The speaker was Mr Dick Jenkins, long time convenor of shop
stewards for the Transport and General Workers Union at the Kirkby
Manufacturing and Engineering Works outside Liverpool, and since its
establishment as a 'Wedgwood Benn' co-op in late 1974, one of its two
directors. With something short of complete conviction I ventured to
suggest that, apart from the support of other production co-ops, there
was evidence of an appreciable new interest from the political Right.
More stoically I went on to point out that the position he had described
was nothing new. Almost without interruption since the first ventures
were launched in the last century, Britain's producer co-ops and similar
enterprises had been the unloved changelings of the industrial scene.
Even the natural sibling affection for them of the consumer co-ops had
been in doubt since the 1880s.

If there was any exaggeration in my rejoinder to Mr Jenkins, it was
certainly very limited and, I would argue, wholly pardonable. The fact is
that at least from the *Communist Manifesto* in 1848 down to Mr
Wedgwood Benn's appointment as Industry Secretary in 1974, British
support for producer co-ops – or for similar democratic enterprises – has
been marginal. On the Left the two main thrusts of the working-class
movement – for the legitimatization of trade unions and their collective
bargaining role, and for public ownership – have been such that
producer co-operation has been seen at best as an irrelevance, at worst as
an embarrassment, even a threat. From the Right, with the questionable
exception of the maverick and romantic (if not partly dotty)
'distributism' of Belloc and Chesterton, there has been little or no
recognition up to the last year or so, of the potential or value of such
enterprises. It is true, as Professor Derek Jones has lately shown that

there is an honourable tradition of sympathy for 'associations of labourers' in the writings of liberal economists. Still, as he has also shown, that sympathy has been overwhelmingly qualified with pessimism. More important perhaps, the attitude of radical liberals has rarely gone beyond support for things like 'works' councils' and profit-sharing schemes, or in effect, the sort of 'cosmetic reforms' reluctantly favoured by the minority business members of the Bullock Committee. That is not, it is true, quite the whole story. For one thing there has been a recurrent, if not continuous, strand of what Lenin would have called 'infantile left deviation' at the edge of the working-class movement: the anarchists, the Guild Socialists, and, since 1918, the Independent Labour Party (ILP) have favoured bottom-upwards democratic enterprises even if they have rejected ownership by the workers. Then, too, neither Marx himself nor the trade unions have been quite as monolithically negative about initiatives in this area as today's attitudes might suggest. Equally, from outside the working-class movement, co-operative and similar production enterprises have been periodically supported and even promoted by Christian Socialists and by a series of paternalistic (or radical) Quakers. It must also be remembered that in the pre-1848 period, and for some little time after, the teaching of Robert Owen (and even to some extent his almost invariably unsuccessful co-operative community ventures) attracted a quite widespread following.

In a general way, however, there is no doubt about the position. During the 125 years which separate the *Communist Manifesto* from Mr Wedgwood Benn's arrival at the Industry Ministry, neither of the two main sides of British politics and British industry, labour or capital, have felt inclined to encourage either democracy at the place of work or worker ownership. So far as capital is concerned no demonstration is required. In the case of labour the briefest glance will suffice.

In effect, all three principal elements in the British working-class movement — the semi-revolutionary Marxist, the straight trade union and the social democratic or Fabian — have collaborated for most of the period since 1848 in seeking to achieve two main objectives: improvement in the material conditions of working people's lives through the build-up of union bargaining strength in law and in fact; and the progressive reduction of capitalist arrangements and the market — through the extension of public ownership. The first is an open-ended objective; and it came first in time. The second could only start to be implemented after government power had been achieved, though the commitment to it came much earlier.

This is no place to rewrite the history of those 125 years; nor am I competent to do so. However, it may be helpful to recall some of the chief events: the formation in 1851 of the Amalgamated Society of Engineers, the first of the industrial craft unions familiar in today's Britain; the first Trades Union Congress (TUC) in 1868; the Acts of 1871 and 1875 which protected unions against prosecution for restraint of trade and legalized peaceful picketing; the founding of the Fabian Society in 1883 and the admission to it of Sidney Webb and Bernard Shaw a few years later; the TUC resolution in favour of land nationalization in 1888; and the symbolically more important vote of 1893 which confined trade union support to parliamentary candidates prepared to commit themselves to the nationalization of the means of production, distribution and exchange; the steady development of the Fabian Society's position in favour not only of public ownership but also, progressively, of bureaucratic industrial administration – culminating in the dismissive and hostile report on co-operative production prepared by Sidney and Beatrice Webb and published as a supplement to the *New Statesman* in February 1914. From then on it is more or less a straight run through, via the new constitution of the revamped Labour Party, with its formal Clause 4 commitment to nationalization in 1918, to Herbert Morrison's public ownership of London Transport in the 1930s and to the nationalization of major sectors of the economy by the Attlee Government after the Second World War.

There is not very much to set against these mainstream expressions of the working-class movement which left democratic production (where it occurred), out in the cold, more or less isolated, on its own. Marx, it is true, made occasional sympathetic noises about co-ops: such as reference to an eventual post-capitalist 'republican and beneficent régime of free and equal producers' – which is scarcely an account of bureaucratic collectivism. Support for the latter can of course be found in his work as well. Nor perhaps, is it surprising, given his interest in the grand drama of history, that the most expressive adjective he uses about co-operative enterprises is 'dwarfish'. But, essentially, Marx saw workers' co-ops as instruments, if not very exciting ones, in the class struggle rather than as ends in themselves.

At the other end of the working-class movement's political span, evidence of more flexible attitudes is of two kinds. There is, first, evidence of *some* trade union support for co-operative production, particularly in the 1870s when the idea of what has been called the 'Working Class Ltd' was briefly popular in certain quarters. The suggestion was that by successfully launching working-class enterprises on quasi-capitalist, quasi-co-operative lines, the 'sons of toil' might succeed – against all the apparent odds – in turning the system to their own advantage. And we can perhaps couple with this the surprisingly

buoyant opposition by TUC 'moderates' at successive Congresses in the
1870s and 1880s to early attempts to commit the movement to formally
collectivist positions: opposition to the Land Nationalization resolution
before that was finally passed in 1888; and opposition to resolutions
calling for political support to be confined to nationalization men before
the eventual passing of a resolution on those lines in 1893.

Second, there is fragmented evidence of 'rightist deviation'; what we
might call working-class Tory attitudes at a more grass-roots level.
Sidney Pollard* quotes a letter published in the *Co-operator* Newspaper
from a Mr William Smith of Bridgnorth in 1869 when the ideas of
'Working Class Ltd' were beginning to gain ground:

> We have seen enough of communism, enough of the Utopian
> ridiculous mummery of socialism. We don't want it. ... Let co-
> operation be what it is. ... Let it initiate no other spirit but gratitude to
> God, loyalty to our sovereign, love to our country and good will to all
> mankind ... in the cause of constitutional competitive co-operation.

It is easy to believe that the local Tory Agent in Bridgnorth would
have made a point of calling on Mr Smith as soon as possible after the
letter was published and seeking to make contact with his friends. In the
absence of Gallup Poll data a century ago, it is impossible to measure
how widely such anti-collectivist and 'Tory' attitudes were held among
working people. However, common sense and history suggest that they
were probably more widely represented than the optimistic or 'infantile'
left deviation from the main collectivist tradition.

The only expression of 'left deviation' which looks now as if it might
have modified collectivist positions is Guild Socialism. It swept on to the
stage and, perhaps more crucially, into Fabian Society committee rooms,
where it stayed for a decade or so from 1912. It thus coincided more or
less with a period of considerable ferment in working-class politics: pre-
war syndicalism; the shop stewards movement of the war itself;
working-class support for Lenin's revolution; the 'revolt on the Clyde',
in which the small, militant Marxist element in the working-class
coalition probably reached the high water mark of its popular support.
The impact of the Guild Socialists was almost certainly enhanced by the
comparative turmoil of the times.

The extent to which Guild Socialism might have modified traditional
collectivism can be clearly defined. Guild Socialists had no quarrel with
the demand for the public *ownership* of the means of production – by

---

* Sidney Pollard, 'Nineteenth Century Co-operation: From Community
Building to Shopkeeping', *Essays in Labour History in Memory of G. D. H.
Cole*, ed. Asa Briggs and John Saville, Macmillan, London, 1967, p. 100.

this time a long standing commitment of all three main elements in the working-class coalition. What they challenged was the orthodoxy of state (bureaucratic) administration of industry. They sought a kind of bottom-upwards system of workers' management and control on a democratic, though union-linked, basis. In today's terms their aim was an organization on Yugoslav lines, though they would almost certainly have rejected the role which the Yugoslavs have assigned to the market.

The chief expositor of Guild Socialism was G. D. H. Cole. His wife Margaret, who was very much involved, has given a fascinating account of the conflict between Cole's Guild Socialism and the orthodox bureaucratic position of the Webbs in her *Story of Fabian Socialism*. Having explained how the Guild Socialists advocated that 'the organization of production should be in the hands of 'guilds of producers run on democratic lines' she goes on:*

> But to the leading collectivists, Webb and Pease in particular, the very notion of management of industry by the workers engaged in it was at that date intolerable, savouring of the many Victorian enterprises in Co-operative Production which, according to them, had either failed disastrously or turned into little closed corporations not differing in any essential way from capitalism.

In a revealing passage Margaret Cole offers this explanation:

> The Webbs had a fundamental faith in the civil servant and the trained administrator; they were natural bureaucrats in the best sense of the word and admitted it. Beatrice said they were Bs, benevolent, bourgeois and bureaucratic, contrasting with As who were aristocratic, anarchist and arrogant – and they were perhaps more than they realised, distrustful of the common man's ability to take important decisions unless he was wisely guided by his superiors and presented with simple and definite choices – at election time for example. 'A discreetly regulated freedom', was a frequent phrase of Sidney's which particularly exasperated the opposition.

But Margaret Cole is nothing if not balanced:

> The Guild socialists, on the other hand, displayed an equally naive belief in the virtues of trade unionists – at least of such as were not hide-bound reactionary officials – and of factory representatives – which they would probably have come to revise if the movement had lasted longer than it did.

---

* Margaret Cole, *The Story of Fabian Socialism*, Heinemann, London, 1961, p. 148.

Furthermore the guild socialists were most of them young, energetic, intellectually very able and articulate, with a strong dash of anarchism in their make-up ... Beatrice's diaries display considerable resentment at their shocking behaviour. 'Freely laughing at ourselves' which Shaw had recorded as a merit of Fabians, did not, she felt, include undergraduate horseplay. They for their part regarded the Webbs as 'pestilent old obscurantists'.

The Story of Fabian Socialism is a most valuable source for any understanding of the Guild Socialists not only because of this account of their debate with the Webbs. For it also suggests their links with other groups which espoused revolution or change. Within the working-class movement the Guild Socialists attempted*

via the trade unions and particularly via their shopfloor based institutions, workshop committees and shop stewards, pit committees and check-weighmen and their like to marry the workers' control theories of the Syndicalists and Industrial Unionists with what its leaders considered worth-while preserving in the orthodox collectivist demand for the public ownership of the means of production, distribution and exchange.

There were also links, if lesser ones, with tendencies outside the working-class movement. They were 'influenced to a greater or lesser degree by a yearning for the status society of the Middle Ages, as recreated above all by William Morris, by the pluralist political philosophers such as J. N. Figgis and by the vision of an individualist peasant proprietor "distributivist" type of society preached principally by Hilaire Belloc and G. K. Chesterton.' It is partly because of these links outside the working-class movement that the Guild Socialists seem relevant to the current revival of interest on the Right in the potential of co-operative production.

Both in the Fabian Society and in the wider Labour movement the Guild Socialists lost their argument with the Webbs. After 1918 they, and Cole in particular, were briefly associated with the short-lived and unsuccessful Building Guilds – and never really survived their collapse. Margaret Cole, however, puts the effective end of their influence rather earlier and ascribes it to a different cause.†

It was the Russian Revolution itself [she writes] which soon spelt the end of guild socialism as an organised movement. Immediately the

---

* *Ibid*, p. 147.
† *Ibid*., p. 185.

Russian factory workers did in fact take over control of factories, and the resultant chaos was so disastrous that the Bolsheviks quickly put a stop to it and introduced centralised discipline.

It is really only now clear that the debate between the Webbs and the Guild Socialists was based on a misunderstanding of the objective requirements of successful factory production. For those requirements include the need for both the consent and the ultimate control and responsibility of the shop floor on the one hand, and the need for efficient management on the other. The Webbs saw the second and not the first; the Guild Socialists saw the first and not the second. Given the half century it has taken for a consensus to emerge it would be absurd to blame either party.

Though briefly the most important and influential, the Guild Socialists are not the only examples of a libertarian Left deviation in the history of the British Labour movement. To some extent, though not in their support for state ownership, they were the carriers of old anarchist ideas from the late nineteenth century. Their rather ill-defined belief in bottom-upwards industrial democracy and workers' control passed on to the Independent Labour Party (ILP). This last tradition survived, though with perhaps more eloquence than support, even in the 1970s.

The British anarchist tradition is chiefly worth recalling because of the long, if accidental, association with it of that outstanding anarchist, Prince Peter Kropotkin. For thirty years Kropotkin was based in Britain, from 1886 until his final return to Russia following Lenin's revolution. He found asylum here as a refugee – in the days when Home Office policies were so marvellously less illiberal than they have since become. So attractive is he that there is an obvious danger of exaggerating his influence, but there is no doubt that he was respected in both intellectual and working-class circles. He addressed the Durham Miners' Gala on at least one occasion, and was described by Bernard Shaw as having the appearance and character of a 'shepherd on the delectable mountains'. He became so respectable that he was commissioned to write the definitive article on 'anarchism' for *Encyclopaedia Britannica*. Yet his influence on the British Labour movement in general and on the Fabian Society in particular seems to have been modest. Certainly little attention was paid to his warnings about state capitalism – which seem nothing if not prophetic today: 'State capitalism', he wrote in his *Britannica* article, 'would only increase the power of bureaucracy and capitalism; true progess lies in the direction of decentralisation.'

As with Kropotkin, so with the libertarian socialists more generally. Their views are so attractive that there is a danger of assuming that they have been much more influential than the facts allow. Take the following, quoted by the labour historian Walter Kendall (in *Workers' Participation and Workers' Control; Some Aspects of British Experience*) from evidence to the 1919 Sankey Commission on the Mines, on behalf of the Northumberland mineworkers by William Straker their Agent:*

> In the past workers have thought that if they could secure higher wages and conditions they would be content. Employers have thought that if they granted these things workers ought to be contented. Wages and conditions have improved but the discontent and unrest have not disappeared. Many good people have come to the conclusion that working people are so unreasonable that it is useless trying to satisfy them. The fact is that the unrest is deeper than the pounds shillings and pence, necessary as they are. The root of the matter is the straining of the spirit of man to be free.

Yet it would be wrong to assume that values reflected in Mr Straker's analysis have ever been widely held in the British working-class movement. There has never really been a libertarian faction on its more moderate, less class-struggle oriented wing. Since the collapse of the Guild Socialists it has been the old Independent Labour Party (ILP) at the extreme Left of the spectrum which has been the only organized faction to favour democratic, decentralized industrial arrangements. Already in 1922 we find that the ILP's new constitution called, very much on Guild Socialist lines, for the 'internal management of each industry [to] ... be in the hands of the workers, technical and manual, engaged therein. ....'† Even earlier, in 1919, Fenner Brockway‡ had written that 'capitalism was inefficient but must be replaced not by state directed nationalization but by industrial self-Government.'

An ILP historian has suggested that it was experience during the 1914–18 war which 'caused many of the ILP to adopt a hostile attitude to the centralized state'. There is also evidence that a shared pacifism had brought many of them under the influence of radical Quaker thinking during the First World War. In any case from the end of the war onwards, alongside their sometimes fanatical commitment to the class struggle, there has been a consistent and honourable ILP record of opposition to centralized state bureaucracy and to the institutional forms of the Russian communists in particular. While the Webbs in the middle

---

*Mimeo.
† Robert E. Dowse, *Left in the Centre; The Independent Labour Party 1893–1940*, Longmans, London, 1966, p. 65.
‡ Fenner Brockway, *Labour Leader*, 6 May 1920 and quoted in Dowse, *op.cit.*, p. 67.

1930s were writing their laudatory account of the new Soviet state, James Maxton and the ILP were denouncing the Moscow trials with extraordinary vehemence.

In the 1970s one of the most articulate and persuasive representatives of this old libertarian Left and ILP tradition is Walter Kendall; by all accounts he is also a man of courage. One particular occasion when he showed his courage was at the Annual Conference of the Institute for Workers' Control (IWC) in 1975. The event coincided with the high-water mark of the influence of the Portuguese communist party in Lisbon. The country's main socialist newspaper had just been closed down and delegates to the IWC conference were evidently anxious to express their opinions about it. By all accounts Kendall was almost alone – and very much in the ILP tradition – when he denounced the closure of the newspaper as an act of communist censorship.

Kendall's position in the current debate on industrial arrangements is, however, much more relevant than his brave stand against censorship in Lisbon. For a man of impeccably Left and working-class credentials, his attitudes are full of delightful surprises. Take the following, for example, from his address to the second International Conference on Self-Management held at Cornell in 1974:

> If all that is required of socialism is ownership of property by a self-producing oligarchical elite, then the Catholic Church has been a socialist institution for 20 centuries. ... If all that is required for socialism is production according to plan, for use and not for profit, under the supervision of an authoritarian command structure, then the prison workshop is the proper prototype of a socialist community.

Kendall is clear that whatever else socialism means to him, it does not mean the kind of arrangements 'for use and not for profit, under the supervision of an authoritarian command structure' which are represented in today's Britain not only by prison workshops but also, for example, by the direct labour departments of the local authorities and (to some extent) by the nationalized industries.

What is particularly refreshing about Kendall is his commitment to both socialism amd freedom. In his ILP pamphlet *State Ownership Workers' Control and Socialism*, published in 1975, he wrote:

> the socialist criticism of bourgeois democracy is not that it provides too much freedom but too little. This involves the need for socialists to face the problem of bureaucracy in mass organisations.

What is more, and in common with only a handful of socialists until very recent times, Kendall has perceived that 'facing the problem of bureaucracy' involves at least some revision of traditional left-wing hostility to the market. He shows this in the following passage from the same·pamphlet:

> The existence of market forces became the Bolshevik equivalent of the Christian doctrine of original sin. To the extent that the infinitely large amount of up to date information can never (even at totally excessive cost) ever be available in a complex economy at a single plan centre, the controlled socialist market fulfils a useful and invaluable function. Soviet mathematicians are reported as estimating that using only desk calculators it would take some 30,000 man years to produce an internally consistent plan for the Russian economy. An academician has claimed that even if one million high speed electronic computers were harnessed to the task, optimal planning of the economy from the centre would still be beyond their capacity.

Kendall, the ILP, other libertarian and anarchist elements in the working-class tradition, Cole's Guild Socialism, are all worth bringing to the centre of the stage in the debate about industrial arrangements – but not because they have been influential; they have not. The practical influence has all been in the other direction – towards bureaucratic socialism, and dismissive of, if not hostile to, any real experiments in industrial democracy. Yet these somewhat isolated voices are worth reproducing for a rather different reason. They can remind the young radical Left that to oppose bureaucratic socialism is not necessarily to betray the working-class movement.

For rather similar reasons, it is worth recalling the attitudes of liberal economists to what in the eighteenth century were called 'associations of labourers'. They, too, have not been influential. Here again they can serve as a reminder to the young radical Right that to support bottom-upwards industrial democracy is not by itself to betray the great liberal tradition. Thanks to some excellent recent work by Professor Derek Jones,* a survey of the relevant evidence is available.

To begin with, there is the fairly well-known, and perhaps suspiciously prophetic assertion of John Stuart Mill,† when still a young man, that: 'The relationship of masters and workpeople will be gradually superseded by partnership in one of two forms: in some cases, associations of the labourers with the capitalists; in others and perhaps finally in all, associations of labourers among themselves'. Nor can there be any doubt about the immense moral and social benefits which he

---

* 'British Economic Thought on Association of Labourers 1848–1974', Derek Jones, *Annals of Public and Co-operative Economy*, September, 1976.
† *Ibid.*, p. 2.

believed would flow from the fulfilment of this prediction: 'the emancipation of women', he wrote, 'and co-operative production are, I fully believe, the two great changes which will regenerate society.'*

Because he was 'soft on socialism' – to say nothing of women's liberation – Mill's views may well be dismissed by the radical Right. But Derek Jones has shown that this support for 'associations of labourers' was strongly echoed, even if with important qualifications, by some of the most eminent of the subsequent liberal economists – by Alfred Marshall, and Sir Denis Robertson, to mention only two. The attitudes of people like these cannot be treated with cavalier rejection.

Marshall was perhaps the most explicit. Derek Jones† quotes from a paper, *The Future of the Working Classes*, delivered by Marshall at Cambridge in 1873, in which he expressed the opinion that 'in many industries production would be mainly carried on, as Mr and Mrs Mill have prophesied, by "the association of labourers among themselves on terms of equality, collectively owning the capital with which they carry on their operations, and working under managers elected and removable by themselves".'

It is clear from the evidence quoted by Jones that Sir Denis Robertson's optimism about an industrial future of this kind was slightly more qualified, as is shown in the passage which Jones quotes:‡

Private enterprise will remain the dominant form of organisation; but … we need not despair of witnessing the slow growth of something worth calling freedom in industrial affairs; even if we know that in any society we are likely to live to see old Bill Bailey will continue to think more about his early broccoli than about the mysteries of cost accounting and young Alf Perkins to take more interest in the prospects of Manchester United than those of cotton cultivation in equatorial Africa.

Associations of labourers and production co-operatives evoked more than expressions of sympathy and support. Various specific comparative advantages, particularly associated with labour productivity and a transcending of class conflict, were postulated for them. Jones quotes several important examples such as the following from Mill:§

The other mode in which co-operation tends, still more efficaciously to increase the productiveness of labour, consists in the vast stimulus given to productive energies, by placing the labourers, as a mass, in a

---

* *Ibid.*, p. 3.
† *Ibid.*, p. 5 fn.
‡ *Ibid.*, p. 5 fn.
§ *Ibid.*, p. 7.

relation to their work which would make it their principle and their interest – at present it is neither – to do the utmost instead of the least possible, in exchange for their remuneration.

Mill was clearly very struck by the counterproductive characteristics and the disincentives to team-work in conventional business structures, and by the contrasting opportunities offered by his favoured alternative. Jones fittingly quotes this amplification of his views:*

> the general sentiment of the community, composed of the comrades under whose eyes each person works, would be sure to be in favour of good hard working, and unfavourable to laziness, carelessness and waste. In the present system not only is this not the case, but the public opinion of the workmen class often acts in the very opposite direction: the rules of some trade societies actually forbid their members to exceed a certain standard of efficiency. ... The change from this to a state in which every person would have an interest in rendering every other person as industrious, skilful and careful as possible ... would be a change very much for the better.

And Marshall was evidently very much of the same mind. From a discussion of likely shop-floor attitudes which producer co-operatives would usher in, Jones quotes the following:†

> for their own pecuniary interests and the pride they take in the success of their own business make each of them averse to any shirking of work either by himself or his fellow workmen.

Mill was almost equally explicit about the favourable effects of co-operation in relation to the class struggle. 'Co-operation', Jones quotes him as writing, '... [is] the real and only thorough means of healing the feud between capitalists and labourers'.‡ As for Robertson,§ we can perhaps infer what he thought of capital labour relations under the existing system from his reference to 'capital in the saddle and labour barking when necessary at his heels'. But Jones also quotes him more explicitly on the dangers of keeping labour in a conflict position:¶ 'if this strength is always to be exercised in opposition then the temptation to use it heedlessly will always be great and on occasions irresistible.'

The advantages claimed by this tradition for productive arrangements based on co-operation shade imperceptibly from the economic to the

---

* *Ibid.*, p. 7.
† *Ibid.*, p. 7.
‡ *Ibid.*, p. 9 fn.
§ *Ibid.*, p. 9.
¶ *Ibid.*, p. 12.

moral. Sometimes it is not altogether clear where the first ends and the second begins. Would the transcending of the class war count as a moral or an economic advantage or both? The question is raised by Mill in emphasizing above all the moral advantages:*

> It is scarcely possible to rate too highly this material benefit, which yet is nothing compared with the moral revolution in society that would accompany it: the healing of the standing feud between capital and labour; the transformation of human life from a conflict of classes struggling for opposite interests, to a friendly rivalry in the pursuit of a common good to all; the elevation of the dignity of labour; a new sense of security and independence in the labouring class; and the conversion of every human being's daily occupation into a school of the social sympathies and the practical intelligence.

Yet for all the various advantages – economic, moral, educational, political and in terms of what might be called personal and collective growth – claimed by this tradition for co-operative production, it remains basically pessimistic. Derek Jones has described the tradition, in the round, as being one of 'sympathetic *pessimism*'. Of course a part of that pessimism was empirical. There were many more early failures than early successes among enterprises structured in the way that the tradition favoured; but theoretical difficulties, Jones has reminded us, were identified by the tradition too.

Both this liberal tradition and, much more forcefully, the Webbs argued that enterprises of this kind would be seriously handicapped because of management problems. Indeed, for the Webbs it was a practical impossibility. True to their own self-confessed bourgeois and bureaucratic colours, and to a deep elitism – Sidney Webb apparently talked about control being exercised by an enlightened body of 'Samurai' administrators – they simply asserted that 'No self-governing workshop, no trade union, no professional association, no co-operative society ... has yet made its administration successful on the lines of letting the subordinate employees elect or dismiss the executive officers or managers.'

The sympathetic liberal tradition, though far from believing with the Webbs that the position was hopeless, pointed to various important difficulties. There was an obvious worry about discipline which Professor James Meade expressed well in the early 1970s† 'There is the basic but not strictly economic question whether a workers' co-operative

---

* *Ibid.*, p. 10.
† J. E. Meade, 'The Theory of Labour-managed Firms and Profit Sharing', *Economic Journal*, March, 1972, p. 426, quoted in *ibid.*, p. 16.

organisation is compatible with the maintenance of the discipline needed to ensure the efficient operation of a concern which employs a large body of workers.'

But there were other worries too. Robertson* was concerned that the democratic process might well not throw up the right men: 'it is not easy to bring oneself to vote for the most capable man among one's shopmates as manager, rather than the best talker or the best fellow.' Marshall† was anxious in case smooth management might be thwarted by shop-floor representatives on management committees: 'the fact that the employees on the committee of such a co-operative business are able to hold their own against their managers in matters of the minutest detail, may often go a good long way towards wrecking the concern.'

The list of worries about management, as expressed by this liberal tradition, is still not exhausted. Both management motivation and morale were thought liable to be lower than in conventional capitalist undertakings. Though expressed in theoretical terms there had been some practical experience, even when Mill was writing, to confirm that many of these difficulties had been confronted in fact.

What was more, according to this same tradition, even if a democratic enterprise surmounted management problems it might well face other special disadvantages. Given what was likely to be at best a lukewarm commercial environment, it would face difficulties of market entry; for similar reasons the raising of start-up capital and finance for subsequent expansion could hardly be other than a struggle. There was also the problem of risk: with their savings all concentrated in one venture the worker–owners of a production co-operative might very reasonably be more hesitant about new investments than their capitalist counterparts.

Finally, there is a recurrent theme to the effect that the mass of ordinary working people might not yet be ready to assume the responsibilities which democratic control involved. British workers (like Africans in the 1950s) might not be sufficiently educated to manage self-government. The corollary, of course, was that more resources should be allocated to relevant educational programmes – to Mechanics Institutes for the British workers, just as in the next century to secondary schools for Africans. The liberal tradition was always, of course, most enthusiastic about anything like that.

Yet a belief in the relevance of educational levels, as a key to the success or otherwise of democratic ventures, could be a source of optimism for the future – as well as pointing to an obstacle in the present. Indeed the non-attainment of appropriate educational and

---

* *Ibid.*, p. 13.
† *Ibid.*, p. 13.

maturity levels by ordinary working people could be an explanation of
co-operative failure but at the same time, because remediable, it offered a
ground for hope in the long term. That at any rate is how Marshall
seems to have seen the position. Jones quotes his powerful argument to
this effect:*

> It will be said that such associations [of labourers] have been tried and
> have seldom succeeded. They have not been tried. What have been
> tried are associations among comparatively speaking, uneducated
> men, men who are unable to follow even the financial calculations
> that are required for an extensive and complicated business. What
> have to be tried are associations among men as highly educated as are
> manufacturers now. *Such associations could not but succeed*
> [emphasis mine]; and the capital that belonged to them would run no
> risk of being separated from them.

Notwithstanding this crucial qualification of Marshall (we shall see
later just how important), it is clear that the weight of this sympathetic
liberal tradition is, as Jones contends, pessimistic. 'Yours is a worthy
objective', these liberal economists seem to be saying to the would-be co-
operators, 'but we don't really expect you to succeed, anyway not in
today's world.'

To complete this review of the intellectual, political and commercial
climate in which British democratic enterprises have operated at least up
to 1974, there are two further sources of support. They are the Christian
Socialists (and associated with them an unevenly helpful Quaker
tradition) and the Catholic 'distributism' preached mainly by G. K.
Chesterton and Hilaire Belloc. Although neither has been widely
influential they are none the less interesting.

There are many reasons why the reformist suggestions put forward
by Belloc and Chesterton under the name of distributism were largely
ignored when first published and have since been almost forgotten. The
Pre-Raphaelite outer garments of peasant smocks, the idealized
mediaeval impedimenta of maypole and village tavern with which their
proposed reforms seemed inextricably tangled, can only have
discouraged 'political economists' from taking them seriously. Then too
there is a pronounced whiff of small shopkeeper 'Poujadisme'; both
socialist collectivism and big business seem to be rejected with equal
ferocity. It is, too, as if some positive encounters with aristocratic
families on the one hand and some negative experiences with Jewish
financiers on the other, have tended to warp their thinking into
snobbish, anti-semitic moulds.

* *Ibid.*, p. 18.

Yet the central idea embedded in Belloc's *Essay on the Restoration of Property*, published by the Distributist League in 1936, seems far from irrelevant in the current debate. He writes there about 'spreading the moral effect of economic independence', and his obvious concern is to reintroduce into industrial society the sturdy yeoman values associated with peasant proprietors. Though he does not, so far as I can discover, use the phrase 'self-reliance', it is a fair guess that this is what he had in mind.

This 'distributist' thinking seems to have envisaged something much more like a unit trust type participation of working people in industrial ownership than direct worker ownership in democratically controlled enterprises. And yet it does point out a question which the Left, in its proper concern for the redistribution of wealth, has always tended to ignore. Should what is redistributed from the rich be channelled, in small parcels, into the personal accounts of the poor − instead of becoming, as the Left has always argued, the indivisible 'social wealth of the community'? Just as most working people seem to prefer higher personal income to increases in the social wage, may they not also prefer increases in their own personal wealth to a corresponding advance in what is socially owned?

Belloc and Chesterton had contacts with the Guild Socialists and G. D. H. Cole. It would be nice to find − though I have not been able to do so − that they offered support to the Building Guilds during their brief existence in the early 1920s. However, their relevance here is mainly as trenchant critics of social or public ownership of wealth and as advocates of an alternative which did not simply ignore the private ownership interests of ordinary working people.

The Christian Socialists, who sprang to life as an organized group after the collapse of British Chartism in 1848, were, of course, very much more high-minded, earnest and teetotal in their approach than Chesterton and Belloc. The leading figures, F. D. Maurice and Charles Kingsley, were Anglican clergymen; associated with them were church-going members of the liberal professions like the two barristers, E. V. Neale and Thomas Hughes (the author of *Tom Brown's Schooldays*). But they were also more active and industrious than Chesterton and Belloc. Inspired in part by the experimental workers' associations in the revolutionary Paris of early 1848, they helped to set up a number of those 'Victorian enterprises in co-operative production' which the Webbs were to disparage so strongly. Along with John Stuart Mill they must also be credited with having attracted Parliamentary support for the Industrial and Provident Societies Act 1852 which, among other things, gave the protection of limited liability to co-operative enterprises.

All or most of the enterprises promoted by the Christian Socialists ended in failure. It is not altogether surprising given the stated aim of Maurice in setting up one of them, a 'tailors' association'.* 'To call men to repentance first', he wrote, 'but then also ... to give them the opportunity of showing their repentance and bringing forth fruits of it. This is my idea of a tailors' association.' Though it is easy to smile at the idea of a mass repentance by the 'sons of toil', yet the Christian Socialists undoubtedly left a mark – and it survives today.

For it is far from fanciful to see a connection between the ideals of the Christian Socialists in the middle of the last century and the actions of people like Spedan Lewis and Ernest Bader (and the Bewley family of progressive Quakers in Dublin) who have handed over flourishing capitalist enterprises to their workforces in more recent times. Because of his explicit religious objectives, and his attempts to encourage religious observances by the work people, the connection with Ernest Bader is particularly strong. And if the John Lewis Partnership is excluded, Scott-Bader is, of course, often held up as the only good – commercially the only really successful – example of the self-governing enterprises in Britain today.

Yet as with Kropotkin, so it is in general with the motley array of splinter groups and divergent factions which we have been reviewing – the ILP, the Guild Socialists, the sympathetic pessimists of the liberal tradition, the distributists and the Christian Socialists. They are on the whole so much more attractive and their ideas so much more refreshing than those of either the capitalist or the bureaucratic socialist mainstream, that there is a danger of exaggerating their influence. Compared with the vast artillery batteries and massed infantry battalions of the organized working class and the opposing fortresses of organized capitalism, it is clear that they are but 'dwarfish' skirmishing forces on the flanks of the great class battlefield – or on bridle-paths away from the march of history. Equally important, and until Mr Wedgwood Benn's appointment as Industry Secretary in 1974, these voices had never been heard at the Cabinet table. There were, to be fair, a few contracts for the manufacture of army boots thrown by the Civil Service to a handful of boot and shoe co-ops in the 1880s, but for the rest the divergent democratic enterprises, like the voices which have spoken up for them, have been officially ignored. This is the unpromising environment for the experience of democratic enterprises in Britain which is examined in the next chapter.

---

* Raymond Postgate, 'Christian Socialism', in *Encyclopaedia Britannica*, 14th ed., 1929.

5

The old British producer co-ops

How have independent, democratically owned and controlled enterprises fared in Britain's unpromising – and unsupportive – environment? Though the old conventional wisdom may have acknowledged a few exceptions – with the corollary that special factors both explain success and preclude replication – the record has been seen as uniformly depressing, if not disastrous. Essentially the conventional wisdom has followed the assessment of Beatrice Webb (then Beatrice Potter): that such enterprises have either failed commercially or failed to remain democratic (or both). An amplification of this assessment, quoted by Derek Jones,* appears in *A Constitution for the Socialist Commonwealth of Great Britain*, published jointly by the Webbs in 1921.

> Democracies of producers, as all experience shows ... have hitherto failed, with almost complete uniformity, whenever they have themselves sought to win and organise the instruments of production. In the relatively few instances in which such enterprises have not succumbed as business concerns, they have ceased to be democracies of producers managing their own work, and have become in effect associations of capitalists ... making profits for themselves by the employment at wages of workers outside the association.

Since democratic enterprises do exist and since it can be fairly convincingly shown that they have tended, anyway since 1918, to become more rather than less democratic, the assessment of the Webbs may be provisionally treated as just plain wrong. On the other hand a fairly dismissive assessment might still be correct on balance. 'Let us accept,' a fair minded observer might conclude, 'that the Webbs were formally wrong. But the record still shows more failure than success. And quite honestly there just hasn't been enough success for reasonable men to look in this direction for their models of industrial reform.'

There is no effective short method of overturning such a position. All

---

* Derek Jones, 'British Producer Co-operatives', in Ken Coates (ed.), *The New Worker Co-operatives*, published for the Institute of Workers' Control by Spokesman Books, Nottingham, 1976, p. 48.

one can do is to re-examine actual experience. But to be re-examined it needs to be broken down. Excluding Utopian Owenite experiments and more or less informal (but often very successful) taxi-cab, fishing boat co-ops and the like there are three different experiences which need to be looked at:

1 The old 'associations of labourers' and producer co-ops, all or almost all of them founded before the First World War.* These are the enterprises with which the Webbs were chiefly concerned. Roughly a dozen of them survive in more or less flourishing shape. I shall refer to enterprises in this category started after 1880 as the 'cloth cap' co-ops.

2 Enterprises linked with the Industrial Common Ownership Movement (ICOM). Most, but not all, are companies which started, like Scott-Bader or Bewley's Cafés, as conventional capitalist undertakings then adopted a more democratic structure. They are mainly a post Second World War phenomenon. If companies outside ICOM, but with characteristics similar to those of ICOM members, are included (like the John Lewis Partnership and Airflow Developments in High Wycombe), there were roughly a dozen operating in the late 1970s.

3 The experience of enterprises which have been salvaged – or salvaged themselves – from the wreckage of capitalist failure. The most famous are the two surviving 'Wedgwood Benn' co-ops, Kirkby Manufacturing and Engineering and Meriden Motorcycles Ltd, but there have certainly been others in the 1970s, though it is not clear how many have survived.

Looked at from a standpoint 125 years after the enactment of the first enabling legislation, the Industrial and Provident Societies Act of 1852, the experience of the old British producer co-ops can be divided into two main phases. The first phase stretches back into the period before the 1850s to earlier Owenite origins and can be somewhat arbitrarily ended in the early 1880s. It is characterized by ambitious (even Utopian) goals, considerable confusion about structural models and objective requirements, many false starts and by a few quite limited successes. By the beginning of the second phase a more or less workable model has been evolved and goals have been drastically reduced. There is a minor explosion in the number of new enterprises and a respectable number survive. However, the mix of forces and opportunities responsible for

---

* The only major qualification is the short-lived, early 1920s, Builders' Guilds experience. The only minor ones are the Stafford Shoe Co-op and the Watford Printers Co-op established between the wars.

this modest flowering was effectively spent by the outbreak of the First World War. Thereafter, with the exception of the Building Guilds, there are no major initiatives to start new co-ops of this type. On the other hand, with a surprising stubbornness and quality of survival, a fair proportion of the old foundations remain in business.

An important type of false start in the first phase can be seen in what Holyoake, the eminent early historian of co-operation, called the 'world amending' goals of the first co-operators. The previous Owenite experiments – at New Harmony and elsewhere – had been similarly motivated. The classic example is provided by the Leeds Redemptionist Society founded in the late 1840s. The Society's aim was the establishment inside Great Britain of 'colonies' in which member–settlers would live together and engage in productive work, both agricultural and industrial on a co-operative basis and in a new way. The Leeds Group was not the only redemptionist society founded in the late 1840s, but it was the only one to get beyond the discussion stage. A small estate was acquired in South Wales and for a few years a colony of settlers worked the land and made a precarious living. They had little experience, the income was insufficient to pay interest on the loans with which the estate had been purchased, and the experiment soon collapsed. Clearly it was both over ambitious and insufficiently hard-nosed.

A similar analysis may be applied to explain the widespread failure of a series of initiatives launched in the early 1850s by the Christian Socialists. Sidney Pollard puts it this way:*

> The divines and lawyers who undertook to change society by means
> of co-operative workshops were not only remarkably innocent of any
> knowledge of the social sciences or of the life of the industrial
> proletariat ... but even of earlier and contemporary co-operative
> efforts.

We can get a vivid, not to say hair-raising picture of what was liable to happen as a result of Christian Socialist initiative from the report prepared in 1851 by the Society for Promoting Working Men's Associations, quoted by Benjamin Jones,† and later by Mavis Kirkham as follows:

---

* Sidney Pollard, 'Nineteenth Century Co-operation: From Community Building to Shopkeeping', *Essays in Labour History 1886–1923 in Memory of G. D. H. Cole*, ed. Asa Briggs and John Saville, Macmillan, London, 1967, p. 93.

† Benjamin Jones, *Co-operative Production*, Clarendon Press, Oxford, 1894, vol. 1, p. 121.

In the first 9 months of our life as a society we set up 3 sets of
shoemakers in association, supplying in 2 instances the whole of the
funds, in the other all but £5. None of the men were picked; we
accepted them just as they came to us. We gave them absolute self-
Government, merely reserving to ourselves certain rights of
interference in any cases of dispute or mismanagement while any
capital remained to us. Each one of these associations quarrelled with
and turned out its original manager within six months; one, the West-
End Bootmakers, went to pieces altogether before 9 months had gone.
The other two struggled on until the beginning of the next year, never
paying their way and continually quarrelling. ... Working men in
general are not fit for association. They come into it with the idea that
it is to fill their pockets and lighten their work at once, and that every
man in an association is to be his own master. They found their
mistake in the first month or two and then set to quarrelling with
everybody connected with the association but more especially with
the manager; and after much blood has been raised the association
breaks up insolvent.

In this case, quite apart from unbusinesslike and over-optimistic
assumptions about human nature, we can identify specific and practical
shortcomings which will crop up again and again: wholly insufficient
preparation and general indiscipline associated with a failure to
recognize the need, within a democratic enterprise, for separate and
semi-autonomous management functions.

A quite different variety of false start is best represented by the
experience of the textile manufacturing co-op founded by the Rochdale
pioneers (and which I have already mentioned briefly). Here is how the
story of this enterprise has been most recently recounted:*

The Rochdale Pioneers established a co-operative cotton factory,
known as the Rochdale Co-operative Manufacturing Society, in 1854.
Despite a severe shortage of capital they were able to start operations
by leasing a single room in an established mill. Most of the
shareholders worked in the Co-operative. The few non-working
members were Rochdale pioneers who had altruistic motives for
joining. The few non-workers were given full and equal voting rights
in accordance with Rochdale principles. Initially the 100 or so
workers in the co-operative were all shareholders.
    In 1857 and 1858 the cotton market suffered a severe price slump.

---

* Andrew McGregor in 'Capital, Rent Extraction and the Survival of the
  Producer Co-operative' (Cornell University duplicated thesis, June 1974).

Despite shortages in capital the co-operative was able to survive the period relatively well. An important factor seems to have been its ability to maintain output. Its adjustment to adverse prices was not through reduced employment but rather through reductions in members' incomes. To quote the *Rochdale Observer*:

> The disastrous years of 1857 and 1858 sorely tried the infant establishment; and although during a period of 15 weeks no sales were effected, or sales only to a trifling amount, yet the hands were never put on short hours, although other mills in the town yielded in this respect to the pressure of the times.

In 1859 the depression in the cotton market was replaced by a boom. The co-operative's record during the depression, coupled with the boom, made it an attractive investment proposition. It began to attract conventional investors, who were not involved in the co-operative movement and did not wish to work in the mill. Furthermore these shareholders were encouraged to join the co-operative to finance a new £34,000 mill.

By the end of 1860 the co-operative had 1,400 shareholders of whom only 200 worked in the co-operative. Thus within a year the co-operative was transformed in principle into a joint stock company. In practice it also operated in an identical fashion to a joint stock company today. The previous policy of distributing part of any trading surplus to labour was abolished. Workers now received just the going wage. All management committees were made up exclusively of non-working shareholders. An important Rochdale Pioneer, Abraham Greenwood, described what had occurred:

> It was the success of the society which attracted to it persons who only cared for the eternal 'divi'. These people brought into the society their money very rapidly thus raising the number of shareholders from 200 or 300 to 1400. It was the new shareholding element which swamped the original promoters.

Here is in the first place, an example of what the Webbs stigmatized as 'degeneration', or less emotively, an external take-over. In principle there is no reason why a co-operative should not protect itself against such risks by restricting votes to worker members. At the time, however, such a restriction was thought to conflict with the fundamental 'open door' policy of the Rochdale pioneers. It was not perceived that while such a policy makes excellent sense for a consumer co-op, it is liable to be self-defeating if applied to production societies without modification. Yet this was only appreciated much later, and outside Britain, by the Mondragon industrial co-ops. They alone have made a success of reconciling a modified 'open door' policy with the need to restrict votes to working members.

McGregor's account of Rochdale suggests a further point. The new shareholders, he tells us, were '*encouraged* to join the co-operative to finance a new £34,000 mill'. The implication is clear. The founder members could not raise that kind of money from their own resources and were not in a position to borrow it from a bank. G. D. H. Cole saw precisely this problem of finance as one of the main reasons why many of the early producer co-ops 'degenerated' into joint stock companies.* And he explicitly includes the case of textile production as an important example.

Judged by results the launching, during the first phase, of enterprises in various branches of the metal trades – as well as a series of co-operative type mining ventures – must be seen as another false start. Benjamin Jones,† the most comprehensive early chronicler of producer co-operation, introduces his chapter on the former with the sentence: 'The history of societies started since 1862 in different branches of the iron trade is mostly one of disaster.' His terse heading for the latter is 'Colliery Failures'.

The most ambitious project in these two sectors, the Ouseburn Co-operative Engineering Works in Newcastle, was also the most disastrous. Started in 1871 following the great Tyneside strike for a nine hour working day, the works were finally forced into liquidation in 1875. Beatrice Webb claims that the trade unions lost £60,000 as a result of the collapse. Jones implies that the losses sustained by the retail and wholesale co-operative societies which had backed the venture were above £25,000. This perhaps *par excellence* is the example of 'Working Class Ltd'.

There is a clear suggestion in Jones's account of sharp practice by the Rev Dr Rutherford, the prime mover behind Ouseburn who became in effect its chairman and managing director. Even without malpractice the project could have had only one outcome. Its story is a cautionary tale of how enterprises of this kind should *not* be launched and managed. By his own admission Dr Rutherford knew nothing about engine-making. More important there seems to have been no real preparatory work, no costings, no market study; most of the early contracts seem to have been priced well below actual costs. Above all, the commitment of the workforce was never seriously engaged in the success of the business.

---

* *A Century of Co-operation*, Allen & Unwin for the Co-operative Union, London, 1945.

† Benjamin Jones, *Co-operative Production*, Clarendon Press, Oxford, 1894, vol. 2, p. 436.

58   *The old British producer co-ops*

Very likely they never came to think of it as in any genuine way 'theirs'. At least twice there were disputes with the workforce about deductions from wages to finance compulsory personal shares.

It can now be seen that the project was far too ambitious. The labour force was built up from nothing to 800 in less than six months. There is no record of how the key management posts were filled – apart from Dr Rutherford's own top position. But even with the best management imaginable it would have been virtually impossible to break into a tough and sophisticated market like marine engines at the pace which the labour force build-up required.

No single new co-operative production venture on the scale of Ouseburn has been started from scratch in Britain since the failure of the Rev. Dr Rutherford's project in 1875. The lessons of that false start do seem to have been learnt. Certainly, the losses sustained in it by the consumer co-ops and the trade unions are partly responsible for the cautious policies which they have adopted in their lending to producer co-ops ever since.

There is no need to elaborate the point. Apart from considerations of capital availability, which Cole emphasizes, by the end of the 1870s it must have become clear to the producer co-ops that new large scale works, particularly in sophisticated or specially competitive areas, were beyond the resources which could be mustered. No projects in mining are recorded beyond the 1870s. In metal working the two enterprises which survived for any length of time, Wolverhampton Platelock Makers and Walsall Locks, were at the dwarfish end of the sector. To its astonishing credit Walsall Locks, which was started following a prolonged strike, survives in the late 1970s.

So at the end of the 1870s, as the first phase of producer co-operation came to an end, a number of negative lessons stood out pretty clearly. The founding of redemptionist colonies as part of a world amendment programme was unlikely to meet with success. Nor was the endowment by philanthropic Christian Socialists of very small-scale artisan centres – tailors' and cobblers' shops, for example. At the other end of the scale, ambitious new projects in engineering, iron and steel and coal mining, had proved failures. Meanwhile one of the few real successes – and one of a minority which had resulted from a genuine and committed working-class initiative – the Rochdale Textile Mill, had degenerated into a joint stock company through faulty rules and a need to finance the expansion which followed success.

Particularly in the light of other evidence, the working-class initiative behind the Rochdale Textile Mill seems worth special emphasis. Workforce commitment is obviously a vital ingredient in a co-operative enterprise. But the key point can perhaps best be expressed in the negative. Experience shows that this commitment is rarely achieved when the initiative comes from outside the main working group. That helps to explain the fatality rate of those Christian Socialist sponsored ventures. Conversely, as the French experience shows, very similar enterprises started by French artisans enjoyed a real measure of success.

If the first phase of British producer co-operative experience is marked by false starts and by failed – sometimes wrong-headed or over ambitious – experiments, the second is one of concentration on a quite narrow range of less ambitious industries and of 'durable' (G. D. H. Cole's expression) if unspectacular success. Three industries, clothing, printing and boots and shoes, account for the great majority. Apart from these, there were fairly numerous ventures in co-operative building and construction with some temporary successes. And along quite different lines of business there was a handful of thriving enterprises of which Walsall Locks is the best example. However, clothing, printing and boots and shoes never seem to have accounted for less than 60 per cent of the enterprises in existence at any one time.

The 1880s and 1890s are the decades of expansion, and more especially the years from 1885 onwards. Derek Jones, who has made the most thorough study, gives figures for producer co-operatives in England and Wales at selected dates between 1880 and 1900 (see Table 5.1).

TABLE 5.1   Producer co-operatives in England and Wales, 1881–93

Year	No.	Year	No.
1881	13	1894	108
1885	27	1895	103
1890	74	1897	112*
1893	113	1900	105

* A total of 112 was again reached in 1903; thereafter though the decline is quite gradual it was never reversed.

Source: 'British Producer Co-operatives', in Ken Coates (ed.), *The New Worker Co-operatives*, Spokesman Books, Nottingham, 1976, p. 36.

To understand the context of that expansion in the 1880s and 1890s we must refer back briefly to the original Rochdale pioneers. There is no question that they saw themselves as promoting co-operation among consumers and producers alike. If anything, in the very early days their long-term goals had more to do with production than consumption: consumer co-operation was chiefly seen as a first step towards the more difficult production co-operation. In short, working people would learn the secrets of shopkeeping but very much with a view to running factory enterprises afterwards. On the other hand, the very success of the consumer stores soon started to colour that original thinking. Once there was a choice between the two there would be an obvious tendency to expand the consumer stores because that was an area in which success had already been achieved. Nevertheless, until the 1880s the movement as a whole remained committed to supporting both kinds of co-operation on a more or less even-handed basis.

Derek Jones has suggested that the movement's commitment to an even-handed policy remained formally intact till the Co-operative Congress at Dewsbury in 1888.* But he has also pointed out that it began to be eroded *de facto* when the wholesale co-operatives, in effect federations of the consumer societies, decided to go in for production on their own account in 1873. He has argued further that the producer interests in the movement clearly recognized the direction in which it was heading when they set up their own, semi-autonomous, Co-operative Production Federation (CPF) in 1882. This, the CPF, is effectively the federal body of what I call the 'cloth cap' co-ops.

There is no reason to challenge Jones's account, but its implications suggest a curious coincidence in time. There is the final swing away by the main movement from its old even-handed policy to one of giving priority to consumer co-operation. At the same time there is the surge of maximum expansion among the producer societies in the second half of the 1880s. Both are preceded by the establishment of the semi-autonomous CPF in 1882. We might conclude that the gain of having their own agency was more important to the producer co-ops than their loss of support in the main movement. This conclusion is supported by the fact that the key figure at the CPF during those years was a most dynamic individual, Thomas Blanford. On the other hand, we cannot be sure that if the main movement had continued to be as enthusiastic about producer as about consumer co-operation the increase in the number of producer societies would not have been larger than it in fact was. A diverse array of events and initiatives lies behind the new societies formed during this period of expansion (see Table 5.2).

Benjamin Jones,† explains the work people's initiative behind the Northamptonshire Productive Society established at Wollaston as having been due to dissatisfaction with prevailing wage rates. He also says that the group had the extraordinary good fortune to secure a government order for army boots, sufficient to keep them going for

---

* Derek Jones, *op. cit.*
† Benjamin Jones, *op. cit.*, vol. 2, p. 402.

twelve months, before they actually started production.

TABLE 5.2

Date founded	Enterprise	Origin
1881	Northamptonshire Productive Soc. (NPS)	Group of boot and shoe workers
1886	Finedon Productive Soc.	Disfavoured workers at NPS
1886	Equity Shoes	Strike at Co-op Wholesale Society
1887	Leicester Co-op Printers	Trade union and co-op initiative
1888	Kettering Book and Shoe Co-op	Co-op store
1893	Kettering Clothing Co-op	Capitalist discrimination

Finedon is only a few miles from Wollaston in the same county. The interesting factor about this case is that it points to the second kind of 'degeneration' against which the Webbs vented their displeasure. The original Wollaston men had evidently hired their neighbours from Finedon to work simply for wages in their co-operative venture. They had refused to admit the Finedon men to membership thus turning themselves, as Beatrice Webb correctly pointed out, into a group of 'small masters'. Understandably, the Finedon men eventually voted with their feet and set up shop on their own.

The origin of Equity Shoes is of particular interest. For here we have an enterprise only slightly less venerable than Walsall Locks, which was also started as a result of a strike. But the strike was not against capitalists – it was against an enterprise belonging to the consumer societies. To be fair to the Co-operative Wholesale Society in which the strike took place, it seems to have made no attempt to stop the formation of a rival business – and even to have given some help. Moreover, the consumer co-ops provided Equity Shoes with its market for many years later.

The roots of Leicester Co-operative Printers are different again. It resulted from initiatives taken not so much by ordinary people themselves as by local working-class institutions. Its establishment was preceded by a series of meetings in Leicester between local trade unions and the flourishing (mainly consumer) co-operatives. In a detailed study of the society, Mavis Kirkham brings out the deliberate and semi-ideological character of the initiative.* The objective was in part the narrower one of drawing the co-operative and trade union movements in Leicester closer together: 'the best mode', a speaker told one of the preparatory meetings, 'by which co-operators and trade unions can be

* Mavis Kirkham, 'Industrial Producer Co-operation in Great Britain: Three Case Studies' (Sheffield University, unpublished thesis, 1971).

brought into closer union is by establishing co-operative industries in which both parties can take equal rights in management.' Wider ideological objectives were also involved. As one participant in the initiative later saw it:

> the continued disputes between employer and employed, between capitalists and workers (of which trade unions can produce much evidence) show that some different mode of solving the problem of capital versus labour must be applied. Co-operative production under the opinion of the most eminent economists promises the best solutions to these difficulties. Under this class of association the Leicester Co-operative Printing Society was established.

What its origin chiefly demonstrates, however, is that the Leicester Co-operative Printing Society should probably not be counted as a genuine example of bottom-upwards industrial democracy. It resembles, on a local level, those German 'commonweal' enterprises – like the Bank für Gemeinwirtschaft – which are owned and controlled by working-class institutions and which, for that reason, are sometimes assumed to be examples of industrial democracy. This impression is confirmed by the enterprise's constitution under which only a minority of its nine directors – 'a minimum of one and a maximum of three' – were to be elected by its workforce. The majority were to be chosen by outside institutions, the trade unions and the consumer co-operatives. Mavis Kirkham's study also shows that within this control framework the management practice of the enterprise was strictly orthodox.

The two Kettering productive societies – Kettering Boot and Shoe and Kettering Clothing – both ultimately owed their origin to the existence of a prosperous consumer store in the town. The store which finally 'made it' in Kettering had been founded in 1866, after a number of earlier failures. By the 1880s it was operating on a strongly profitable basis and a number of its more dynamic members, particularly a Mr W. Ballard, the Secretary, evidently became well disposed to the idea of using some of the profits to encourage co-operative production. Mr Ballard is quoted as saying forcefully that it would be a great mistake to invest the store's profits in capitalist business since that would simply strengthen 'the sinews of the enemy'.

In this situation it was apparently the successful establishment of Equity Shoes in nearby Leicester in 1887 which acted as the spur in the setting up of the Kettering Boot and Shoe co-op a year later. Help with starting capital and advice in co-operative principles was supplied to the founding boot and shoe makers by the Kettering store. The new enterprise found a ready market for its products in the prosperous network of co-operative retail shops. So far as I can discover it enjoyed real if unspectacular success from the moment of starting production for nearly two generations. Moreover, despite the part played by the Kettering store, from the outset control was firmly in the hands of the workforce. It is one of the few enterprises the genuine democratic character of which is conceded even by Beatrice Webb (if only rather surreptitiously in a Table at the back of her *Co-operative Movement in Great Britain*).

The motivation behind Kettering Clothing, founded in 1893, was different; although the relevant background of the Kettering store was the same. Henry Lloyd, an American enthusiast for co-operation, who visited Kettering in the 1890s has given this account of it:*

> This new enterprise had its immediate suggestion in a boycott of the co-op store by a firm of manufacturers in Kettering. The store had added a clothing branch to its other departments and sought to purchase its supplies from the local manufacturers. But they would not sell, because the co-op store was the rival of one of their principal customers in Kettering. Some of the employees of this firm were members of the co-op store; and upon this refusal they said to their fellow members that if assisted they would organise a co-operative manufactory to supply the clothing needed. ... The start was made with 12 workers, 7 of them men who had been discharged by the local firm. They were drilled in co-operative ideas and methods by Mr W. Ballard of the store for 12 months before beginning.

As with the boot and shoe co-operative, so this new enterprise seems to have had no trouble selling its output to the consumer societies. In its case too, and from the outset, control seems to have been in the hands of the workforce. And there is a very similar record of modest success down to the Second World War. At times indeed its success seems to have been more than modest. Henry Lloyd reported that its shares were selling for above their par value at the end of the 1890s – and points to the danger that outsiders might gain control. However, that did not happen. It survived as a genuine co-operative continuing in business until after the Second World War.

What stands out most clearly from this brief account of the origins of half a dozen of the producer co-ops in the 1880s and the 1890s is that the founding initiative came in all cases from working-class people or working-class institutions. People from outside the working class – like the 'divines and lawyers' of the Christian Socialist movement – were not

---

* Henry Lloyd, *Labour Co-partnership*, Harper Brothers, London, 1898, p. 139.

directly involved in any single one of these initiatives. Their working-class and 'cloth cap' character is brought out by two other points. With the exception of the Wollaston boot makers who managed by a stroke of luck to secure an army contract to get going, all depended more rather than less on institutional working-class markets. The two Kettering enterprises and Equity Shoes sold the bulk of their output to the co-operative stores from the beginning and more or less continuously until the Second World War. For Leicester's printers (though the dependence is less marked), it was the trade union and co-operative movements together which supplied most of the orders in the early stages. What was true of markets was also largely true of starting capital; virtually the whole of it was put up by working-class people and institutions.

Yet to stress their working-class character is not to suggest that we are dealing here with any real militance or serious revolutionary or 'world amending' aims. Trade union officials in Leicester had doubtless read Mill and Marshall. Mr Ballard in Kettering might urge investments which brought no comfort to the enemy, but as a contemporary observer put it: 'there was in this newer form of producer co-operation no grand challenge to capitalist industry; hardly more than a plea to be allowed to live side by side with it.' Marx would doubtless have argued that even if more militant objectives had been the rule, the forces at the disposal of these new enterprises were far too dwarfish to make any challenge realistic.

No, the working-class character of the new co-ops is important because it was restrictive. There is little or no evidence of any serious efforts by these new businesses to being in middle-class and professional skills or to broaden out the base of their appeal or their support. That indeed is the main reason why we can think of them as 'cloth cap' co-ops. Mavis Kirkham's excellent study of Equity Shoes brings out the point exactly: a deep rooted suspicion of anyone with other than the most authentic 'cloth cap' credentials. Thus it was that the shoe makers who set up the Equity enterprise insisted in their constitution that their 'committee of management' − in effect their board of directors − should include none but 'practical men'. Thus it was almost twenty years before that committee of management could bring itself to appoint someone with the title of Manager. Thus it was that none of the first four holders of that post left on speaking terms with the committee. These attitudes reflect in part a sort of primitive republicanism and confusion about the necessary function of 'management' in any productive organization with more than a handful of people; but they also unquestionably reflect a distrust by the working-class operative who uses his hands, of the characteristically middle-class 'operative' who does not. This, I think, is the key sense in which this second generation of producer co-ops was essentially working-class and 'cloth cap' in character and also in which that character was restrictive. For, inevitably, it narrowed their horizons and limited possible growth. The French experience, at least up to the post-1945 period, provides evidence of very similar attitudes.

The number of co-operative enterprises of this kind in England and Wales went into a very gradual decline in the 1900s. About the exact figures there is some uncertainty; about the trend none. The following series gives Derek Jones's* estimates of the number of 'cloth cap' co-ops in England and Wales for selected years down to 1971 (the 1973 figure is my own interpretation of Industry Department data): 112 in 1905; seventy-one in 1913; sixty-four in 1924; fifty in 1936; forty-four in 1950; thirty-seven in 1960; twenty-six in 1970; sixteen in 1973.

I have called them 'cloth cap' co-ops, and it has seemed right to exclude from the 1973 figures recently established enterprises: a co-operative association of architects and two taxi-cab co-ops of owner drivers (which though similar in form are very different in character). I have also closed the series in 1973 to avoid confusion when examining the appearance of the new 'Wedgwood Benn' co-ops in 1974.

The first point to be made about the decline shown by the figures is that in reality it has been astonishingly slow. For the fact is that excluding the new co-ops of the 1970s and the short-lived Building Guilds of the early 1920s, the number of new enterprises of this kind started since 1914 is negligible. It follows that of the population of these enterprises which existed in 1913 not less than 20 per cent were still alive and at least adequately profitable sixty years later. Any population in which the birth rate is nil is bound to decline. To be surprised by the *smallness* of the number of 'cloth cap' co-ops which survived in 1973 is like being surprised at the small number of Zoroastrians in today's world. What is surprising is just the opposite — just how large the number of survivors is.

Once the point is taken that the number of new recruits into the ranks of the 'cloth cap' co-ops has been almost negligible since 1914, the British record begins to look almost respectable — and becomes almost comparable with that in France. Claude Vienney† has shown that between 1884 and 1960 a total of 2,250 producer co-ops were founded in France. Just under one in four — 520 — were alive and functioning in 1960. Thus the big difference between the experience in the two countries is not the survival rate but the fact that in France the pool of

---

* Derek Jones, *op. cit.*, pp. 36 and 41.
† Claude Vienney, *L'Economie du Secteur Co-operatif Français*, Editions Cujas, Paris 1966.

co-ops has been continuously replenished by new starters.

The surprisingly strong survival quality of these old 'cloth cap' co-ops is suggested by other evidence as well as by a comparison with the French experience. In Table 5.3 Derek Jones has compared, for the year 1963, the average age of small private capitalist companies and of the co-ops:

TABLE 5.3   Average ages of small private companies and British producer co-ops in 1963

	Oldest quartile	Median	Youngest quartile
Capitalist	55	22	10
Co-op	75	66	52

In other words the 'cloth cap' co-ops extant in 1963 were decidedly more venerable than their capitalist counterparts. The figures imply a further point: a higher proportion of 1914 'cloth cap' co-ops than of 1914 small private companies were still soldiering on fifty years later.

Ten years on, in 1973, according to the Department of Industry, the 'cloth cap' co-ops which survived, together with their turnover and labour force were as shown in Table 5.4.

TABLE 5.4

	Turnover £	Employees
Printers		
Blackfriars Press (Leicester)	N.A.	N.A.
Bristol Printers	36,000	15
Derby Printers	91,000	26
Hull Printers	230,000	59
Leicester Printers	377,000	94
Nottingham Printers	78,000	21
Watford Printers	219,000	62
Boots and shoes		
Avalon Footwear (Kettering)	475,000	119
Equity Shoes (Leicester)	916,000	196
NPS Shoes (Wollaston)	303,000	68
St Crispin Footwear (Wellingboro')	268,000	80
Clothing		
Ideal Clothiers (Wellingboro')	1,247,000	632
Queen Eleanor (Kettering)	412,000	138
Sunray Textiles (Coalville)	382,000	72
Other		
Leicester Carriage Builders	119,000	48
Walsall Locks	408,000	174

As well as the capacity to survive Table 5.4 reflects, I think, both their continuing working-class character and lack of dynamism. By 1973 all but two were concentrated in those three sectors − clothing, footwear and printing − in which markets controlled by the consumer co-op movement and the trade unions remained important. Thus it is not altogether surprising that when he wrote his history of British co-operation in the early 1940s, G. D. H. Cole could refer to them as 'satellites' of the consumer movement. In commercial terms they were. And despite some diversification into new markets in the early 1960s − and some cosmetic changes in the form of modernized names − that is largely what they remained in the last years of the 1970s.

The absence of any real dynamism is shown not only by the negligible number of new starts in the sixty years following the outbreak of the First World War; it is also revealed by a comparison of the 1973 labour force figures with those for earlier years. The average labour force of the 1973 survivors was just over 100 − the same as in 1913. Between the two dates it never rose above 175. The fact that the peak was achieved in 1945, when forty-eight of these co-ops had a total workforce of 8,218 (roughly 173 each), may perhaps reflect government contracts during the Second World War.

This impression of stagnant survival can be overstated. The redoubtable Walsall Locks has absorbed small capitalist businesses, as well as at least one other co-operative, during its more than 100 years of existence. Equity Shoes, among others, has diversified not only out of its traditional markets in the co-op stores but even into exports. Against this the character of Equity Shoes may be reflected more authentically by its main product line: good, stout walking shoes for middle-aged and older women in which, apparently, fashions change but slowly.

The 'cloth cap' co-ops which survived well into the post-1945 period (and even more so those which still survive in the late 1970s) are, in fact, something of a rare phenomenon in a market economy. They have survived *without* expanding and even, to an extent, while contracting. It is a performance which defies the supposed law of 'get on or go bust'. They have simply soldiered on, making the minimum of necessary adjustments.

These old producer co-ops have undoubtedly been working-class in origin and character, but were they truly democratic in the sense that control and ownership were vested only in the workforce? The straight answer is 'no'. For none attempted to ensure that there was an identity between the workforce on the one hand and those who owned and controlled the enterprise on the other.

Characteristically they have been amalgams both of inside and outside ownership and inside and outside control. Likewise the workforces have included both shareholder members and workers with no shares – and thus no membership. The outsiders involved have included institutions, like trade unions and retail co-op societies, as in the case of Leicester Printers, and individuals: typically local sympathizers and retired members of the workforce.

Hence, there is a marked absence of structural purity. At the same time the researches of Derek Jones suggest that various trends can be identified, such as changes of control, defined by membership of management committees. Jones has produced the following series of the average percentage of management committees actually composed of workers: 34% in 1890; 53% in 1935; 60% in 1948: 55% in 1958; 49% in 1970.

Up to 1948 these figures seem to reflect a pressure from worker members to reduce the influence of outsiders but a decline of interest thereafter. This second trend seems to be echoed by a gentle reduction in the proportion of the co-op's workforce who have bothered to take up membership – and buy shares – since the Second World War.* Jones's researches show a fall off in this percentage from 63 per cent in 1948 to 53 per cent in 1970. As one would expect, as proportionate workforce membership fell so outside shareholdings grew: from an average of 76 per cent in 1948 to as high as 84 per cent in 1970.

What structural, sociological, or other factors lie behind these and other changes in the ownership and control mix of the old 'cloth cap' co-ops? Some of the more important ones may be worth examination.

To begin with, when such co-operative enterprises remain basically static (as most of these have done for years) there will be an inevitable tendency for the proportion of shares owned by non-workers to increase – unless the rules say otherwise. For no new shares will be created; and retiring members will have no particular incentive – and perhaps no readily available mechanism – to sell their holding to newcomers. Jones's published figures include no long series for share ownership.

Structural factors may also tend to reduce participation by the workforce in a more direct way. Profit-sharing rules for example, may provide an active disincentive to workforce members from extending membership rights to others. The incentives may be all the other way: towards hiring a group of second-class wage earners to work alongside them. This was one of the sources of 'degeneration' identified by the

---

* In his earlier unpublished PhD thesis 'The Economics of British Producer Co-operatives', Jones showed that this decline in worker membership was paralleled by a decline in the proportion of share capital owned by workers: from 25 per cent in 1948 to 18 per cent in 1968.

Webbs. It happened in the treatment meted out by the Wollaston boot makers to their less fortunate brethren from neighbouring Finedon. A less crude example is recorded in a history of Walsall Locks* published in 1923: 'The members refuse to elect other members as shareholders as it would to some extent reduce their bonus for half the non-member bonus is retained and added to the reserve fund.' Obviously, where the rules permit more than one category of worker, this kind of thing is bound to happen; but, of course the rules could lay down one category of worker–member only.

Structural features are not, however, unchangeable. There is at least one excellent example in France. The workforce of La Verrerie Ouvrière d'Albi was successful in the 1930s in reversing the original position of external majority control and taking power itself. There may be similar cases in British experience, and they may partly explain the increase between 1890 and 1948 in the degree of internal control in the old British producer co-ops which Jones's figures bring out.

However, we should also beware of thinking that structural features and changes are the whole story. The decline in British co-op participation since 1950 is probably due mainly to sociological factors. Speaking to Mavis Kirkham in 1971 the manager–secretary of Walsall Locks, Mr Rose, clearly indicated that it was wages, above anything else, which exercised the workforce. 'Now', he told her (the implication was that things had been different in the past), 'members want to know what it is at the end of the week. They are not interested in the "divi" in six months' time.' If Walsall Locks is at all typical, it would seem that the 'weekly wage packetism' which so dominates British shop-floor attitudes in private and public industry has spread to the old producer co-ops as well.

One further aspect of the old 'cloth cap' co-op experience needs to be mentioned briefly. As creations of the working-class movement it is scarcely surprising that in most or all cases they have followed policies of maintaining the closed union shop. But union membership has not just been a solidarity gesture – as we might expect it to become in a fully democratic and self-governing enterprise. In the consumer co-ops, co-op banks and enterprises owned by the Co-operative Wholesale Societies, there have, *vide* the origin of Equity Shoes, been periodic strikes. I suspect the same to be true of the old 'cloth cap' co-ops though my researches have not yet thrown up a concrete example. On the other hand there is specific and direct evidence, in Mavis Kirkham's study of the Leicester Printers, that the unions in the old 'cloth cap' co-ops

---

* R. Halstead, *The History of Walsall Locks and Cartgear Ltd 1873–1923*, Birmingham Printers, 1924, p. 17.

enjoyed their familiar bargaining and negotiating role. This is no surprise in view of the 'impure' structures of the co-ops and the fact that their workforces have normally contained a smaller or larger proportion of unenfranchised non-members. For wherever membership (and thus a share of ownership and control) is only partial, the need for the traditional bargaining activity of the unions will survive.

Yet the place of the union in a co-op may be unlike as well as like that in a conventional concern. The evidence is provided by the curious union position at Walsall Locks. There, if I have understood the position correctly, the union is an independent* one but it may only be joined by those working for the co-op. There is not a mandatory closed shop, but in practice 90 per cent of those eligible to join do so. Conceivably in a transitional worker-owned and controlled sector the Walsall Locks way of dealing with union membership might be one to be followed more widely; the independence of the enterprise would be protected but the possibility of a divergence of interest between shop floor and management would also be acknowledged.

Before summing up the performance of these old co-ops, the short-lived Building Guilds of the 1920s require a mention as they fit in better here than at any other place in an account of the British experience. They are worth mentioning if only as a cautionary tale: basically they show how easy it is for a precipitate, ill-prepared and externally determined push into co-operative structures to go wrong.

In the early months of 1920 post-war economic optimism was riding high. So was the rhetoric of building a world fit for heroes; and in bricks-and-mortar terms demand was starting to outrun the capacity of the construction industry – with the consequence of a sharp upward push in building prices. With the main aim of getting more houses built, Lloyd George's government introduced new payment arrangements for local authority housing in 1920. The town halls' contribution to building costs was limited to a fixed sum. The Exchequer in London was to cover the difference, however great, between this sum and the price of the finished article. It was an open-ended invitation to the building industry to take up house building contracts on a cost plus basis.

These were the exceptional circumstances which provoked groups of ordinary building tradesmen to set up guilds in centres all round the country but particularly in parts of London and in the Manchester area, during the second half of 1920. G. D. H. Cole, himself fairly closely

---

* It is not, as a matter of fact, affiliated to the TUC. It would be interesting to know whether a request for affiliation, were it to be put forward, would be accepted.

involved in the events he describes, argues that one of the main aims of building workers in forming these guilds was to keep prices *down*; unlike the capitalist contractors they would not be greedily looking for windfall profits.* A considerable number of active guilds were quickly established and contracts negotiated with the local authorities.

Generous provisions for interim payments against work in progress were written into these contracts, so the financial needs of the guilds were relatively modest. Moreover, since the contracts were effectively drawn up on a cost plus basis (whether or not the 'plus' element was small), and since, therefore, the guilds could hardly lose, loans could be advanced to them with virtually no risk. The guilds quickly formed a loose umbrella organization – the National Building Guild – which managed to secure a substantial loan from the Co-operative Wholesale Society. That, plus an unquantifiable amount of individual workers' savings, was sufficient to supply the guilds with the limited capital they required.

The episode of the Building Guilds is like a very brief short story. It has a perfectly recognizable beginning, an unmistakable end, but very little by way of a middle. In the summer of 1921 the policy of Lloyd George's government abruptly swung away from those subsidized cost plus contracts. They were discontinued. So were the provisions for interim payments which had so helpfully scaled down the financial resources the guilds had had to muster. Faced with this new situation, with its money suddenly at risk, the Co-operative Wholesale Society prudently called in its loan to the National Building Guild. Immediate disaster was only averted by the arrangement of standby credits with Barclays Bank.

But the inevitable end was only postponed. By the end of 1922, Cole relates, the situation had become impossible. Barclays put in a receiver and during 1923 the National Building Guild was wound up. As many as sixty-three affiliated local guilds – working on over 200 separate contracts – were wound up at the same time. 'Many hundreds of operatives', Cole writes, 'lost their savings.'

Cole acknowledges that there had been gross mismanagement at the centre. Yet even if management had been of the highest quality it is hard to believe the result would have been different. A sudden political decision to put local authority housing contracts on a cost plus basis – and to insulate the town halls from the consequences of this reckless folly – provides no sort of proper basis for the establishment of totally new industrial structures, particularly in an industry as fickle as

---

* Cole, *op. cit.*, pp. 286 and 287.

building. In any case the cost plus decision was bound to be reversed – and it was as certain as anything could be that the next change would come sooner rather than later.

Not unreasonably Cole argues that neither he nor the other Guild Socialists who were sucked in to help the National Building Guild had ever advocated a set-up of its kind. They had urged industrial democracy and workers' control, but they had always insisted that these should come about within a framework of public ownership – and not on the basis of independent, co-operatively owned local guilds. Still we can now see that whatever their ownership arrangements these particular enterprises were doomed. History shows that, quite apart from the need for skilled management, new industrial structures of this kind only work after the most careful preparation and when large numbers of those involved are fully committed to the long haul towards achieving success. The first condition was never approached in the case of the Building Guilds; the second was at best very partially satisfied.

In assessing the performance of the old British producer co-ops we can reasonably designate the Building Guilds a special case. The same is surely true – at least if we confine ourselves to what might have relevance in today's world – to those very early, world amending experiments in co-operative production. The failure of the Leeds Redemptionist Society's 'internal colony' in Pembrokeshire, tells us nothing, for example, about whether Rolls-Royce might sensibly be reorganized on a co-operative and democratic worker–ownership basis. Nor does the fact that a particular group of mid-nineteenth century clergymen lacked the knowledge and social engineering skills to promote self-governing workshops of craftsmen–artisans. Nor finally does the over-ambitious and predictably disastrous adventure of the anyway slightly dubious Rev Dr Rutherford with his Ouseburn Engineering Works in Newcastle.

If we confine ourselves to the performance of the much less ambitious, less cranky and more work-a-day 'cloth cap' co-ops – such as Leicester Printers, Walsall Locks, the two Kettering co-ops and Equity Shoes – a fairly uniform picture emerges. For the survivors it is an undramatic picture of modest commercial success and of a fluctuating but respectable degree of workers' control and ownership. In other words, the two main blanket criticisms of the Webbs are clearly false, at least as blanket criticisms. The survivors have shown that they are not doomed by their structures to commercial failure; nor do their structures, impure and imperfect as we have seen them to be, lead inexorably to a creeping capitalist degeneration.

However, it might still be reasonable, on the bald face of their overall history, to adopt a fairly dismissive attitude; it cannot be seriously claimed that any real winners have emerged. Moreover, while 20 per cent of the total producer co-ops of 1914 were still in business sixty years later, the other 80 per cent had fallen by the wayside.

I would argue, on the other hand that the only legitimate verdict on the experience of the old 'cloth cap' co-ops is one of 'not proven'. Owing to their constitutional imperfections their experience really tells us nothing about what might happen in fully bottom-upwards democratic enterprises. As the environment has been so generally hostile − and because they have made no sort of commitment to the goals of growth − the undramatic character of their commercial results is not surprising. The assessment of Alfred Marshall seems the most appropriate; in effect he argued that associations of labourers had not really been tried, because they had invariably been lacking in management and professional talent. I have no wish to disparage the dedication and hard work which the managers of the surviving co-ops have put in over the years. Nevertheless, it remains true that they have never sought to recruit the highest levels of management skill. Hence, they provide no test of what a democratically structured, and self-owning team of the best management coupled with the best shop-floor skills could achieve. Their record is like that of a cricket eleven, with solid batting and sound fielding, but without any top-class bowlers.

6

The ICOM and similar companies

When we move from the old 'cloth cap' co-ops to the companies associated with the Industrial Common Ownership Movement (ICOM) we move into a different tradition and a different century. The old 'cloth cap' co-ops are best perceived as the step-children, neglected or worse, of the nineteenth century working-class movement. The seed-bed from which ICOM has grown is the essentially middle-class tradition of progressive if paternalistic business management, fertilized to a greater or lesser extent by Quaker business radicalism. Today's survivors among the old co-ops were virtually all founded in the 1880s and 1890s. With one exception, today's ICOM and ICOM-type companies took on their present shape − or were founded − not earlier than the 1950s; the exception is the John Lewis Partnership which took on its new shape in the late 1920s.

If we ignore John Lewis for the moment (and with a 1977 turnover of £435m and a workforce above 23,000 its inclusion would swamp all other figures in an overall total) and if we ignore too a rash of new initiatives in late 1977 and early 1978, the ICOM and ICOM-type companies numbered a total of ten, employing together some 1,200 people and with a combined turnover of about £20m in early 1977. As we have already seen this number had been reduced by one, when Rowen Onllwyn ceased trading, before the end of the year. As we shall also see, at least two other companies − Landsman's Co-ownership and Sunderlandia − had been forced to reduce their workforces by the end of the year. However, at the start of 1977 the position was roughly as illustrated in Table 6.1.

Though for some purposes the ten enterprises in Table 6.1 can usefully be considered together, it is more convenient for my analysis to group them in three sub-categories. Category one covers the first four enterprises in Table 6.1 former capitalist concerns which were 'high-mindedly' given to their collective workforces by their former owners. At the other end of the 'alternative origin' scale, and ranging in size from what Marx might have called the dwarfish to the very dwarfish, come the last four companies which were all set up from scratch in more or

TABLE 6.1   The ICOM and similar enterprises early 1977

Name	Product	Annual sales £	Work force
Scott-Bader	Plastic resins	15·0m	450
Bewley's Cafés	Cafés, tea, coffee	1·8m	400
Michael Jones	Jewellers	458,000	30
Air Flow Developments*	Industrial systems	2·5m	200
KER†	Plant hire	200,000	25
Landsman's	Industrial caravans	300,000	36
Sunderlandia	Building	225,000	27
Trylon	Plastic mouldings	290,000	15
Rowen Onllwyn	Out-door furniture	90,000	17
'Little Women'	Retail store	N.A.	8

* Only an 'associate' member of ICOM. All others are full members.
† KER Plant Co-ownership Ltd (acronym for General Manager, Keith Edward Robertson); in 1978 name changed to Northampton Industrial Commonwealth Ltd.

less democratic form. In the middle is Landsman's Co-Ownership Ltd. Like those in the first sub-category Landsman's started as a conventional concern owned and controlled by its founders, David and Anne Spreckley. However, the Landsman's workers were not presented with the company as a gift; they had to buy it from the Spreckleys in rather the same way that the Zambian state bought control of the mines on the Zambian copper belt from the Anglo-American Corporation of South Africa and from American Metal Climax of the US.

The commercial performance of the four 'high-minded' companies since their respective transformations has been at the very least respectable. Taken together with the much longer experience of the John Lewis Partnership (John Lewis was sold to a Trust which owns it collectively – not given), their record makes clear beyond any reasonable doubt that if the owners of a successful business decide to hand it over to the workforce, there need be no serious worry that these changes will have an adverse effect on economic performance.

However, that is to put the lessons of the commercial experience of the 'high-minded companies at their lowest. In the case of the two largest – John Lewis Partnership and Scott-Bader – the record has been much more than just respectable. Between 1928 and the mid-1970s the labour force of the John Lewis Partnership expanded more than fifteen times (from 1,500 to over 23,000) and the increase of its sales in terms of constant prices was even sharper. In the case of Scott-Bader, between 1953 (when Ernest Bader the founder handed over 90 per cent of the company's stock to the community of the workforce) and 1976 sales in current prices increased more than twenty times. Of course, for most of the relevant periods large-scale retailing and industrial chemicals have been strong growth sectors in the economy. Still it is clear that each company has outperformed the 'average' enterprise in its sector.

Airflow Developments Ltd who manufacture instruments for testing industrial air systems, domestic ventilation units and industrial fans in High Wycombe are also something of a commercial success story. Their turnover more than doubled between 1973 and 1977 and in early 1978 they were employing some 200 people. It is claimed that productivity increased quite sharply between the early and late 1970s. Starting from a strong position in the home market the company had also begun to move vigorously into export markets.

Bewley's Cafés in Dublin and Michael Jones, the jewellers in Northampton, both had to cope with decidedly unfavourable conditions during the mid-1970s. Michael Jones was confronted with the sudden hoist, up to a rate of 25 per cent, in the value added tax charged on its products, as a result of Mr Healey's budget in 1975. Bewley's Cafés which specializes in tea and coffee blending and includes retail tea and coffee shops, a bakery, a chocolate-making unit and a dairy farm as well as actual cafés, had to contend with tough government price restrictions in addition to a difficult market. These problems resulted in temporary losses for both companies though by 1977 their operations were once again on a profitable basis.

One final enterprise may be added to this sub-category. For KER the relevant record was really too short in 1977 for any reliable assessment to be made. The company was only started in its present form in mid-1976 though all the indications in early 1978 were that it had made a good start. Moreover, there is no reason to doubt its contention that, with the contraction of the building and civil engineering market, there was an increase in the proportion of builders who chose to hire plant rather than to own it. KER may well be worth watching with particular attention over the next few years. Taxi co-ops of owner-drivers are increasingly showing rather good results; there may be a fair chance that a plant hire co-op of bull-dozer owner–drivers will do the same.

What about the non-commercial record of these 'high-minded' companies? In what way, if at all, have the new structures affected people's attitudes in their work and their feelings about it?

To begin with we should not expect too much too soon. In those companies with any length of experience the consequences of structural changes have been gradual. Some would also contend that the changes have been incomplete (and insufficiently radical) and that the workforce has to a large extent been cushioned from them anyway.

It is easy to see, for example, that a switch from non-workforce shareholding to *collective* (unindividuated) workforce ownership may not make that much difference from the shop floor's viewpoint, in practice and at least in the short term. The collective of worker–owners at Scott-Bader will obviously have *some* difference of feeling and motivation derived from the knowledge that extra effort on their part will no longer serve mainly to enrich the Bader family. The same is true of the 'partners' at John Lewis and of the collective common owners at Michael Jones, Bewley's Cafés and Airflow Developments.

Yet the probability that ownership changes of this kind will only affect people's attitudes to a limited extent is reinforced in the case of these 'high-minded' companies by the existence of entrenched constitutional clauses about profit distribution. In none of them does the workforce enjoy a discretion to appropriate to itself a really large share of net profits in the form of a bonus on wages.

Critics would contend that the same kind of argument is in order on questions of final control. They would claim that the supposedly sovereign body of the workforce does not really enjoy the final discretion which sovereignty should entail. True, in all cases, the rule of outside shareholders has been seen off the premises; true too that elected and representative institutions have been created and set in their place. However, the critics would argue that the real positions of power are still beyond the control of the representative bodies. At a formal level they would be right. The workforce in these enterprises does not – perhaps I should say still did not in 1977 – enjoy full powers to hire and fire the directors and the top management. Moreover, their constitutions in the late 1970s would have to be changed if their workforces were to acquire these powers. To take one extreme example, under the present constitution at Scott-Bader, Godric Bader, the son of Ernest, the founder, is Company Chairman for life. (Incidentally Godric's name may throw some light on the character of his father, Ernest. Surely it cannot be a coincidence that Godric was also the name of the only financier ever canonized by the Roman Catholic Church. But that, of course, is something else.)

But notwithstanding the force of these criticisms, it would be a mistake to go anything like all the way with the hard line trade union, working-class leadership Left when it tends to dismiss the structural changes in these companies as window-dressing. For one thing the influences now at work in these companies, whatever their formal power arrangements, are profoundly different from those in a traditional capitalist undertaking. For another their positions are not static; there have been several constitutional changes at Scott-Bader since Ernest made the main gift of stock in 1953; and all have been in a more democratic direction. Third, there is good, specific evidence of behaviour and attitude changes which cannot easily be explained except in terms of the altered structures. Michael Jones, Scott-Bader and Bewley's can all point to occasions when the workforce has been prepared to forego wage increases at least on a temporary basis. In other words they can point to evidence of much greater identification with the enterprise's long-term goals – and thus much greater defensive strength in difficult times – than is normal in a capitalist concern. To get the flavour of what these structures can begin to mean it may be sensible to look more closely at one of the enterprises. Partly because it is not at all well known outside Dublin, I will take the example of Bewley's Cafés.

The Bewleys are a family of Irish Quakers. Records show that an ancestor of the two present generations was already in business in Dublin, dealing in sugar and tea in a small way, as early as the 1840s. In the beginning, the growth of the business was quite gradual. The first café was not opened before the 1880s. In 1977 there were five of these (and a sixth in the planning stage) which double up as specialized tea and coffee shops, plus a bakery, a small chocolate-making operation and a dairy farm at Boyvalley in County Kildare. Though the word 'Cafés' is used in the Bewley's name, old-style coffee shops is probably a better description. The inside appearance of the branches in central Dublin is more reminiscent of a modest version of Simpsons in the Strand, London – or of a restaurant car on an Edwardian train – than of a contemporary café. All the Bewley's activities together employed 400 people in 1977 of whom the largest single group consisted of waitresses.

At least during the leadership as Chairman and Managing Director of Victor Bewley, who retired at the end of 1977, the company always had a reputation for excellent employee relations. In 1976, its atmosphere was unmistakably paternal and light years away from the thrusting, elbowing world of modern competitive capitalism. Victor made no secret of the fact that he was more interested in people than profits. In the Quaker tradition of voluntary good works he spent much of his time watching over the affairs of the Irish gypsies, the 'travelling people'. Yet with the exception of a difficult year, referred to earlier, Bewleys has always made a profit. Wages slightly above the prevailing rate have normally been paid; and the operation was obviously well managed – at least up to the late 1970s. Over the years prudent reinvestment policies have built up capital values. The 1976 balance sheet showed fixed assets of over £600,000 and the company's net worth was well in excess of £$^1/_2$m.

Two sets of changes were brought about at Bewley's in the early

1970s. First, ownership was given by the Bewley family to the work force. More exactly, the company's shares were transferred to a new company, the Bewley Community Ltd, which is limited by guarantee and which holds the shares in trust for all those working in the firm, past present and future. Essentially this form of collective ownership in trust follows models which had been pioneered by the John Lewis Partnership and Scott-Bader and which have also been more or less copied by Michael Jones and Airflow Developments.

Alongside this came changes in the direction of greater democratic control, greater participation. Any member of the Bewley's workforce became eligible for membership of Bewley Community Ltd. Such membership gives to the employees what is, in effect, a right of veto over any major changes in the company's structure – and an invulnerable line of defence if the prospect of voluntary liquidation, or of a take-over, should loom. Basically this is a safeguard mechanism. The community performs much the same function for Bewley's employees as their representation on top-tier boards performs for employees of West German enterprises; the only important difference is that the Bewley's employees have the majority vote and thus the final say.

In respect of employee involvement in day-to-day management, the changes were less radical. A company council was set up consisting of heads of department and elected departmental representatives in equal numbers. This normally meets monthly, under the company chairman, and may concern itself with anything it chooses. On the other hand members of the Bewley family continued to form a majority on the board of directors, which remained responsible for filling, by appointment and not election, any board vacancies. On paper, therefore, the family retained almost complete control of day-to-day management.

Before considering the effects of these changes it is worth saying something about their motivation. A belief in the value and potential of people, coupled with a radical Quaker sense of social justice, seem to be the main relevant driving forces behind Victor Bewley – who was unquestionably the prime mover. In the case of the ownership transfer he is quite explicit: all the company's employees had contributed to build up of its capital worth, so that for its ownership to remain in the family's hands conflicted with social justice. He is explicit too about the main motives for introducing greater democratic control and employee participation: he saw it as the road to the personal and collective growth, the personal and collective maturing, of the workforce.

One further piece of evidence about the motivation behind the early 1970s changes at Bewley's needs to be mentioned. The *collective* ownership by the working community of the company's capital reflects a quite deliberate decision. The alternative of individuated ownership, along Landsman's Co-ownership lines, was rejected on purpose. For the company's new articles lay down as one of its aims 'to encourage thinking in terms of the welfare of the community in which we live, rather than a desire for personal gain at the expense of others.' Individuated ownership, it was felt, would involve a temptation to sell which, if yielded to, was thought all too likely to produce sales at the expense of others.

The 'high-mindedness' of this motivation, however admirable, may be a little much for some tastes, but it is balanced by the very real and practical benefits which seem to have flowed from the changes; and by the very cheery, quite unchurchy, manner of Victor Bewley himself. He is certainly the most relaxed, and easily the funniest, of those who have presented a family company to its employees. In contrast to Ernest Bader he neither looks nor behaves like an Old Testament prophet.

The best evidence that very concrete changes in attitude have flowed from the structural reforms at Bewley's was briefly referred to much earlier, but it is worth recounting in detail. The most relevant point of background was the introduction by the Irish Government in 1973 of strict wage and price controls. National wage increases were decreed. Prices could only be raised with official approval. Moreover, there were invariable delays in securing approval. Bewley's, among others, was caught: prices could not be raised fast enough to keep pace with wages; the profit and loss account moved into the red. As it did so, yet another official wage increase was about to fall due.

Victor Bewley, as Company Chairman, was in no doubt that, though operations were running at a loss, the prospective increase should be paid. All his instincts, and the company's traditions, pointed in that direction. However, some of the younger board members urged that the company's council be consulted even if final responsibility for reaching a decision lay with the board. In any case nothing could prevent the council from discussing the matter.

It did. And the view that emerged was apparently almost unanimous, being voiced as strongly by the elected representatives as by the heads of departments. If at all possible, the council urged, the wage increases should be foregone. Quite apart from anything else, to forego a rise would enable the workforce to 'do something for their company'. Moreover, or so it transpired, this view was not confined to council members; it was more or less solid throughout.

The upshot was that the wage increases were *not* taken, with two qualifications. At the bakery, a union shop, the workers would have been in dispute with their trade if they had agreed not to accept the increase. It was also a part of the decision that any employee who felt that he or she really needed the extra money could take it as of right and without any questions. Only a tiny minority did so. Moreover, among the bakery workers, a large proportion decided that their extra money should be quietly lent back to the company for the duration.

As it happened, the company's financial fortunes started to mend fairly soon afterwards. By the time of the next annual accounts operations were again on a profitable basis; arrears of wage increases were then paid in full. Yet, all the same, it seems fair to emphasize, as Victor Bewley did when he told me the story, that no one could have foreseen this outcome when the original decision to abstain was taken.

It is easy to see what Bewley meant when he cited this episode as evidence of the collective growth, the increased collective maturity of the company's workforce. Equally it shows how the attitudes reflected should greatly enhance the defensive strength of an enterprise during bad times. But Bewley made clear to me, at the same time, that he personally was as much or more interested in individual growth and development as he was in the collective variety. He delighted to produce examples of real involvement, initiative, responsibility by individual members. Sometimes these were effectively 'suggestion-box initiatives' of a kind fairly familiar in traditional business, but often they went a good deal further and involved sustained follow-through action voluntarily undertaken in the company's interests by humblest members of the shop floor.

However, perhaps the single strongest impression I took away from talking to people at Bewley's in late 1976 was that the situation was not static – things were on the move; forces, upward pressures from the waitresses and others on the shop floor, had been deliberately set in motion. No one could be sure what the pace of future changes was going to be, but no one could be in any doubt that they would be in the direction of greater democratic involvement in decision making, of greater influence for the company council ever if the formal supremacy of the board remained.

The increasing influence of the company council at Bewley's was shown in the events which led up to the 1976 decision to launch a new café operation in Dunlaoghaire, just outside Dublin. Opinion on the board was divided with the younger members in favour of the new initiative, the older ones broadly opposed. The issue was transferred for discussion to the company council. Majority opinion there, once the cases on both sides had been put, was unambiguous. The council sided with the younger, less cautious, members of the board. Rather as in the case of the 1977 Indian elections the people's voice was heard and was decisive; though whether the two decisions will be vindicated by their results remains to be seen.

Because of its more relaxed style, and the personality of Victor, the atmosphere at Bewleys seemed different to me from that in the other 'high-minded' companies − Scott-Bader, Michael Jones, Airflow Developments. It is probably true that there was also at Bewley's in the late 1970s a less cautious, a more positive commitment to encourage real democratic involvement even at the expense of short-term economic success. On the other hand, given that their structures, and the forces at work in them, are so similar it is probably reasonable to look at them as a single species or sub-species and to take Bewleys as basically typical.

Looked at together these 'high-minded' common ownership companies could perhaps best be seen in the late 1970s as a mini-Yugoslav sector in the economy. As in Yugoslavia, so in those companies, individual ownership had been eliminated and democratic influences from the bottom upwards were gradually becoming stronger. As all this happened, we might add, the relevance of traditional unions was becoming progressively weaker; of course they were still around in Yugoslavia as well as in the companies. But their traditional adversary role was gradually being superseded, or withering away. They were becoming more like a branch of the Workers' Educational Association, or an extra arm of the Factory Inspectorate and less like the general staff of a militant working class. This process looked in 1977 as if it would continue in those companies − in step with the evolution of the relationship between shop floor and management. As the former came to enjoy more than just a right of veto over really major decisions and became the arbiter, with final responsibility over wide areas of policy, so the old union functions would finally disappear.

However, the key questions about the 'high-minded' companies associated with ICOM are rather different. They are about the régime of collective ownership and about the very high compulsory reinvestment of profit into the collective ownership account. Is this model, of collective ownership and high compulsory reinvestment − in none of the ICOM companies mentioned is it less than 60 per cent − the best one? Would a better model include at least some degree of individual ownership and greater freedom over profit distribution?

The high compulsory reinvestment of profits should in the normal way enhance the financial strength of the enterprise. That, in turn, so the argument might run, will enable more people to enjoy the benefits of working in the democratic common ownership sector, either through expansion in the existing enterprise or through its investment in the promotion of new common ownership companies. Something on these lines is in fact spelled out by Scott-Bader as the rationale for its policy of high compulsory profit retention. To be fair to the company it has, too, been most generous and energetic in assisting with the promotion of new common ownership concerns as well as involved in its own expansion.

The main arguments against this justification of high compulsory profit retention are robust common-sense ones. The first is that because their individual shares of profit can be at best modest, the incentive for the workforce to make any profits at all will be very much reduced. In tandem, the second argument is that a workforce which democratically controls other aspects of policy but has very limited discretion over profit allocation will inexorably push up wages and salaries at the expense of final profits. The incentive will be to ensure that as large a proportion as possible of the company's value added is taken in the form of wages, with as little as possible remaining for profit. Either way, on this line of reasoning high compulsory profit retention in a collective account is liable to be self-defeating; the collective account may retain its large share of profits, but it will be a large share of a declining total.

There is a more theoretical argument against such arrangements. The argument is that, beyond what is justified by common prudence (by the need to insure against hard times), any imposed rules about profit allocation are liable to be wrong in the precise sense that they will produce distortions and prevent optimum decisions being reached. Differently such imposed rules, if woodenly applied, will prevent the capital market from operating efficiently (though it is, of course, far from clear that it does so anyway). If a common ownership company invariably puts a high percentage of profits to reserve, if its own opportunities for productive investment are limited, and if its rules prevent the reinvestment of these reserves in outside enterprises, then the efficiency of the capital market will be to that extent reduced. We shall see later how this objection can be largely overcome − and how it has been in the Mondragon co-operatives of Basque Spain. I mention it here, however, because it occurs constantly in the literature.

However, it is probably reasonable to regard the imposed rules about profit allocation in the 'high-minded' companies as transitional relics of their previous regimes, and to expect that the democratic forces released from the bottom upwards may eventually lead to their revision. However, the system of collective ownership, the rejection of any degree of individual worker shares, looks as if it is a more permanent feature of these companies. Of course it also receives some sort of endorsement from the rather parallel set-up in Yugoslavia. Is it an advantageous feature or not?

The 'incentive objection' can be applied as strongly or almost as strongly to collective ownership as to the imposed arrangements for profit allocation. Workforce members will have little incentive to maximize profits which are reinvested or retained on collective account because, apart from extra job security, they will individually derive no material benefit when that happens. Collective ownership of this kind could, therefore, become a major disincentive to profit maximization – and could well be self-defeating in that its main objective is to increase the company's financial strength. (I say nothing here about the moral and social objectives of collective ownership.)

Uneasiness about the advantages of full collective ownership and of the total elimination of ownership shares in reinvested or retained profits is strengthened in the case of a mixed economy (though not, of course, in Yugoslavia's) by considerations of comparative job attraction. If there are two democratically structured companies between which a new entrant may choose, and if one allows a degree of individual ownership in retained or reinvested profits while the other does not, then, if all other things are equal, the new entrant is likely to choose the first rather than the second. If considerations of life income and savings taken together count positively for him at all, he is indeed logically bound to do so. His lifetime income and savings in the first company must be greater than in the second. Of course, none of this means that the solution at the opposite end of the spectrum – complete individual ownership of retained and reinvested profits – is the right one. There are grave objections to that too. But it does suggest that *prima facie* there is something faulty about the complete collective ownership régimes which these 'high-minded' ICOM companies have all chosen.

It may thus appear that the optimum structure of a democratic enterprise is likely to involve some blending both of individual and collective interests on the one hand, and of short-term and long-term interests on the other. If that is right, then the most successful structure is likely to include first, some combination of individual and collective (indivisible) ownership, and second, it will require some direct link between the interests of the current enterprise workforce and the enterprise's long-term future. It is hard to see how this second condition can be met other than through some individual shares in reinvested and retained profits.

However, the key point here is that the founders of these 'high-minded' ICOM companies all chose a solution at the collectivist (even if democratic collectivist) end of the spectrum. I suspect that moral, social and religious arguments, rather than economic considerations, determined their choice. Having themselves achieved (or inherited) success in the private ownership world of capitalism they seem to have felt, whether oddly or unsurprisingly, that there would be something disreputable about even a degree of personal ownership in the new régimes which their actions ushered in. In the case of Bewley's there is an explicit reference to possible links between personal ownership and exploitation. In the case of the others a generalized 'high-mindedness' plus a latter day version of nineteenth-century Christian Socialism was probably the governing factor.

Is 'high-minded' collectivism likely to mean much, as a source of motivation, to ordinary working people in today's world? I suspect not. And I suspect that that, as well as the disincentive effects on profit maximization of collective ownership, is why with a few possible exceptions, the common ownership philosophy on Scott-Bader lines has never really generated much enthusiasm at shop-floor level. Of course, cultural and social factors are also involved. It is not only that the 'high-minded' ICOM companies have been stamped by their middle-class origin. The common ownership philosophy of 'high-minded' democratic collectivism has in effect been handed down to the shop floor by its middle-class initiators at the top. Its source at the top must make for some resistance to its assimilation at the bottom, but I suspect too that the slightly holier-than-thou flavour of the philosophy may not have been much help either. It is in any event a fact, observable at all general gatherings of ICOM companies, that this enterprise structure seems to evoke much stronger positive feelings from management than from the shop floor.

In the end, or so it seems to me it is this, the comparative failure of the companies to evoke, with their 'high-minded' democratic collectivism, a really strong response from the shop floor − in contrast to their considerable success in 'turning on' executive and professional employees − which is their most striking feature. In a way which is similar but precisely opposite to the old 'cloth cap' co-ops, it suggests they have been handicapped by a class bias in their appeal. The old 'cloth cap' co-ops, on this analysis, were weakened by their working-class centricity and by their suspicious and defensive attitudes to executive and professional people. These 'high-minded' companies, quite apart from any structural defects, have been weakened by their middle-class centricity and their inability to put themselves across effectively to the shop floor. These class biases may not have been intentional but I would contend that they have been none the less potent for that. The extent and the degree of these class biases can be exaggerated; there are examples of quite successful management being recruited into or emerging from within the old 'cloth cap' co-ops. There are numerous examples −

though we looked only at Bewleys in detail − of enlightened shop-floor responses in the 'high-minded' companies. Moreover it is easy to be Utopian about the degree to which any organizational structure can succeed in really generating enthusiasm amongst the shop-floor members of an enterprise team. Sir Bernard Miller, the former chief executive of John Lewis Partnership, has argued that at any one time only about one-third of the worker−partners properly understood the way the enterprise worked. But he also contended that that proportion was sufficient to set the dominant tone and to make the structures work. We may argue that if John Lewis had less of a middle-class flavour − and perhaps if its ownership arrangements were partially de-collectivized − that 'actively aware' percentage would increase; but we want to avoid suggesting that there is any set of arrangements which would generate a sustained enthusiasm throughout the entire workforce all the time.

Still, it seems valid to suggest that the 'high-minded' companies have no more succeeded in transcending the class bias of their origins than have the old 'cloth cap' co-ops. It also seems reasonable to suggest that if class bias could be transcended then much more successful results would be in prospect.

What, then, is a fair general verdict on the performance of the collectively owned and 'high-minded' ICOM companies? It seems reasonable to argue that all things considered, they have not done too badly. They have suffered from serious handicaps, structural defects, unintentional but very real class bias and, in marked contrast to Yugoslavia, an almost total absence of government or any outside social support. Yet their commercial record is good − in some cases very good. Moreover as social communities, despite their class bias, they have nothing to be ashamed of. And for the wider public they have surely been justified by their pioneering experimentation with new industrial forms. If such success can be achieved, despite the handicaps and imperfections, the argument might run, how much greater would be the potential if the handicaps could be overcome and the imperfections corrected.

When we move on to what is a comparative assessment of the ICOM companies started from scratch − Trylon, Rowen Onllwyn, Sunderlandia, 'Little Women' − we move from the dwarfish to the very dwarfish and from a relatively homogeneous sub-group to a very varied one. Only Sunderlandia employed more than twenty people in 1977, and 'Little Women' employed only eight. On the other hand what is interesting and possibly important about 'Little Women' is its origins. I shall, therefore, say something about it, as well as about Trylon, Rowen Onllwyn and Sunderlandia in this brief sub-section.

Trylon is a child, a full child and a sturdy child, of Scott-Bader. Though long since fully independent in financial and other ways, it lives where it was conceived in the family village of Wollaston, outside Wellingborough in Northamptonshire. In its constitutional form, with collective unindividuated ownership vested in a holding company which is also a charity, it is an almost exact replica of its parent. In its whole character too it reflects that 'high-minded' democratic collectivism which is the hallmark of Scott-Bader. Fixed interest loans from Scott-Bader enabled Trylon to be born. It was nursed through its difficult early years by Roger Sawtell, a man with considerable management experience in conventional business and a strongly committed Quaker.

After initial losses, or establishment and market-entry costs, Trylon was continuously profitable for the last eight of its first ten years, and by 1976 had paid off the Scott-Bader loans and built up a net worth of close on £40,000. The evolution of its sales, profits and workforce looks very similar to that of any successful small capitalist concern which set up in the mid-1960s. The basic statistics are as shown in Table 6.2.

TABLE 6.2   Profitability of Trylon 1966–76

Dates	Nos employed	Sales £	Pre-tax profits (loss) £
1966–7	2	270	(4,469)
1967–8	5	7,798	(4,845)
1968–9	6	31,701	458
1969–70	8	49,714	4,274
1970–1	9	90,832	6,157
1971–2	11	127,220	21,076
1972–3	14	155,081	17,478
1973–4	15	207,400	16,738
1974–5	15	247,149	14,437
1975–6	15	290,000	18,000

With the right product – plastic and fibreglass moulds – at the right time, with strong and professional leadership in the early years and with a deliberate policy of only very gradual expansion, Trylon demonstrates that if those conditions are met, there is nothing inherent in a democratic structure or collective ownership which prevents the successful launching of an enterprise of this kind.

What is more interesting and special about Trylon is that its experience seems to confirm what those earlier theoretical considerations suggested. In particular the decline in profitability between mid-1972 and mid-1976 seems to have structural as well as market causes. More competitive market conditions were, apparently, being experienced from 1972 onwards. On the other hand the company's second General Manager, Mike Angerson, who took over from Roger Sawtell in 1972, was in no doubt when I spoke to him in 1976 that other factors are involved as well.

The point which Angerson emphasized was that, given the collective and indivisible ownership arrangements, there is little direct incentive to maximize profits. Thus selling prices, he explained, had probably not been pushed up to their safe limit; and thus Trylon had also to some extent chosen, as theory suggests would be rational, to prefer something extra on wages to something extra on profits. Angerson's version also tends to confirm that for an enterprise structured like Trylon, and once reasonable profitability has been achieved, there is no very strong or direct motive for expansion. He added that if expansion were to be decided upon for altruistic or ideological reasons, then it would almost certainly rather take the form of dividing up the enterprise into two parts – and encouraging each to grow to about the present Trylon size – than that of adding to the existing company. Evidently the benefits of working in a quite small group are clearly perceived and valued.

More generally, Angerson implied that the sovereign workforce at Trylon saw no particular benefit, once profitability has been achieved, in pushing itself heroically hard to increase profits or, for that matter, incomes. In other words there is an element of preference for a more relaxed pace of work and atmosphere even at the cost of some personal income (as well as some profit). I am not arguing that this preference is wrong or irrational; even from the viewpoint of the wider public community this preference on the part of Trylon's sovereign general meeting may well be beneficial – in reducing the occupancy rate of beds in mental hospitals as well as claims of a less specific kind on the Health Service. What I am suggesting is that Trylon's structure probably encourages its general meeting to opt for a 'quiet life' at a relatively lower level of profitability and value added than might be the case if an alternative structure, with partially individuated ownership, had been chosen.

I would guess finally that for a variety of reasons – its structure, its small size and implied commitment to 'small is beautiful', the nature of its origin, the character of its first general manager, Roger Sawtell, its products – Trylon is likely to have more appeal to people with middle-class outlooks than with traditional working-class attitudes. Or, perhaps more correctly, the former are likely to feel more at home there than the latter. In this respect too it resembles its parent Scott-Bader.

Although, as we have already seen, Rowen Onllwyn ceased trading during 1977, its experience is instructive for a number of reasons.

Moreover it would be altogether misleading if the enterprises covered in this book were to consist entirely of survivors – and included none which had withdrawn from business. For such a selection would result in a false picture of the typical experience of these enterprises both historically and in the late 1970s. Many more have been started than have survived for any great length of time. Of course, the same is true of conventional capitalist enterprises, but that should not be allowed to obscure one of the most important lessons which emerges from this study as a whole: unless enterprises of this kind can form themselves into tightly knit and mutually supportive groups – and ICOM in the late 1970s was not such a group – their expectations of long life cannot be considered good.

In fact, from its origin in the 1960s to its achievement of bare profitability in 1973, Rowen Onllwyn clearly had to struggle to survive at all. It is true that there were then a few easier years in the mid-1970s, but it is now clear that the relaxed and fairly easy-going atmosphere which I found there when I visited the enterprise in 1976 concealed a weak and precarious market position. Looking back over its history it is clear too, now that it has gone into liquidation, that its position was never strong. On one occasion it was forced to make a total product change from night storage heaters to out-door furniture. Because of a particular bad debt its workforce was once reduced to two people. Where Trylon's progress was smooth, Rowen's was up and down like a switchback and sometimes almost hair-raising. In some respects it is a heroic history, with more parallels in France than in Britain.

Rowen Onllwyn's origin and early history have been fully described by Roger Hadley* so the barest outline will suffice. The initiative came from an older 'Rowen' or Robert Owen enterprise, Rowen (Glasgow) which was started by a group associated with nuclear disarmament in the early 1960s and finally went into liquidation in the early 1970s. The South Wales Coal Board and the South Wales National Union of Mineworkers (NUM) were also very much involved in getting it set up; for it was conceived as an enterprise which would, among other things, offer retraining and employment to semi-disabled ex-miners. Various intellectuals, notably Bertrand Russell, also lent moral support to the undertaking. So did Scott-Bader; and the Scott-Bader model of collective ownership and a dual company structure – with the controlling company registered as a charity – was followed. An external consultative committee was also set up with strong representation from the South Wales NUM.

---

* Reprinted in J. Vanek (ed.), *Self-Management: the Economic Liberation of Man*, Penguin, Harmondsworth, 1975.

The new company managed to obtain old National Coal Board (NCB) premises, at Onllwyn and Seven Sisters outside Neath, initially at a nominal rent. Its starting capital was entirely raised by public donation. After a number of minor false starts it eventually concentrated on producing the same night storage heaters as were being turned out by Rowen (Glasgow) in Scotland. Its starting labour force consisted mainly of ex-miners. Commercial management was provided by Frank Gregory, a joiner by trade, but a man with considerable commercial experience in the furniture industry.

After a major crisis, caused in part by a large customer's sudden bankruptcy, in part by a sharp contraction in the market for night storage heaters in the late 1960s, Rowen Onllwyn managed to build itself up again. Street furniture – benches, seats, litter bins – became its main product; the local authorities its main market. It was successful in reaching a mutually beneficial agreement with a leading design and sales company in this field, Orchard Seating of Wallingford. And it even won export orders, selling street furniture to France. With the switch of product, Frank Gregory reverted to his old trade as a joiner. The company's leadership and top management was provided, until his resignation in early 1977, by a young ex-welder, William Burnett, who worked originally with Rowen Glasgow. Under Burnett's régime profits of a few hundred pounds were first achieved in 1973. This figure was increased to £1,400 in the year to end-February 1975 and to £4,650 a year later.

There was a strikingly relaxed atmosphere at Rowen Onllwyn when I visited the enterprise in late 1976. Though there were big differences of age, there were none of cultural background or values inside the enterprise. There was a solid identification (to which the high proportion of ex-miners may well have contributed), with the long term goals of the enterprise – a decent level of profitability, so that Rowen could stand on its own feet, a genuinely democratic control of the management by the general meeting and the assumption by the general meeting of final responsibility for important decisions and policy. Yet the company's economic goals, much as at Trylon, did not seem to extend far beyond a decent level of profits and a reasonable wage. There was no real pressure to produce high profits or to go for significantly improved wages. Given the company's structure and the composition of the workforce that, as at Trylon, seemed rational enough; but it was evidently not enough to ensure survival, and it may partly explain why Burnett himself decided to leave the enterprise at the end of 1976. He said he was bored.

However, the important lesson from Rowen Onllwyn's experience is not that collective ownership may not produce the most dynamic of economic goals, though it appears to confirm that lesson only slightly less strongly than Trylon's experience. The most pertinent lesson from this common ownership enterprise in South Wales is the rather different one already referred to in the book's opening section. It is that an enterprise of this kind may have to part formal company with the unions – whatever the claims of working-class solidarity. At the lowest level, as Burnett saw it, the union might simply prove irrelevant once genuine bottom-upwards control had been achieved. In the more extreme situation, as happened at Rowen, a continued acceptance of union directives on wages and conditions might turn out to be incompatible with survival. What makes the Rowen case particularly interesting is that the composition of the workforce and its origins gave it particularly strong ties with the unions.

At Rowen there was a specific agreement with the local NUM that its wages would remain in line with those paid by the NCB to corresponding grades of its surface workforce. In the background too was NUM representation on Rowen's 'consultative committee' of well-wishing outsiders. A readiness to confront the union in an unusually direct fashion was therefore required when the company's general meeting decided, in the early 1970s and following the first of the NCB–NUM wage agreements of the Heath government, that it could not increase its own wage rates in line. The general meeting made clear, in explaining its attitude, that it could not accept final responsibility and at the same time remain subject to decisions of outsiders. The NUM evidently took umbrage – though it never seriously attempted to impose the wage increases. Thereafter, naturally enough, its involvement with the company was minimal.

The significance of this independent stand by the general meeting at Rowen Onllwyn should not be exaggerated. After all, when confronted with a threat to its survival, any shop-floor group may behave in unorthodox ways. There have been examples in capitalist business of a readiness not to press wage claims and to break ranks with union-negotiated rates when the existence of the enterprise is threatened. All the same, Rowen adds a nugget of support to the theory that in a genuinely bottom-upwards structure the relationship between the shop floor and outside unions, outside collective bargainers, is liable to change. We have already seen similar evidence at Bewleys. As we shall see later there is also some corroborative evidence in the French experience.

We look next at the brief early experience of the 'Little Women' co-operative store in Sunderland. 'Little Women', which is basically a grocery, is registered as a co-operative, but it is a producer rather than a consumer co-op in the sense that it is owned and controlled by those who work in it rather than by those who buy groceries there. Financed by private loans and by a bank overdraft it started trading in December 1976. In 1977 its eight worker–owner members were all young mothers; because of the claims upon them in the home, no one worked more than part-time and a nursery was provided above the shop where one of the duty team looked after the children of mothers on the shift. One of the main aims of the founders of 'Little Women' was precisely to provide an opportunity for part-time work – and concurrent child minding – for young mothers.

The first really striking point is, however, that the young mothers of 'Little Women' began by paying themselves just 25p an hour and had not increased this figure to more than 35p by the end of their first year. It became clear from the preparatory projections that the available starting capital would be insufficient (unless spectacular and immediate commercial success was achieved) to stand the resulting losses if hourly pay rates were aligned with those of Lord Allen's Union of Shop Distributive and Allied Workers (USDAW); the funds would have run out well before the shop could seriously hope to be on a profitable basis. In fact, the commercial results of the first year were distinctly encouraging; average daily sales roughly trebled between the first quarter and the last. Still, the key points are first that 'Little Women' could never have got off the ground at all if union-negotiated wage rates had been adhered to; and, second, that that did not deter a small group of working-class women from going ahead.

Yet in the overall context of the current debate about the case for encouraging and strengthening an enlarged co-operative sector, the significance of 'Little Women' may in the long run turn out to be wider and rather different. Of course, though the signs were positive, after only one year it was too early to say whether the venture would be a success. On the other hand, there were features about its pre-start up history which made it unusual, if not unique, in 1970s British experience; and which have parallels with the now standard history of new industrial co-operatives associated with Mondragon in Spain. These features would still be worth considering even if the 'Little Women' venture should fail.

The origins of 'Little Women' make it unusual in post-war Britain for two main reasons. First, the thrust to get it established came not 'from the top' or 'from outside' but from within the group which eventually started working in the shop. It was a necessary, even if not a sufficient, condition of its establishment that these women pushed it along from the first suggestion to the day the shop opened; had they not shown this commitment nothing would have happened. Second, and if only indirectly, each member of the promoting (and then working) group had a significant capital stake, as well as an income interest, in the venture. Both points need amplification.

While the drive behind the establishment of 'Little Women' came from the women themselves, other preparatory ingredients were also necessary. It is probably true that the idea of a co-operative venture came from outside the group. It is certainly true that various, essentially middle-class outsiders provided various kinds of technical assistance which could not have been easily contributed by members of the group: helping with the preparation of cash flow projections, for example, and putting the women in touch with possible sources of finance. Since the start of trading, there have been small amounts of similar help – interpretation of stock figures, assessment of trading results and so on. However, in these respects too, the parallel with what happens when new co-ops are started in the Basque country is fairly close.

The women's indirect capital stakes in the venture took the form of guarantees by their husbands of a bank loan and a bank overdraft. These were also secured by a mortgage on the freehold of the 'Little Women' shop premises. The guarantees, nevertheless, were certainly perceived as real commitments and it was only after something of a struggle that the women persuaded their husbands to sign them. The consequence is that if the venture were to fail and if the sale of the premises were to yield less than the bank debt, then the husbands would become liable for the difference. The psychological importance of this commitment and risk can scarcely be exaggerated. Obviously it gave the women an interest in the venture which went well beyond next week's wage packet. Once again we have here an indirect parallel with Mondragon.

In the context of the current debate the importance of 'Little Women's' special features can scarcely be exaggerated. For it is often argued first, that the prospective working group cannot provide the main thrust in the setting up of a new co-operative; and, second, that working people in this country will always be unable or unwilling to put their own capital at risk. 'Little Women', dwarfish as the enterprise may be, shows that neither of these two positions are necessarily valid. I would in fact argue the opposite and suggest that no new co-operative undertaking should normally be set up unless the prospective workforce takes a major role in the promotion exercise and makes a meaningful contribution.

For a variety of reasons it is much more difficult for me to write objectively about Sunderlandia, the common-ownership building enterprise in Sunderland, than about any other of the ICOM companies. I was one of the company's three original promoters and probably, since

I had more time to work on it than the other two, most responsible for the original conception. For its first three and a half years to mid-November 1976, I was working there full time – and continued to do so on a part-time basis, as well as retaining other important links, thereafter. Quite apart from any difficulties in the way of objectivity which stem from this personal involvement and responsibility, the company's character at the beginning of 1978 was far from stabilized and its future far from certain. In effect after showing a substantial improvement during the first two years of its operations down to mid-1975, Sunderlandia's performance then deteriorated sharply at least up to the beginning of 1978. During 1977 it was forced to run down its workforce from roughly thirty at the start to roughly twenty at the end. Then, in early 1978 a new manager came in with the brief that he should keep going if possible pending an improvement in market conditions. But no one could be sure how many further enterprises would be swept away before better times emerged. Moreover, because of a series of initial mistakes, for which I was mainly responsible, and because of its record of losses, Sunderlandia's position in the early months of 1978 was far from strong. For all these reasons no confident predictions about its future were possible.

The original conception of Sunderlandia can, however, be told quite straightforwardly. Apart from the concept of a building enterprise, there were two main and separate ingredients. There was, first, a fairly radical democratic and common-ownership structure. Second, though entirely within the enterprise, there was a once-and-for-all, on-the-job and part-time release apprentice training programme which was designed to offer skilled employment opportunities to young Sunderland school leavers who were already then, in 1973, on the dole in large numbers. The necessary capital finance was to be provided in the form of loan stock, subscribed in part by the promoters, in part by outside sympathizers and friends. To begin with, the market was to be found in the modernization of old Sunderland houses, particularly 'Sunderland Cottages'. Because of the availability of substantial public grants at that time, demand for this work exceeded the supply of building capacity to deal with it.

The training arrangement scheme was based in part on a model followed in Britain during the war, in part on models evolved in developing Africa. The important characteristic of both was that they aimed to increase the ratio of apprentices to artisans in order to maximize the output of skill. In the original working papers this ratio was set at between four and five apprentices to one artisan, though the actual figure when operations began was closer to three to one. All these ratios were lower than those used either in Britain's war-time Master

Apprentice scheme or in the African models, but they were much greater than is currently normal in the industry – namely one apprentice to four or five skilled men. While on the subject of training I should add that before the start of production all the prospective joiner, bricklayer and plastering apprentices (though not the prospective apprentices in the ancillary trades) attended a seven-week course at the local technical college which cost the company around £7,000.

The radicalism of Sunderlandia's structure found concrete expression in a number of ways. To begin with there was no question of any permanent hold on power by the promoters. The constitution, more formally the Articles of Association, laid down that after the first annual general meeting (AGM) the promoters would find themselves in a minority on an otherwise elected board; that after the second AGM only one of them would remain a board member as of right; and that from the third AGM onwards none would enjoy any specially privileged position at all. Of course, one or more might be elected to the board, but there was no stipulation to that effect. In other words the constitution was informed by the democratic, libertarian, Left tradition. The Scott-Bader model of entrenched, colonial governor-type powers was consciously eschewed.

The same democratic, libertarian tradition determined that the franchise among the workforce be as open as possible; in principle the Articles laid down that anyone who had worked for Sunderlandia for three months was eligible for membership and that, unless there were good reasons to the contrary, all those eligible must become members. Moreover the apprentices who, because of the initial emphasis on the formation of skills, accounted for a large part of the total workforce, were not to be excluded from the franchise. I should not conceal that a majority of the qualified'tradesmen who joined Sunderlandia were initially opposed to the inclusion of the apprentices in the franchise. Rightly or wrongly, they were eventually persuaded to agree.

It was, I think, the same concern to achieve a genuine, non-bogus democracy, which assigned to the elected board of directors the only delegated authority of the General Meeting. Management was referred to in the company's Articles, but the authority of management was not established or defined. This reflected a specific concern that if powers were formally accorded to management, then the elected board might evolve into a purely symbolic, House of Lords type body. Yet many would argue that it also betrayed an inadequate grasp of the necessarily separate functions of management and of the need for formal management authority; they might suggest that for these reasons it amounted to a major error of judgment. With the benefit of hindsight I would certainly agree with these criticisms.

There was an element of radicalism too in aspects of Sunderlandia's financial arrangements. For though starting capital was provided by fixed interest loan stock there was also provision in the Articles for capital contributions from all the company's worker–members. In effect, the Articles laid down as a final target level for members' capital contributions a sum equivalent to six months' wages at current rates. However, there was also provision for this target to be modified and for the commencement of any capital contribution scheme to be postponed until well after the start of trading. In the event, if I may anticipate for a moment, the General Meeting later established a standard capital contribution to loan stock of £1 per head per week to be deducted from wages. By the first months of 1977 those who had been with Sunderlandia since the early days had contributed slightly over £100 each to its capital, though the bulk of these contributions had been withdrawn by the end of that year.

Another important area in which the company's Articles were specific and radical was that of differentials. Excluding apprentices, these laid down that differentials should not exceed 2:1 before tax. Moreover, well before the start of trading, it was agreed between the promoters and the building tradesmen who had come forward to join, that all non-apprentice worker–members would be paid the same. That common rate was fixed at £45 per week at the end of June 1973, or roughly one third above the minimum union level for that time. One reason for fixing the rate at this comparatively high level was the near-unanimous view that bonus working was the bane of the conventional building industry and that bonuses would not, therefore, normally be paid.

The Articles were also specific about union membership. Apart from a provision to cover objections on conscientious grounds, those who joined the company would have to join the relevant union. The most important reason for this insistence was the feeling that the unions had been responsible for an enormous improvement in wages and conditions and that people who joined the industry but not the union would thus be like passengers who joined the bus but declined to pay the fare.

Finally the company's Articles laid down a definite allocation of profits. Interest on the loan stock was, of course, treated as a cost. After providing that 20 per cent of any net profit must be applied to good causes outside the company, the remainder was to be divided in equal parts between the worker–membership as individuals and the worker–membership as a collective. In other words, 40 per cent of any net profits would have to be reinvested in Sunderlandia while the worker–members would be entitled as individuals to an equal sum.

If the special training effort associated with the launching is excluded, we can see that Sunderlandia's constitution reflects an amalgam of ideas. Commitment to a genuinely democratic, bottom-upwards and almost libertarian enterprise structure was perhaps the most important, but there is also evidence of a strong commitment to social justice embodied in the wage differential arrangements – and to some extent in the training effort. There was clearly too some attempt to modify, by the partially implemented scheme for capital contributions to loan stock, the seamless collective ownership of the 'high-minded' ICOM companies, and of Rowen Onllwyn and Trylon. And there was a rather more generous allocation of profits to individual worker–members than in those companies.

This constitution, it should be emphasized, was the work of the company's three promoters and particularly, as I have indicated, of myself. It was *explained* with a greater or lesser degree of detail to all those who applied to join. It is probably also true that, with the exception of the disagreement over the apprentice franchise, no formal opposition to any of the main provisions was expressed in the early stages. Against this, the extent to which those who joined felt really committed to the enterprise or its structure is another question. They had not initiated it. Nor had they provided the main thrust to get it going. And they were certainly not committed to it in a way which might, as in the case of 'Little Women' or of the Mondragon co-ops, carry the risk of capital loss. It is also doubtful whether the ideas of either a bottom-upwards enterprise structure, or of social justice, were sufficiently appealing in themselves to provide much in the way of enterprise solidarity or extra motivation. If we add that the role of management was left undefined and unbuttressed with formal authority, and that the new company had assumed a most unusually heavy burden of apprentice training, it can be appreciated that Sunderlandia was in for a quite tough struggle when it started trading in July 1973.

The Sunderlandia labour force shown in Table 6.1 was 27. That was the figure at the beginning of April 1977 – it was also the lowest figure since the start of trading. In the beginning total numbers had been between forty and fifty with just over thirty apprentices, but by the end of 1973 the apprentices had been thinned out and their ratio to tradesmen narrowed. Then, from the beginning of 1974 to the autumn of 1975 total numbers remained roughly stable, with just over twenty apprentices and a rather smaller number of tradesmen. However, towards the end of 1975 there was a further reduction, once again mainly of apprentices, but also including two non-apprentices. As a result the ratio between tradesmen and apprentices underwent a further shift. And during 1976 while total numbers oscillated between just over thirty to around forty-five, the tradesmen-apprentice ratio varied between about $2^1/_2$:1 and $3^1/_2$:1. In early 1977 total numbers fell below thirty for the first time.

There was, too, a sequence of variations in the company's work programme. For the first six months the modernization of Sunderland properties, normally for owner occupiers, constituted the bulk of the company's work. 'Modernization' usually involved the building of a new kitchen and bathroom, a new 'back-end' attached to Sunderland's charming and very serviceable single-storey cottages. Between twenty and thirty jobs were successfully completed. However, it had been clear from the outset that this market would not last, since the improvement grants available from public funds were due to be reduced from 75 per cent to 50 per cent in mid-1974.

Nevertheless, Sunderlandia was fortunate in managing to negotiate with a local housing association – before the end of 1973 and before the reduction in the level of grants – an important contract to modernize twenty terraced houses at Newfield, in rural County Durham. This, with three contracts to build large new vicarages for the Church Commissioners within reach of Sunderland, provided most of the work from the beginning of 1974 to mid-1975. Unlike those of most other agencies, the budget of the Church Commissioners was apparently impervious to the building cycle.

Finally from mid-1975 to early 1977, the largest part of the company's work was of two kinds. First, there were three more contracts to modernize blocks or clusters of old properties (as at Newfield) but second, the company undertook and completed the design and construction of a new development, with a total of eleven house units on its own account. The houses were designed by Michael Pearce, a fellow promoter of Sunderlandia and the company's production supervisor from the start. All but one had been sold by the end of 1977 and both the designs and their execution were widely acclaimed.

Before turning to the economic results produced by Sunderlandia, something needs to be said about the evolution of the company's board of directors, about the question of management, and about the performance of the general meeting. In the case of the board, the electorate of the General Meeting quickly showed its independence – and the reality of the company's bottom-upwards power structure – by declining to re-elect me in the autumn of 1974. But the main break – and assertion of power from the bottom – came a year later when not one of the original promoters was even nominated for board membership and when the incoming board was dominated by tradesmen. On the other hand, that situation did not last either; within six months of their election four of the chosen tradesmen had quit the company. My fellow promoters, Michael Pearce and Peter Smith, were both re-elected as directors in successive by-elections early in 1976.

The re-establishment of Michel Pearce on the Sunderlandia board in early 1976 was reinforced later in the year when the company's General Meeting passed a resolution formally designating him as General Manager and assigning various powers to the post. By early 1977 there was also a growing feeling inside the company that subordinate management posts, manned by general foremen, should be introduced below the general manager on the larger sites, and that happened in Sunderlandia's largest site in June 1977. In other words, the initial error of failing to define management posts and management authority was finally corrected.

We have already seen how the sovereign assembly of Sunderlandia's General Meeting asserted its power. More disturbingly, and at least up to the end of 1976, it had shown little inclination − unlike its counterparts in other co-operatives − to adopt attitudes significantly different from those of the traditional shop floor. In particular, up to the end of 1976 it had shown little restraint on questions of wages; and very little in the way of serious commitment to improving productivity. I say 'more disturbingly' because it is clear that disaster is the only probable result if those with the power choose to use it without restraint and without regard to any but the most short term consequences.

Against this background the economic performance of Sunderlandia over the first three and a half years of its existence can now be quickly summarized. In round figures the results were as shown in Table 6.3.

TABLE 6.3   Economic performance of Sunderlandia, 1973–6

Dates	Turnover £	Trading loss* £
1973–4	130,000	(5,500)
1974–5	195,000	(1,400)
18 months to end 1976	360,000	(14,000)
1975–6 at annual rate	240,000	(9,350)

* After interest and depreciation. Though final figures for 1977 were not available when this was written, it was already clear that the results might well be worse than in the previous year.

Common sense as well as a comparison with the earlier Trylon figures suggests that the results of the first two years were not far short of respectable. Indeed if, as in the case of Trylon, trading losses to mid-1975 are regarded as mainly a concealed cost of 'market entry' we should not be particularly disturbed by these. At mid-1975 it might have seemed reasonable to believe that, whatever the conceptual and other errors in its establishment, and however over-ambitious its initial training programme, the company had succeeded in breaking into the market and in establishing a position of near equilibrium. Stretching the evidence a little one might even go on to 'explain away' the subsequent losses by referring to the especially tricky nature of modernization contracts and point out that building enterprises with much more experience than Sunderlandia lost large sums when engaged in that kind of work in the late 1970s.

Now it is certainly true that up to the end of 1977 Sunderlandia never succeeded in making profits on modernization contracts which covered more than one or two units. It is also true that it lost more money on one of these contracts alone than the total of its accumulated trading losses for its first three and a half years. Partly because it is systematically difficult for all the work to be specified in advance – which militates against efficient programming – and partly for other reasons, these modernization contracts undoubtedly involve special hazards for the builder. Moreover, for the period from mid-1975 to early 1978 the bulk of Sunderlandia's workforce was engaged in this work.

With the benefit of hindsight it also appears to be true that the company's results were adversely affected from the beginning by the decision to make a complete break with the bonus systems of payments which are normal in the industry. The building tradesmen had been emphatic in their opposition to any productivity-related bonus system from the very first discussions before trading started. They argued that such arrangements set people against each other and resulted in poor quality workmanship. So the decision was taken to pay roughly one-third above the normal industry rates and to forego a bonus entirely. On the other hand, both the results and casual observation suggest that for much of the time Sunderlandia was paying bonus levels of wages without getting bonus rates of work. Quality, as the tradesmen argued, was doubtless improved, but then above a certain minimum threshold a building enterprise like Sunderlandia is not paid any extra for any extra quality.

Yet, since it operated from the start, the absence of any productivity-related bonus scheme cannot explain the deterioration in Sunderlandia's performance after mid-1975. My own feeling is that in so far as it was not due to the modernization contracts, that deterioration resulted mainly from a sharp increase in antagonism between the company's blue- and white-collar workers from mid-1975 onwards. This heightened antagonism was reflected in the composition of the board elected in late 1975. In a show of strength a new 'working-class leadership' took over. The fact that the majority of the new board had resigned and quit the company within six months of their election must suggest that the arrangements which allowed this take-over were faulty. For my part I remember feeling in the hopeless position of someone who has moral responsibility but no authority. I also remember feeling that I had never worked in a team in which mutual trust was so low.

What lessons, if any, does Sunderlandia's experience proffer? It seems first to confirm that, at least above a very small size, attempts to work without a properly defined management system and authority are doomed. Indeed it seems to confirm too that however much democratic power from the bottom upwards needs to be real and genuine – if the whole exercise is not to be dismissed as a confidence trick – this must be compatible with management's authority. Libertarian democracy cannot, in other words, be the single overriding value because democratic power has to be reconciled with the requirements of efficient management.

Sunderlandia's experience seems also to show that a new democratic enterprise needs a serious commitment to it by the people involved, blue-collar as well as white-collar. In particular the commitment has to include a recognition that, in a democratic enterprise, the normal adversary attitudes of shop floor to management are not merely inappropriate – they may well be suicidal.

However, having said that, and having criticized the Sunderlandia shop floor quite explicitly and sharply, I must emphasize once again that the initial errors were not theirs and that they were in fact mainly my own. Those initial errors, it may well be argued, prevented the company from reaching a position of profitable trading in a reasonable period of time and thus caused demoralization and resentment to set in. It could further be argued that, like those Christian Socialist enterprises in the 1850s, Sunderlandia's main importance lies in the fact that it shows how such enterprises should *not* be started. As the person mainly responsible for initiating the experiment, clearly I, rather than the building tradesmen, must take the main responsibility for the poor results which followed.

We can now consider the experience of these four 'standing start' ICOM companies – Trylon, Rowen Onllwyn, 'Little Women' and Sunderlandia – as a whole. On the face of it, all but Sunderlandia succeeded in attracting the loyalty of their workforces and in eliciting from them attitudes which transcended the traditional adversative position of the shop floor. As well as Sunderlandia's admitted mistakes, its larger starting size may well be an important factor. One deduction might be that if democratic enterprises are to be started from scratch, really small beginnings have a better chance of achieving success.

I am sure there is no doubt about the truth of that. However, I also believe that the necessary loyalty and commitment can be ensured in ways which make starting size less important and which do not condemn new democratic enterprises to the most dwarfish terms. What I have in mind is the start up model more or less followed by 'Little Women' and evolved in detail, as we shall see later, in the Mondragon co-operatives. According to that model there are at least two necessary conditions for starting a new democratic, co-operative venture. One is that a majority of the prospective workforce should play an important part in getting if off the ground. The second is that through a meaningful capital stake each of the starting work-group should have an interest in the success of the enterprise which goes substantially further than next week's wages.

A quite separate lesson about growth incentives is to be drawn from the experience of these 'standing start' companies. Trylon's experience provides very strong evidence that collective, unindividuated ownership may fail to encourage expansion and profit growth. Some may feel that this is no bad thing but, as the Mondragon experience will show, a group of co-ops is perfectly able to commit itself to growth if it so chooses; there is nothing in the democratic structures themselves which is irreconcilable with sustained expansion.

Finally there is the very specific evidence from Rowen Onllwyn that a genuinely democratic enterprise is not free to remain subordinate to any outside body except possibly to a co-operative federation. For the experience of Rowen Onllwyn makes clear that to maintain this subordination, for example to a union, may put survival at risk; and Rowen's experience also makes clear just how vulnerable these isolated enterprises are.

Landsman's Co-ownership, the last of the ICOM-type companies examined in this chapter, was forced largely by adverse market conditions to cut back its activities very sharply in the autumn of 1977. Having started after the Second World War as a business engaged exclusively in hiring out industrial caravans, it had later expanded into manufacturing them as well. In late 1977 it was forced to close down the manufacturing side of the business, to reduce its workforce from thirty-five to twelve, and to revert to hiring operations alone. These were understood to be quite unambiguously profitable in early 1978 and the prospect of resuming manufacture once market conditions improved was certainly not ruled out. However, that prospect was, of course, entirely speculative.

However, the chief interest of Landsman's is not so much that its 1977 experience demonstrates once again just how vulnerable isolated enterprises of this kind are bound to be; it is included in this chapter for rather different reasons. First, it shows that a conventional private business (or by implication a state owned one) can be transformed into a co-op owned by its workforce, not only by gift or official *fiat* but by a gradual process of being bought out by its employees. In other words, those who advocate the enlargement of a worker-owned co-operative sector do not have to rely on acts of magnificent charity by extraordinary figures like Ernest Bader, or on the chance presence at the Industry ministry of some one as single-minded as Mr Wedgwood Benn. The whole process can take place on a much more mundane and workaday basis – as a business transaction, like buying a kipper at the fishmonger, or more exactly like buying a house on a mortgage or a new car on hire purchase. Second, what we have here is an example of a business sold to its workforce not as a collective unit but as an aggregate of individuals; what resulted was not collective ownership as at Scott-Bader and elsewhere, but individual worker ownership.

Landsman's was started in the village of Buckden outside Huntingdon, by David and Anne Spreckley shortly after the Second World War. The company's initial business of industrial caravan hire quickly became prosperous and the enlargement of its activities to include manufacture took place in the early 1950s. By the early 1960s it was employing between thirty and forty people.

The initiative for the change to Landsman's Co-ownership came from the Spreckleys. They were enthusiastic about the related ideas of worker–ownership and industrial democracy and knew of the pioneering work of Ernest Bader (for Buckden is within easy motoring distance of Wollaston). But though the Spreckleys admired what had happened at Scott-Bader, they firmly decided against the 'gift model'. For one thing, so David argued, that model was never going to be universalized; there were not nearly enough 'high-minded heroes' for the number of gift transformations to exceed a handful. Thus, they felt that if the main aim was to launch a valuable (because widely replicable) social and economic experiment – rather than to make a grand gesture – it was more sensible for the labour force to buy the company rather than to be given it.

The transaction they worked out was simple, in its essentials at any rate. Two notionally distinct processes had to take place: the workforce had to buy Landsman's; it also had to acquire voting control. The first was accomplished essentially by converting the original Spreckley-owned equity shares into fixed interest stock and by assigning all future profits to the workforce, mainly in the form of new shares. The second was accomplished by assigning relative voting weights to the new workforce shares and to the Spreckley-owned fixed interest stock. This was done in such a way that, assuming a reasonable level of profit after meeting all expenses (including financial charges), the control of the company would move gradually out of the Spreckleys' hands and into those of the new co-owners.

All that happened. The Spreckleys old shareholdings were valued at their market price on 'transformation day' (equivalent to 'vesting day' when a company is taken into public ownership) and converted into fixed interest non-transferable 'A' shares, redeemable over a period. From the same day profits accrued not to the Spreckleys but to the workforce 'co-owners' in proportion to their earnings over the same accounting year. These profits were mainly issued to the workforce in the form of new 'B' shares (in normal years about 60 per cent), and only partially in cash. Finally, each Spreckley fixed interest 'A' share was assigned 50 per cent of the voting power of the new 'B' shares. Profits and 'B' share issues were such that the 'B' shares achieved majority control in five years.

There were defects of detail, which the Spreckleys acknowledge, in this model, but the main point to emphasize is that it worked. It worked gradually and without the changes causing any disruption. And because the company remained sufficiently profitable, it worked in a way which was financially quite painless from the workforce's point of view. At no time did any wages have to be foregone to enable the workforce to acquire their ownership of the business. Indeed because 40 per cent of their profit shares were normally paid in cash, the workforce was better off after the transformation, both on current and capital account.

The transformation worked in another sense. The Spreckleys reckon from their experience that, starting from the 'normal' shop-floor attitudes, it takes three years or more for the ordinary person to acquire the new outlook appropriate to a worker–owner who shares in final control over the responsibility for the enterprise. Of course, a classroom-type knowledge of the arrangements will come earlier; shop-floor workers will be able to give correct answers about the new arrangements to visiting journalists from a very early date; but real understanding, defined as something which can relevantly modify attitudes and behaviour, will only come later.

The Spreckleys cite numerous examples of attitude changes, all reflecting a much greater identification with and responsibility for, the company's interests: an end to pilfering reflected in the abandonment of actively irresponsible attitudes. When an assistant manager left in the late 1950s it was found that there was no need to replace him because in large measure people had assumed responsibility for monitoring their own performance. Needless to say for a company of Landsman's size – its workforce has never moved out of the thirty to forty range – the elimination of an assistant manager's wage can have a positive effect on profits.

From the shop-floor point of view the transformation enabled the company's employee–members to accumulate most worth-while capital stakes. For obvious reasons of cash flow and liquidity protection, the rules only allow gradual disinvestment over a period of up to five years if someone leaves before retirement. On retirement, on the other hand, a worker–owner is entitled to take out his or her entire capital stake. The cleaning lady who retired early in 1977 took out more than £1,200. The capital stakes of the more highly skilled workforce members with a similar length of service were, of course, because of their higher wage rates, substantially larger than hers by the same time.

One feature of their model which the Spreckleys will now acknowledge was wrong was that they failed to provide for any compulsory and indivisible reserve funds. The argument which dissuaded them was clear enough: they saw it as inequitable that the work of any particular generation of co-owners should contribute to the wealth of the next. But they now concede that pragmatic considerations in this case should have greater weight than purist theoretical ones. Without indivisible reserve funds it may be very difficult, if not impossible, for one generation of co-owners to pay itself off on retirement by finding any but conventional capitalists to buy the business. In which case, of course, the worker–ownership experience can last for one generation only. That is a problem, incidentally, shared by many of the plywood co-ops in the north west of the US.

There are other objections to arrangements which exclude indivisible reserve funds. New investment may well be discouraged. The impact of any losses will be experienced much more directly and sharply – since individual capital stakes will have to be written down. Moreover the absence of any indivisible reserve funds is probably an extra disincentive to expansion. On the basis that 'small is beautiful', some may regard it as a plus rather than a minus. All the same, those who believe in an enlarged co-operative sector cannot logically opt for a model which actively discourages expansion. On the other hand, the Spreckleys and their fellow Landsman's co-owners recognized in 1975 that the absence of any provision for allocating a share of profits to indivisible reserve funds is a mistake; thereafter *ad hoc* decisions were taken in an effort to correct it.

Yet the Landsman's model is manifestly more important for its positive lessons than for its defects. It shows that a gradual and business-like transformation is possible and that, providing the enterprise remains adequately profitable, the workforce can buy it without foregoing any present wages and indeed with benefit to themselves on both current and capital account. Equally important it shows that slowly, after the formal and financial transformation, attitudes start to change in the direction of an increasing degree of shop-floor responsibility; it would be most perverse to contend that that was not a change for the better.

Of course, it may be said that if the workforce has been the financial gainer from the transformation, the Spreckleys have been the losers. In a sense that is true. In 1964 the Spreckleys exchanged their total ownership of profits past and future for a fixed sum (covering the past) and no more than their own wage-related share in future profits. If an unchanged Landsman's had been as profitable as the transformed model then the Spreckleys would clearly be richer than they are. But that is to bring only money into the calculus. Certainly the Spreckleys behave as if they have had a great deal of satisfaction out of a most worth-while experience; I have never heard them express any regrets.

The more serious point about the transaction by which the workforce bought out the Spreckleys is rather different. Public opinion recognizes that existing owners may in principle be bought out – as in the case where a business comes into public ownership – without doing flagrant violence to private property rights. Of course, there may always be disputes about a fair price – especially where the putative value of future profits is involved. In principle, however, an equitable bargain between willing buyers and willing sellers can be struck. The Spreckleys have shown that this can happen in practice between a workforce and private owners, just as much as between the state and private owners – indeed there is no reason why it should not happen between a workforce and the state.

These positive aspects of Landsman's experience are not, it seems to me, seriously invalidated by the events of 1977 when, as we saw earlier, the company was forced to revert back to caravan hire alone and to cut the workforce by two-thirds. External market factors, rather than the company's structure or transformation history, were the main cause of those decisions. It is true, of course, that its capacity to ride out market difficulties would have been greater if indivisible reserve funds had been built up from the start. It is also true that a complicating factor in 1976 and early 1977 was a basically ideological withdrawal by David Spreckley from his position of Managing Director into an advisory role – a withdrawal which was reversed in late 1977. However, the main point about the events of 1977 is that it was the company's isolation which made it so specially vulnerable; had it been part of a strong and mutually supporting group (like the Mondragon co-operatives), it might well have succeeded in weathering the market downturn.

One final point is worth adding in answer to those who will assert that the company's difficulties in 1977 provide powerful support to the argument that workers' savings should never be put at risk alongside their jobs. When Landsman's manufacturing operation was closed down the factory in which that had taken place was sold quickly and well. As a result the value of its 'B' shares was reported in early 1978 to be fully intact. Thus neither those who were forced to leave the company, nor those who remained, in fact lost their savings.

7
The 'Wedgwood Benn' co-ops

The so-called 'Wedgwood Benn' co-ops, the Meriden Motorcycle enterprise, the now defunct *Scottish Daily News*, and the co-operative conglomerate, Kirkby Manufacturing and Engineering (KME), are the three largest examples of a new phenomenon within the British co-operative scene: the employment protection or anti-redundancy co-ops. (Opponents might call them the Canute co-ops because they have attempted to defy the tide of capitalist change.) They are not the only examples. Apart from Fakenham Enterprises which, like the *Scottish Daily News*, though after a much longer struggle, is now also defunct, there have been other examples of the same phenomenon in Britain: Leadgate Engineering at Consett in County Durham and an enterprise called Bardrec Ltd in Lanarkshire which makes highly specialized screws. As we shall see later there are also examples in France.

In all these cases the co-operative enterprises were launched, following a longer or shorter period of delay, after the close down of an earlier capitalist business. In all cases (except possibly one), the thrust and leadership which eventually resulted in the establishment of the co-op came from the shop floor. Yet in no case – unlike the position at the end of the last century – does there seem to have been any strong initial feelings in favour of the co-operative form. On the contrary, there is good evidence that the workforces would have preferred – and certainly have settled for – continued employment under capitalist arrangements, had it been possible to persuade former owners to reverse close down decisions or to invite new capitalists to move in.

It is hard to imagine a less promising set of starting conditions: you have previous capitalist failure; you have the disruption caused by a hiatus of longer or shorter extent; you have the re-born enterprise working within structures of no one's very enthusiastic choice and of which none has any direct experience. What may be surprising in the circumstances is not so much that the *Scottish Daily News* and Fakenham Enterprises have failed, but that the casualty rate has not been higher.

Apart from their relatively large size, the 'Wedgwood Benn' co-ops are special cases of the general phenomenon of the anti-redundancy co-op only in a rather narrow sense: their rebirth would almost certainly never have taken place had it not been for determined action on their behalf by Mr Wedgwood Benn when he was Industry Minister between the end of February 1974 and July 1975. Each was the beneficiary of substantial government grant money or loan money or both. In each case too, government funds were made available against the explicit advice of the official Civil Service. Moreover, it is easy to credit the reports that Mr Wedgwood Benn had some difficulty persuading his fellow Cabinet members that any public money at all should be risked in this way.

I shall do little more than mention the *Scottish Daily News*. Its experience as a co-operative – barely six months between May and November 1974 – was really too short and too turbulent for any reliable lessons to be learnt. I would also suspect that the involvement of Mr Robert Maxwell, however indispensable financially, was deeply unsettling and must have been a real obstacle to the development of a genuinely co-operative form.

However there are two special points about the *Scottish Daily News* which may be worth emphasizing. The first is that all those employed on the reborn enterprise invested money, normally a percentage of the redundancy payments which they had received from the old *Scottish Daily Express* when that closed down, into the new venture. There were some 600 on the co-op's payroll. What they put in together came to roughly £200,000 so that we are talking about an average of a little over £300 each. It is easy to see that such investment must have strengthened their commitment to making their venture a success. And it is obviously sensible when 'redundancy co-ops' are attempted that redundancy money from the former employers should contribute to the required finance. This has in fact become almost a rule in similar cases occurring in France.

On the other hand, whatever extra commitment these workforce capital contributions may have generated, it was clearly insufficient to make the difference between success and failure. I suppose that in their advice about the possible newspaper Mr Wedgwood Benn's Civil Servants must now be judged to have been proved correct: market conditions, they told him, were too unpromising for there to be any real chance of success. On the other hand, in at least two published accounts, there has been strong criticism of the journalists for their failure to develop a distinctive style and character for the paper – with at least the implicit suggestion that, had they done so, the result might have been different. In the end there is really no method for assigning proper weight to these other factors in any full explanation of why the *Scottish Daily News* failed. Yet it would be perverse to argue that its co-operative structure was the only, or even the main, cause.

In contrast to the *Scottish Daily News*, and at least by the end of its third year, Meriden Motorcycles Ltd (the co-op successor of the original Triumph Motor cycle enterprise), looked as if it had a very fair chance of medium-term survival. To begin with it had a product, the Triumph Bonneville, with a strong market and one which seemed able to capture the imagination of consumers and producers alike. Second, by the end of 1977, it had emerged from an early almost 'primitive Christian' phase during which it had been assumed that conventional management could be largely dispensed with. A team of five professional executives had been appointed. Third, the co-op appeared to have attracted a real measure of shop-floor loyalty. Despite the fact that its wage rates were well below those prevailing in the neighbourhood, its productivity was significantly higher than under the previous capitalist régime and its labour turnover was almost negligible. So, despite audited losses for the first two and a half years of its existence, a cautious optimism about the co-op's future seemed to be in order.

A look at the background to the Meriden experiment takes us back to early 1973 when the Tory government made a grant of £4.8m of taxpayers' money to Norton Villiers Triumph (NVT) to assist with the rationalization of the British motor cycle industry which was clearly in poor shape. The Meriden works formed the Triumph division of the NVT operation. When rationalization plans were drawn up by management in 1973, it was decided that production at the Meriden site should be rapidly phased out and motor cycle manufacture concentrated at the company's two other plants: the former BSA factory at Small Heath in Birmingham and Norton's own works in Wolverhampton. These plans also provided that, after a short run down phase, the entire Meriden work force of 1,750 should become redundant.

The announcement of these plans to trade union representatives of the Meriden workforce in September 1975 produced an immediate response. Work was for the time being continued as normal, but no finished motor cycles were allowed to leave the premises and the removal of other stocks, or of any machinery, was prevented. A long struggle part work-in part sit-in, had begun.

There is no need to rehearse in any detail the long sequence of events which intervened over a period of eighteen months from the announcement of the rationalization plans by Mr Dennis Poore, the NVT Managing Director in September 1973, to the start of trading by

the new Meriden co-op in March 1975. Ken Fleet* has provided a full
account in his contribution to *The New Worker Co-operatives*. But two
points stand out in this period and are worth emphasizing. First, the determination and solidarity of the workforce under the leadership of their
senior shop stewards convenor, Mr Dennis Johnson: there can be no
doubt that there would have been no co-op had the workforce not
shown an implacable refusal to accept the close down. Second, it must
surely also be true that the co-op would never have existed if Labour had
not won the election in February 1974 and if Mr Wedgwood Benn had
not been appointed Industry Minister. As it was a package of just under
£5m of taxpayers' money (including £750,000 of straight grant and
£4.2m of concessionary loans) it was eventually approved by the
Cabinet – subject to certain conditions. With this money it became
possible for the manufacture of motor cycles to be resumed at Meriden
and this happened, under the auspices of the new co-op venture, in
March 1975.

We know that the co-op lost money from March 1975 to September
1977 – an audited £1.2m in the first year – proportionately rather less so
over the next accounting period of eighteen months. We know too that
its difficulties were such in early 1977 as to make necessary a support
operation. Sir Arnold Weinstock and his General Electric Company
agreed to come forward and help the co-op with management and
finance. The financial help took the form of a cash advance by GEC of
£1m against 2,000 stockpiled Meriden motor cycles, or £500 per cycle.
Management help was headed by Mr Bill Morgan, GEC's Assistant
Managing Director, with half a dozen professionals in support. By the
end of the year the stockpile of motor cycles had been cleared and GEC
had fully recouped its £1m. Moreover, shortly before the year end, and
after considerable soul searching, the co-op had appointed its own
management team. So the need for professional GEC assistance fell
away. Mr Morgan was reported as saying that by the time of GEC's
withdrawal at the end of 1977, the co-op had succeeded in 'pulling a
workshop into a full fledged business'. From both sides in early 1978 –
from the co-op and from GEC – there were expressions of respect for the
other; certainly, there was no suggestion that the break with GEC
reflected disillusion on the company's part.

The other key development in 1977 was that the co-op was enabled,
with a further £500,000 of taxpayers' money, to purchase the marketing
side of its business from NVT and thus to become responsible for the

---

* Ken Fleet, 'Triumph Meriden', in Ken Coates (ed.), *The New Worker Co-
operatives*, published for the Institute for Workers' Control, Spokesman
Books, Nottingham, 1976, pp. 88 ff.

selling, as well as for the manufacture, of its motor cycles. The retention of responsibility for marketing by NVT had, in fact, been one of the main conditions on which the original money was made available in early 1975, and for the two following years the co-op acted essentially as a production sub-contractor to NVT. Whatever the theoretical justification for these arrangements they seem to have worked badly for both parties: the co-op claimed that the build-up of its stockpile in early 1977 was the result of inefficient selling by NVT; the company countered predictably that it was due to erratic production by the co-op. In this sort of situation it is rarely possible for an outsider to get at the truth, but if the Meriden co-op is to be taken as a valid test of whether enterprises of this kind can succeed, then it is clearly necessary that it should be responsible for the entire operation – for selling as well as production. Certainly, in early 1978 the co-op's management and its elected leaders were both saying that they had felt far less uneasy about the future since responsibility for sales has been assumed.

With its new professional management team satisfactorily installed and apparently accepted, and with its capacity fully booked to the late summer, Meriden Motorcycles Ltd seemed in early 1978 to have created the conditions for steady work and cautious development. Whether that was going to happen appeared to depend on two sets of questions, one external the second internal to the co-op. Externally, the questions were about the strength and duration of the market for the Triumph Bonneville motorcycle; internally the questions were about whether the co-op could extend its already significant productivity gains and could do so to the point where an adequate margin of profit was achieved.

In 1978 optimism at Meriden about the demand for the Bonneville rested on the contention that this was a quality product with its own special market. With annual production running at something over 16,000 motor cycles they were clearly not producing for a mass market. Moreover they were not tooled for a mass production exercise. The assembly lines at the Meriden works are controlled by hand and not by machine. The co-op argued that it was precisely this factor – a quality production which could be sold as a hand-made one – which ensured them their place in the market. They claimed further that their dealers in the US – who were still taking more than two-thirds of the co-op's total output – had expressed confidence that the American market would remain strong for at least five more years. They also pointed to the evidence of market strength provided by new orders from elsewhere, from Canada and Australia and from Western Europe and the Middle East.

Assuming that the predictions about an assured market for five years into the early 1980's turn out to be right, then the co-op's leaders were presumably also right to argue in early 1978 that Meriden enjoyed a brief breathing space. But they were fully aware too that if a new or significantly modified model was to be developed for the markets of the middle 1980s, then design studies would have to be under way by 1979 and considerable capital funds would have to be found. So what were the prospects, looked at in early 1978, that that co-op might be able to raise a fair part of any development budget from its own cash flow?

The realistic answer seemed to be that such prospects were not too good. It is true that at the start of its fourth year in March 1978 the co-op could point to considerable improvements compared both to its earlier years and to its former operations as a division of NVT. Under NVT's régime, a labour force of 1,750 have been producing 750-800 motor cycles per week, or roughly twenty-one per man year. In March 1978, the corresponding figures were a labour force of 650 and a weekly output of around 350, or roughly twenty-six per man year. It was also suggested in early 1978 that the co-op's market position was becoming strong enough for some differential price increases to be contemplated.

However, as against these positive factors there was a very real and understandable pressure from the bottom upwards for increased basic wages. Leaving aside a productivity bonus shared equally by the entire non-management work-force, the wage rate paid across the board to everyone was still no more than £58.80 in early 1978 — or roughly £10 less than corresponding wage levels in the area. It seemed probable that if and when a fair margin of profit was achieved (or even before) the pressure for higher basic wages — to catch up with the neighbourhood as well as to offset inflation — would become irresistible. The limits within which funds might be diverted from the cash flow for future development seemed, therefore, to be quite narrow.

On the other hand, my own view would be that even if Meriden Motorcycles Ltd only survives for the market life of its present model, this experiment has been enormously worth-while and has fully justified the taxpayers' money which has made it possible. The co-op seems to me to demonstrate that ordinary working people in the UK of the 1970s can evolve democratic enterprise structures which have a fair chance of success: they can come to recognize that professional management is just as necessary in a co-op as it is in a capitalist operation; they can come to behave with unusual forebearance and responsibility in the matter of wage rates and to identify quite closely with longer-term enterprise goals. This success, limited as it may be, must encourage optimism about what could be achieved if the co-op was not operating as an isolated venture but was part of a mutually supporting and mutually financing group, as at Mondragon. This relative success suggests too that it would be wrong to argue, if Meriden eventually fails, that that was because of some inherent weakness in their democratic structure as such. It is much more likely to be due to a combination of special factors together with the co-op's isolation. A co-op solution must always be a vulnerable solution, on this hypothesis, if it is attempted on a single enterprise basis.

Partly because it attracted special attention from the start of the co-op's existence, partly because of its inherent importance, a final word needs to be added about wages policy. The single basic rate of £58.50 paid to all members of the workforce (aside from the professional management team) in early 1978 has already been mentioned. A single rate, eliminating traditional differentials between the skilled and the unskilled, has in fact been a key feature of wages policy since the co-op was launched. Until early 1978, the only major modification of this policy was that associated with the decision in late 1977 to appoint a fully professional management team. It was a mark of the co-op's increasing realism and maturity that when that decision was taken it was also decided that the team should be paid competitive rates.

There was also, it is true, a brief experiment with differential productivity bonus rates for the more and the less skilled outside of the management team. Under the first productivity bonus scheme approved by the co-op's General Meeting, some 250 of the more skilled received a £4 weekly bonus before any other bonuses were paid – with any available balance divided equally between the workforce as a whole. However, early in February 1978 the workforce reversed that decision and any productivity bonus money was thereafter shared out equally. In other words the forces favouring enterprise solidarity seemed stronger at Meriden, when that vote was taken, than those favouring differentials.

It would not be altogether surprising in the longer run, and if profitability is achieved, if the forces favouring differentials grow stronger. However, the co-op's low turnover of labour seems to suggest that at least during its first four years of struggling to survive, Meriden's enterprise solidarity was a source of strength rather than weakness. Certainly the co-op's elected leadership was anxious to stress the positive aspects of no differentials early in 1978. This leadership, consisting of the co-op's elected board, was also refreshingly down-to-earth when asked if there were any plans for them to be paid directors' fees. 'We would not last for twenty-four hours if we tried that,' I was told.

Early in February 1978 workers at Kirkby Manufacturing and Engineering, the conglomerate enterprise outside Liverpool and the third 'Wedgwood Benn' co-op, were addressed in a meeting behind closed doors by Mr Robert Kilroy-Silk, the Labour MP in whose constituency the co-op is situated; the Press was not admitted. The source of the initiative which gave rise to the meeting was not disclosed, but there was no doubt about the main thrust of Mr Kilroy-Silk's message: the co-op must not expect any further grants of taxpayers' money; it would have to stand on its own feet or go under.

A plausible view about the genesis of this meeting traced it back to the government in general and to Mr Wedgwood Benn (as the co-op's original 'fairy godmother') in particular. Roughly a year before, in January 1975, Kirkby had received a new grant of £860,000 of tax-payers' money to bolster what was left of the original £3.9m grant which had enabled the co-op to start trading in the first place. It had shown losses in two sets of published accounts – well over £1m for its first fifteen months and roughly £300,000 in the year to April 1977. Moreover, at the meeting in early February 1978, it was conceded by Mr Jack Spriggs, one of the co-op's two Directors, that the results of the year to April 1978 were unlikely to show a significant improvement compared with those of the previous twelve months. Fearing that the further set of audited losses would precipitate a further request for additional grant money from the co-op, the government, in the plausible view circulating in Liverpool at the time of the meeting, had dispatched Mr Kilroy-Silk to announce in advance that such a request would be turned down.

Thus, whereas in early 1977 (at the time of GEC's support operation at Meriden), the prospect at Kirkby had looked to be the brighter of the two, a year later the position had been reversed. For though Kirkby had shown greatly improved results for the year to April 1977, it had evidently not managed to extend that improvement a year later to the point of becoming profitable. And though, as we shall see, it could point to substantial productivity gains and greater workforce flexibility compared with both its own early period and with the position under the pre-co-op capitalist régimes, it was doubtful whether these had gone far enough for anyone to be very confident about long-term survival. Early in 1978, some argued that the co-op, while it might soldier on a while longer, would succumb sooner or later to the 'Merseyside Disease' – a particularly virulent strain of the general British complaint of low manufacturing productivity. Others with more optimism suggested that the rationalization measures already in hand, together with the prospective upturn in the economy, would be sufficent to ensure at least medium-term survival. There was no reliable method of choosing correctly between those two predictions.

In some ways Kirkby's prospects had looked more promising than Meriden's not only in early 1977 but from its start of trading in January

1975. The hiatus between the end of capitalist production and its resumption under co-op auspices was less than half as long at Kirkby as it had been at Meriden. There was also continuity of key management figures. Then too Kirkby was fully responsible for its own selling from the start and this avoided some of the special problems which beset Meriden.

However, that is not to say that Kirkby's path was easy in its early days. It had to contend with a formidable array of obstacles both from the start of trading and before. To understand these we must go back briefly to its previous history as a capitalist undertaking and to the events that led up to the original grant of £3.9m of taxpayers' money. The story has been told in some detail by Professor Tony Eccles* in his excellent contribution to *New Worker Co-operatives*. Only the main points will be covered here.

The original KME factory and offices were built on the edge of the Kirkby Industrial Estate just outside Liverpool by Fisher Bendix in 1960. The complex was planned on a generous scale. The largest single building has an area of just over 300,000 sq. ft and was designed for an eventual labour force of 3,000. Domestic appliances were mass produced during the early 1960s and the initial success was such that by 1964 the factory was employing three full shifts and working round the clock.

However, this good start was not maintained beyond the mid-1960s. First Fisher Bendix itself, then the three companies which followed it in succession as owners of the Kirkby plant – Parkinson Cowan, Thorn and International Property Development (Industry) (IPD)(I) – all made losses. The fourth and the last IPD(I) not only made losses; eventually, in July 1974, it went into receivership.

Difficult market conditions may well have been an important factor in this dismal record, but it seems clear that other problems more specific to Kirkby were also involved. After the mid-1960s the labour force never looked as if it would begin to approach the target 3,000 level. As numbers tended to contract so the weight of fixed overheads became more burdensome. More important, there seems to have been little real commitment on the part of successive owners to find a way forward which would ensure profitability and thus the continuity of employment at Kirkby. Meanwhile, on the other side, the successive owners were faced with a tightly organized and fully unionized shop floor with both defensive and militant attitudes. And the 'Merseyside Disease' cannot have helped.

---

* Tony Eccles, 'Kirkby Manufacturing and Engineering', in *ibid.*, pp. 141 ff.

Moreover, the product mix was changed and changed again. By mid-1974 its main engineering items were not washing machines or any of the other sophisticated domestic appliances associated with the earlier days of Fisher Bendix, Parkinson Cowan and Thorn but domestic radiators, night storage heaters and contract pressing work. One other, less congruous product was brought in by IPD(I) from a loss making operation in Surrey during the pre-receivership year: soft drinks.

One further point of background should be stressed. Over the years and under the leadership of the plant's two convenors of shop stewards, Jack Sprigg of the Amalgamated Union of Engineering Workers (AUEW) and Dick Jenkins of the Transport and General Workers' Union (TGWU), the tightly organized labour force had become a determined body of men. Twice during Thorn's régime, in June 1971 and January 1972, the workforce had been successful, by taking determined industrial action, in thwarting or modifying management plans for employment reductions or closure. It was scarcely surprising, therefore, that the official receiver was forced to negotiate with the men as soon as he appeared on the plant premises in the second week of July 1974 – and was forced to agree to at least a postponement of his planned redundancies in return for a work-sharing agreement.

The detailed sequence of events from the arrival of the receiver in July 1974 to the start of trading as a co-op in January 1975 need not concern us. In effect the labour force, through its two convenors, kept up tremendous pressure on Mr Wedgwood Benn to make possible the setting up of the co-op. At the same time a succession of officially commissioned studies and advisory opinions, culminating in one from the Industrial Development Advisory Board, argued more and more pessimistically about the prospects of success.

However, the pessimists were overruled and the government announced its grant of £3.9m to the prospective co-op on 1 November, 1974. The figure was well below the £6.5m which the men had first asked for. Moreover, since £1.8m would have to go at once to the receiver and a further £100,000 to IPD(I)'s parent as an advance on rent, there was a balance of no more than £2m to cover working capital needs and the predictable trading losses which would be the minimum price of market re-entry after a confused trading hiatus. Finally, it was a condition of the government's grant that the co-op would not be permitted to borrow against its assets. Funds were clearly going to be very tight.

The first point to emphasize about the co-op's operating experience is that it was a very close-run thing that liquidation was avoided during the first eighteen months. Had a substantial reduction in the rate of operating loss not been achieved towards the end of the first year, Kirkby would quickly have followed the *Scottish Daily News* into history. The rate of loss at the beginning was as high as £30,000 a week; the first accounts, dated April 1976 showed a total loss of £1.156m – or an average of roughly £25,000 per week – for the initial fifteen month period. However, on the basis of an improving performance in the second half of 1976, the co-op was able to secure a modest increase in its available financial resources. It succeeded in negotiating its release from the no-borrowing conditions attached to the original government grant, and it managed to arrange a £350,000 overdraft with one of the commercial banks. Then, in the spring of 1977, it used its political influence to extract a further £866,000 of taxpayers' money from the government. Cautious optimism seemed justified when the accounts to April 1977 showed that the average weekly loss had been cut to approximately £6,000 and that cumulative losses were still below £1.5m. There had been, the co-op was entitled to claim, a substantial improvement. How had it been achieved?

Looked at from a product point of view the main explanation of the improvement was clear enough. The April 1976 accounts had shown that domestic radiators contributed 49.9 per cent of total sales during the first fifteen months; by the end of the year that figure had risen to 65 per cent of significantly higher total sales. In fact, the co-op claimed that by the end of 1976 radiator output was running at roughly 13,000 per week compared with 7,000 in the pre-receivership capitalist days of IPD(I). Output in the co-op's secondary lines – night storage heaters, soft drinks, contract steel pressings, ventilation equipment – was said to be at least as high as it had been at the end of the capitalist era. Moreover, the substantial increase in output claimed by the end of 1976 had certainly been achieved with a virtually unchanged workforce. The numbers remained around 750. In other words, quite apart from a real marketing success – in re-entering its old domestic radiator market and then almost doubling sales at a time of building industry slump – the co-op appeared to have achieved significant productivity improvements. How had that happened?

From discussion at Kirkby at the end of 1976, it seemed clear that specific changes in work practice were involved. Two in particular were emphasized. The first had to do with dinner- and tea-break arrangements. Under the co-op's régime the shop floor had agreed to operate on a 'flexi-break' basis so that the machines could go on running without interruption. When a similar arrangement had been proposed under the previous capitalist régime it had been categorically rejected.

The second example of work-practice change quoted at Kirkby at the end of 1976 was equally sharp. Under the co-op, the entire workforce had agreed to work flexibly in the precise sense that when work was not available 'in trade' people might be switched to other, normally unskilled tasks — like filling bottles with soft drinks. Moreover, these new arrangements had already been enforced in practice, as well as having been agreed in principle, before the end of 1976. In the summer of that year a group of seven tool setters had refused, notwithstanding their agreement in principle, to switch on to soft drink production when their own work was temporarily not available. On the initiative of Mr Jack Spriggs and Mr Dick Jenkins, who had become the co-op's two Directors (as well as continuing in their old roles of shop steward convenors), these seven tool setters were dismissed. Outside the factory gates, their union declined to back their complaint of unfair dismissal against the co-op; when they took the complaint to an industrial tribunal it was thrown out.

Two points are worth adding to this account of how the co-op achieved significant changes of work practice — and thus significant productivity gains — compared with the previous capitalist régime. The first, which was put to me with some emphasis at Kirkby by Mr Jenkins, was that he and his fellow stewards would have fought tooth and nail if the former capitalist owners had really tried to introduce similar changes. The second is less encouraging in its implications for the co-op and seems to have been confirmed by the later record in 1977 and 1978. Mr Jenkins also made clear to me at the end of 1976 that even after those changes in work practice, his chief concern was with the manning levels. If it was true that a reduced labour force could manage on its own during lunch breaks, it was presumably also true that substantial overmanning remained. The 'Merseyside Disease' had been ameliorated but was far from cured.

That, at any rate, seems to be the most plausible explanation of the fact that after the sharp improvement in the co-op's perfomance in the year to April 1977, it failed to achieve any real improvement in results during the following twelve months. There were even unconfirmed reports from Liverpool that the agreement to work flexibly was not always being honoured in practice. Further there were more general reports of shop-floor resentment against the enterprise's two shop steward convenors who had become its directors as well.

However, what seemed clear, early in 1978 after Mr Kilroy-Silk's announcement to the co-op of no more taxpayers' money, was that unless there were further changes inside the enterprise it could not be expected to survive on a long-term basis. Some benefit could, it was true, be expected to come from a decision (which had evidently just been taken), to close down two of the secondary production lines – the incongruous soft drinks and the night storage heaters. There were indications, too, early in 1978 that the co-op's leadership had accepted the need for voluntary redundancies. And, of course, there was a reasonable prospect that at least by the end of 1978 demand for the co-op's products would have improved beyond anything in its first three years. All the same there was an obvious question as to whether this combination of factors would be sufficient to ensure survival. More generally there was a question as to whether the co-op could expect to survive unless there was a genuine commitment to work co-operatively by working out of trade when necessary and in other ways.

Casual observation certainly suggests to me that in this respect – the degree of genuine commitment to co-operative working and the general level of trust – Kirkby's achievement up to early 1978 was a good deal less than Meriden's. Perhaps that is one of the advantages which Meriden gained from its single unified wage rate – with its professional management team, when appointed, the only exceptions. At Kirkby, by contrast, a more or less conventional wage structure was maintained from the start. Moreover, Kirkby's accounts for both April 1976 and April 1977 show that its elected Directors, Mr Spriggs and Mr Jenkins, received director's fees of £3,000 each at the end of both accounting periods in addition to the normal wages. No similar fees have ever been paid to the Meriden directors. Although it is easy to believe that Mr Spriggs and Mr Jenkins have had to work much harder – and under much greater pressure – since they became directors as well as convenors, it is also easy to see that such fees can cause resentment and create mistrust about motives in a struggling worker's co-op.

However, to be fair, Kirkby has almost certainly suffered from two handicaps, compared with Meriden, for which it cannot be blamed. Situated outside Liverpool as it is, it can hardly fail to be exposed to the 'Merseyside Disease'; second, it is obviously harder for the Kirkby workforce to become attached to domestic radiators – or any of the other elements in its product mix – than for the Meriden workforce to become attached to its motor cycles. Given these difficulties, the Kirkby achievement may even be superior to that at Meriden. Certainly, and despite its uncertain future, its achievement should not be dismissed as negligible.

8
The French experience

In the mid-1970s the old French industrial co-ops began to attract attention from politicians and other non-specialists for the first time since the end of the Second World War. The French President, Giscard d'Estaing, spoke encouragingly about what they were trying to do, and of possible changes in French law, at a conference of the International Co-operative Alliance (ICA) in Paris in September 1976. Towards the end of the same year the co-ops received approaches from M. Mitterand's Socialist Party. Further, early in 1977 the leading French trade union grouping, the communist controlled Confédération Générale du Travail (CGT), requested a high-level meeting. The old French industrial co-ops, which are linked in the Confédération Générale des Sociétés Co-opératives Ouvrières de Production (SCOP) were suddenly encouraged to think that their doings might be of interest to someone outside their ranks.

A part of this sudden interest could, of course, be explained by special factors. In the mid-1970s France, like Britain − and indeed other countries − began to experience more than just isolated cases of workers' resistance to factory closure. L'Affaire Lip, when the labour force at a watch-making factory in eastern France refused to accept a close down, was widely covered in the French and international Press. A co-operative solution had been one of the possibilities canvassed − though it was not in fact the adopted one. But Lip was only one in a long and continuing series. From the start of 1975, the SCOP offices in Paris began to receive requests for help from groups of workers faced with impending shut downs at the rate of thirty a year; nothing approaching that number had ever been received before.

However, there were other and perhaps less ephemeral strands in this renewal of interest in the old French industrial co-ops. Of course, few if any French socialists were prepared to admit that public ownership and nationalization were proving largely disastrous; still less were the mass of ordinary French working people who saw the public sector basically as a source of steady wages and job security. All the same, there does seem to have been a genuine and quite novel desire on the part of some

French socialists to find out more about the co-ops. At an individual level, there was a trickle of young French engineers, professionals and managers, who suddenly thought that work in an industrial co-op might be more stimulating – and might allow greater freedoms – than working in the capitalist or public sectors.

Since the French industrial co-ops have been significantly more successful in both quantity and quality than their British counterparts, this renewal of interest has been reflected on the British side of the channel as well. There have been a number of newspaper articles – even some British political interest. However, there are dangers as well as advantages in this renewal of interest.

The first danger is that co-ops will be thought to provide a fully-fledged blueprint for a genuinely democratic ownership and control of industrial organizations. If they do not – as is likely (for they have not been traditionally set up with that main goal in mind) – then the cause of genuinely democratic ownership and control is likely to be set back rather than advanced. There will be a temptation too, pandering to current fashion, to present their achievement and history in over rosy colours. Equally there will be a danger of underestimating the enormous obstacles which would have to be overcome if the present marginal contribution of these co-ops to French economic and social life is to be significantly extended.

It must be clear at the outset that the French industrial co-ops should not in fact be mainly seen as conscious models for the democratic ownership and control of enterprises. They should be seen first for what they historically are: namely workers' or working men's enterprises. The key word on the SCOP title should be seen as Ouvrières and not Co-operatives. It is no accident that they only became co-ops towards the end of the last century. Before that they were known as Associations Ouvrières – like John Stuart Mill's associations of labourers' – to distinguish them from Associations Patronales. In other words their identity as associations of working men preceded their identity as democratic co-ops. Even today, with a minority of exceptions, it is their 'cloth cap' and artisan character – rather than their democratic structure – which largely defines them.

If we understand them primarily in this way we shall avoid disappointments and mistakes. We shall not expect them to be too democratic, nor expect too much from the fact that their success has been decidedly superior to that of their British counterparts. Nor will we be surprised if, despite this important relative superiority, the experience of the French co-ops does no more than point rather uncertainly to what might be achieved with the best possible enterprise structures.

In 1975 there were 537* enterprises affiliated to SCOP in Paris employing an estimated 30,000 people. These figures suggest a group of small- and medium-sized enterprises with average employment per co-op just less than sixty. In fact a much sharper picture of the co-ops appears if we arrange them in a size pyramid. Employment figures are not available, but 1975 sales figures are shown in Table 8.1.

TABLE 8.1   Sales figures for SCOP enterprises 1975

Sales (Frs m)	No. of co-ops
400 +	1
200 +	1
100 +	2
50 +	3
25 +	9
10 +	32
4·5 +	52
1·25 +	137
Up to 1·25m	300

Source: SCOP

The pyramid makes it immediately clear that the majority of co-ops affiliated to the SCOP in 1975 were mini-enterprises. Additional data from the SCOP offices suggests that the average sales for the 300 smallest co-ops were no more than Frs 500,000 − or the equivalent of just under £60,000. In those an average of twelve to fifteen employees is probable, perhaps fewer. For the next group, with sales ranging from Frs 1.25m to 4.5m (roughly £150,000 to £500,000), employment hardly exceeds 70.

Thus the pyramid suggests that in 1975 more than 80 per cent of the SCOP co-ops probably employed under seventy people, and well over 50 per cent fewer than fifteen. At the other end of the scale less than 20 per cent of all these enterprises employed more than seventy people. As for the co-ops at the top of the pyramid, at this stage it is enough to say they comprise one large enterprise plus 100 or so others ranging from barely medium to good medium-sized. In employment terms the scale of these 100 was probably from around fifty to 1,000 employees. The single really large enterprise, the Association des Ouvriers en Instruments de Precision (AOIP), was employing nearly 4,500 people by 1977 though the figure for 1975 was rather less.

Both by numbers and by sales almost half of the co-ops in 1975 were building and civil engineering enterprises. The relatively modest fixed capital needs for starting a building business are doubtless a partial explanation. Traditions of artisan 'companionage' are also important

* The latest figure, for March 1978, was 556.

and maybe the fact that these co-ops have also enjoyed advantages —
such as exemption from tendering below a certain price level and from
obligation to supply bonds — both from central government and from
local authorities. A complete sectoral breakdown of all the 1975 affiliated
enterprises is not available, but the distribution of 373 is said to be
reasonably representative.

TABLE 8.2

	No. of enterprises	%	Sales (Frs m)	%
Building and CE	186	49·8	1,229	47·1
Printing, etc.	56	15·0	172	6·6
Services	47	12·6	176	6·7
Engineering, etc.	36	9·9	771	29·5
Food and agriculture	10	2·6	31	1·2
Leather and textiles	16	4·2	103	3·9
Glass	5	1·4	80	3·0
Furniture	6	1·6	6	0·2
Quarries, etc.	4	1·1	13	0·7
Other	7	1·8	29	1·1
Totals	373	100	2,610	100

Source: SCOP

If we exclude engineering, services and glass for a moment, the
low-technology, artisan and generally 'cloth cap' character of these co-
ops becomes clear enough. Engineering and glass are both rather special
cases. The two largest co-ops by turnover are in the engineering group
and together account for 75 per cent of the sector's sales. Similarly, the
fifth largest co-op by turnover makes glass bottles and it accounts for
more than 75 per cent of the glass sales figure.

The only really surprising element in the table is 'Services' made up of
a small group of co-ops which are much more 'middle-class' in
character. They consist mainly of enterprises started after the Second
World War and are characteristically involved in activities like town
planning, architecture and market research; in Britain they would
almost certainly have been formed as partnerships or private companies. The stronger industrial co-op tradition in France, plus the less
stereotyped and less woodenly Marxist politics of radical young French
professionals, probably explains why a certain number set themselves up
as co-ops.

Almost as striking as the dominance of building and civil engineering
enterprises among these co-ops is the numerical importance of those

which by the mid-1970s were middle-aged or older. The SCOP reports that over one third of those affiliated enterprises in 1978 were founded before 1945. Table 8.3 gives the more detailed figures available covering the entire membership of the Confédération as it stands in 1978.

TABLE 8.3

Starting date	No. of co-ops	%
Pre-1914	61	11
1914–45	123	22
1945–75	240	43
1975–8	132	24
Total	556	100

Source: SCOP

The character of the SCOP confederation is probably determined by its older member enterprises to an even greater extent than the figures in Table 8.3 imply. That is partly because each of the five co-ops with the largest turnover were pre-1939 vintage; but it is also partly because of the sectoral distribution of the new post-war enterprises. If we exclude very recently formed 'job saving' co-ops and middle-class service 'partnerships', almost all of the post-war creations affiliated in 1975 were small building and civil engineering businesses. (The only major exceptions are two provincial daily newspapers which transformed themselves into co-ops at the end of the Second World War.) Because of their narrower industrial spread, the post-war co-ops still seemed in the mid-1970s to carry less weight than the pre-war ones – although there were some signs that this might be starting to change.

This brief sketch of the old industrial co-ops in France in the mid-1970s immediately makes clear that they are, relatively, much stronger than their British counterparts. In Britain, even if we pull together all three separate elements – the 'cloth cap' co-ops, the ICOM companies and Mr Wedgwood Benn's creations – we have a total of some thirty enterprises employing fewer than 3,500 people. The corresponding figures in France are more than 500 enterprises with a workforce of approximately 30,000.

It is also worth stressing the fact that the UK enterprises are divided by their origins. The old 'cloth cap' co-ops are mainly affiliated to the Co-operative Production Federation. Enterprises which were originally capitalist companies, or have been founded as common ownership ventures since 1960, are associated with ICOM. The two surviving

Wedgwood Benn creations, at Meriden and Kirkby, are not – so far as I know – affiliated to anyone.

There *are*, of course, co-ops of the 'Wedgwood Benn' job-saving type in France, there are also co-ops which started life as private companies but were then handed over to their workforces. The difference is that in France enterprises of these two kinds are affiliated, alongside the industrial co-ops which date from the last century, in a single confederation. The main reason is that the old French industrial co-ops have been much stronger, at least since the First World War, than their British 'cloth cap' counterparts.

It is sometimes argued that the superior record and strength in France is mainly due to the building co-ops, and it is further argued that these building enterprises result mainly from the special favours extended by the French state for most of the last ninety years. However, figures suggest that not more than half of the relative French superiority can be explained in this way. For if all the building co-ops are excluded from the SCOP confederation totals, the French co-op labour forces remains roughly five times as large as the British figure; and the ratio of enterprises is still nearly 9:1.

Underlying the difference is the fact that Frenchmen have been forming co-ops continuously and without major interruption throughout this century. By contrast, in Britain the numbers of 'cloth caps' co-ops peaked soon after 1900 (when they were not far short of the French total), and have declined ever since, The immediate reason is that, with a handful of exceptions, no new enterprises of this kind were started in Britain between 1914 and 1960. Why did Frenchmen go on starting co-ops after 1914 while in Britain such initiatives dried up? Even a limited answer requires a brief look at the French historical background.

As in Britain, the early history of the French industrial co-ops, Les Associations Ouvrières as they were originally called, is largely one of the false starts and disasters. In a series of waves, the first in 1848, the second in 1863 and the third in the 1880s (if we exclude the short-lived and revolutionary workers' enterprises set up under the Paris Commune in 1870) several hundreds of workers' enterprises were founded. The great majority failed.

The first Association Ouvrière was founded in Paris as early as 1834 by a group of craftsmen – jewellers who worked in gold (l'Association Ouvrière des bijoutiers en doré). Its creation was the work of artisan – craftsmen inspired by the 'philosopher' of workers' enterprises in France, J. P. Buchez. One can imagine a closely-knit group of skilled craftsmen inspired by the ideals of the 'republic in the workshop' and by beliefs in social justice and self-improvement. Their enterprise seems to have been reasonably, if undramatically, successful. In many ways it is an admirable prototype for the artisan 'cloth cap' enterprises which were to form the bulk of the French industrial co-ops – yet it remained the only example of its kind up to 1848.

The first impetus behind the 1848 wave of Associations Ouvrières was, of course, the impetus of revolution.* 'With ardour and generosity of spirit, but also with the illusions natural to that time, working people rushed to form associations. Several hundreds were founded, and in nearly every trade. . . . But very few survived.'

Revolutionary ardour, if a generalization may be permitted, rarely provides a firm and reliable basis on which an enduring enterprise can be built. If an operation depends on quite exceptional and sustained enthusiasm on the part of relatively large numbers of people, it is unlikely to last long. M. Hubert-Valleroux does, it is true, show that there were some heroic exceptions. He mentions an association of tailors, all of whose members managed on a wage of no more than Frs 2 per day for an eighteen month period, and he does so in language which makes clear that Frs 2 then would buy a good deal less than 25p today. He recounts too the extraordinary struggles of a group of spectacle-makers whose enterprise, started in 1848, eventually became large and prosperous and survived well into the twentieth century. On the other hand, he offers a second explanation, as well as the tough going, to explain why the great majority of the enterprises of 1848 were so short-lived.

The reason, he tells us, is that many succumbed to the temptation of accepting loans and grants from the French authorities. When they did so, he argues, the independent spirit of the Association was undermined and the end normally came fast. This reason also explains the widespread failure of the next two waves of Associations in the 1860s and 1880s. In the early 1860s, he tells us, most of the new foundations were created because of the availability of soft loans from the government of Napoleon III. In the early 1880s the source of loans was different – the legacy of a wealthy well-wisher, a M. Benjamin Rampal – but the results were much the same. In neither case, or so he argues, were the new enterprises based on any genuine workers' commitment from the bottom. There are obvious parallels with those disastrously un-successful enterprises launched by the London Christian Socialists in the 1850s – and there are obvious lessons for our own day. Still, the chief point is that the Rampal legacy seems to have been the last major source

---

* P. Hubert-Valleroux, *Les Associations ouvrières et les associations patronales,* Paris, 1899, p. 14.

of false starts in the history of the French co-ops.

Thereafter what we observe is a modest number of new starts each year, based on genuine initiatives and commitment from the bottom. Sometimes these initiatives followed strikes, as at Walsall Locks and Equity Shoes in the UK. The more normal pattern was one of independent initiatives by groups of craftsmen or artisans. Moreover, unlike what happened in the UK, these annual batches of new starts have continued in France down to the present day. Further, since the annual birth rate has normally been higher than the death rate among existing enterprises, for most of the twentieth century the total number of French co-ops has been rising. Table 8.4 gives figures for selected years.

TABLE 8.4   Number of French co-ops (selected years)

1901	119	1939	478
1914	251	1944	520
1919	274	1947	703
1922	336	1959	514
1928	284	1966	494
1933	385	1975	537

According to Claude Vienney, 2,250 co-ops were started between the mid-1880s and 1960 – an average of roughly thirty each year. On the other hand, as he also points out, on average no more than twenty-three survived. This gives a net annual growth rate of seven co-ops for the seventy-five years to 1960.

Vienney distinguishes between periods when the growth rate has been relatively high – the years before 1914, the aftermath of both World Wars, the Depression of the 1930s – and those during which it has been that much lower. The enormous mushrooming of new co-ops after the defeat of the Germans in the Second World War certainly *is* interesting: it perhaps reflects in part feelings of inter-class solidarity generated by the shared experience of Occupation and the Resistance,

In contrast to Britain, the really striking point is the extent to which, notwithstanding periodic variations, a continuous tradition of co-operative enterprise formation has survived among ordinary French people. The majority of the new formations have been quite small operations started from the bottom. Perhaps this tradition has survived in France because the values of peasant self-reliance have remained more widespread among the French than among the British. Or perhaps it is that the influence of the trade unions and of Webb-style bureaucratic socialism has been less pervasive in France. Perhaps it simply reflects the bolder, more libertarian and more revolutionary traditions of the French

Left and an abiding attachment to the ideals of the 'Republic of the Workshop' (which has long since burnt itself out in Britain), both on the shop floor, and among the barons of the General Council of the TUC. But, whatever the reasons, the result is the survival into the last quarter of the twentieth century of several hundred small artisan co-ops in France which make up the bulk of the SCOP confederation membership.

As the SCOP pyramid showed, more than half of the confederation membership in the mid-1970s consisted of small or very small enterprises. As many as 300 of the 537 affiliated co-ops had average sales of not more than Frs 500,000 (£60,000). Unless they were 'cooking their books' for tax or other purposes they cannot have been employing on average more than a dozen people.

This large group, together with most of those in the category next above (with sales not exceeding £500,000) can perhaps best be understood as the co-op equivalent of the small family business (or, in the case of the really small building enterprises as the equivalent of the 'lump'). A fairly typical example might be Le Co-op Serrurerie Picarde (the Picardy Locksmiths Co-op). This enterprise had sales of Frs 1.25m (or roughly £150,000) in 1975 – making it 237th in the turnover table of SCOP co-ops that year. It earned profits before depreciation and leasing charges of Frs 86,000. Dating from before the First World War, Le Co-op Serrurerie Picarde produced these 1975 results with a workforce of sixteen, of whom ten were co-op members. Its position in the turnover table shows that there were more smaller co-ops than the Picardy Locksmiths than there were larger ones in that year.

Another example is the Le Co-op Imprimerie Angevine (The Angers Printers Co-op) which also had a labour force of sixteen in 1975, although twelve were co-op members. The value added in printing seems to be higher than the locksmithing, for the Angers Printers achieved 1975 sales of Frs 1.5m and their comparable profit was Frs 178,000.

The mid-1970s picture in France is of several 100 similar or even smaller widely-scattered co-ops. Many, like the Picardy Locksmiths, have reached their third or even fourth generations of members. There are little co-operative enterprises of painters (and of other specialized building workers), I was told in Paris, with continuous histories stretching back to the 1890s. A co-operative of Paris gardeners (Co-op Jardiniers de Paris) is shown among the enterprises affiliated to the SCOP confederation's predecessor in 1899. It was still soldiering on, with a labour force of twenty-one and with sixteen working members, in 1975, when it achieved a turnover of Frs 2.2m with profits, before depreciation and leasing charges of Frs 323,000.

Obviously, a model which might be of use to British Leyland is not to be found by studying the Picardy Locksmiths or the longlife gardeners co-op in Paris, but we *may*, of course, be looking for other things as well. We *may* be looking for models not so much to replace as to supplement the family business. Or, in the building industry, we may be looking for ways in which something creative might be done about 'the lump'. It is true that these small artisan and 'cloth cap' co-ops have not achieved much in the way of 'growth', but then nor have a large number of small family businesses – nor, for that matter, have the more informal groupings of the 'lump'. And the small artisan co-op, quite apart from its appeal to the advocates of 'small is beautiful', has the great advantage of spreading the values of both individual self-reliance and mutual group solidarity.

On the other hand, it is clear that the small artisan co-ops cannot provide any sort of model either for British Leyland or for medium-scale manufacturing industry. For they have been either unwilling or unable to build themselves up to compete in national rather than local markets. There is, however, a handful of enterprises, at the top of the SCOP pyramid, which have grown into leading enterprises in their sectors in France. The best examples of these enterprises given in Table 8.5 are probably the 'big five' which achieved the highest sales figures in 1976.

TABLE 8.5   The 'big five', their main industrial activities, sales and estimated employment figures, 1976

Name	Activity	Sales (Frs m)	Estimated employment
AOIP	Telephone equipment	603	4,000
ACOME	Copper wire	263	675
Hirondelle	Building	164	1,000
Avenir (Lyons)	Building	170	1,000
VOA	Glass bottles	104	500

Source: SCOP

Though the technologies within which these five enterprises work can be graded as more or less advanced, there is no doubt that all compete successfully with the top performers in their respective industries. L'Association des Ouvriers en Instruments de Précision (AOIP), has been one of France's leading producers of telephone equipment for many years – perhaps even, without stretching a point too much, since the First World War. La Verrerie Ouvrière d'Albi (VOA) on the other hand has only recently 'arrived' as a modern enterprise and its secure position as a leading producer of glass in France really only dates from the mid-1970s. Evidence of the competitive position and professional quality of the Paris-based Hirondelle is provided by its success in, for example, winning a large chunk of the contract to build the third Paris airport, Charles de Gaulle. As for l'Association des Ouvriers en Materiel Electrique (ACOME) based in northern Normandy near Mont Saint Michel since the Second World War, it has proved itself to be an important leader and innovator in the French copper wire industry. It was the first French enterprise in its sector to switch to plastic coated wire, and it was responsible for introducing a special kind of wire for car circuits which eliminates engine interference with car radios.

Yet it is not only that the 'big five' have reached positions of industrial leadership. More important in this context is the fact that they all started small and with working-class leadership. AOIP was the initiative of a group of artisan instrument-makers in Paris in 1896. Over the first year it could provide enough work for only one man; over its second for only five. Hirondelle was launched by a small group of bricklayers and concreters in 1920 and, like AOIP had to struggle with great tenacity in its early years to get established. La Verrerie Ouvrière d'Albi came into existence after a ferocious strike and lock-out in the 1890s. Its original working-class credentials could hardly be challenged even by the most hardline zealot. The origin of ACOME, which dates as a co-op from the 1930s, was the bankruptcy of an earlier capitalist undertaking. Here again the original leadership was unquestionably working-class.

In the case of the four biggest, the transition from struggling to growing seems to have been a gradual, cumulative process. Employment figures are some sort of yardstick in the case of AOIP. Its payroll of only one in 1896 had increased to 183 by 1914, to 600 by 1930 and by the mid-1950s stood at 1500. At what point did the crucial changes occur? The best date in AOIP's case might be 1914. That year the co-op committed itself to building its own professional and technical school – not a decision which you would expect from a small artisan-type enterprise.

There are, similarly, gradual employment increases in the records of Hirondelle, Avenir and ACOME, but more research is needed to establish convincingly and precisely when they emancipated themselves from the limited horizons of their origins. All three had done so by the late 1950s, but research would probably show the crucial events took place a good deal earlier – in Hirondelle's case perhaps as early as the late 1920s.

Yet it is the Albi glassworkers who experienced the most dramatic transition. It was an astonishing and in some ways highly encouraging sequence of events. To understand what happened we have to go back to the co-op's origins in the 1890s.

Roughly 15km north of the cathedral town of Albi, in the Tarn department of southern France, is the little industrial centre of Carmaux. One of its most important enterprises in the 1890s was a capitalist glassworks employing between 200 and 250 people. The works was probably sited there because of relatively cheap fuel from neighbouring coal mines. In the mid-1890s, a period of considerable industrial unrest and class conflict in France, the entire workforce came out on strike. This was quickly transformed into a lock-out as the owners attempted to batter the working people into submission.

But the workforce would not give in. Their struggle attracted attention and support in the Tarn department and outside and their cause was espoused by Jean Juarès, the young Socialist deputy for Albi, and through him various others prominent in the French Left. Substantial funds were subscribed for the workforce, but when the strike and lock-out had lasted more than a year without agreement, a 'workers' glassworks' was decided upon as the best solution. Further funds were subscribed. Because of the particular hostility of the business community in Carmaux it was decided to site the new works in Albi. It is said that both during the building phase (which the glassworkers themselves largely undertook) and for many years afterwards the majority of the former Carmaux workers made the journey to Albi and back daily and on foot. And this story need not be disbelieved. The early annals of the French industrial co-ops are filled with epics of heroism which are difficult to credit only because of the very much changed conditions of today. In any case, the new works started production in 1897 with an output of roughly 3m bottles. A graph in its 1975 annual report shows that production has only been interrupted once since then – towards the end of the Second World War.

With origins of this kind the workers in the new factory at Albi might well be hostile to business and business values; and that is evidently what happened. I have heard it claimed that for some years the enterprise refused to avail itself of normal banking services. That may be a myth, but it is clear that at least up to the end of the Second World War La Verrerie Ouvrière d'Albi remained a centre of militant working-class attitudes. This explains why, despite official support by the Vichy régime for co-operative endeavours, the works closed down briefly during the Second World War.

The extreme class militance of the Albi workforce softened with time and was generally milder in the post-1945 world. All the same the enterprise, like the majority of its fellow co-ops in France, retained many traditions from its past. For example, it remained remarkably egalitarian in its wages and salary differentials: up to the early 1970s the maximum differential is said to have remained 2.5:1 against roughly 7:1 for comparable enterprises. Moreover the management, professional and office staff were kept down to a minimum, probably averaging no more than 25 per cent of the figures for similar undertakings.

Other inherited traditions also came to be seen later as inimical to growth and modernization. For example a forge was maintained at the works and occasional blacksmithing work, instead of being placed with specialists outside, was done on the premises. Promotions, such as they were, tended to be made from within, so the enterprise was starved of new blood. In many ways it must, to be fair, have been a most attractive and supportive place to work in: people rarely spoke sharply to each other; feelings of family-like solidarity prevailed. On the other hand though the production of glass bottles continued to rise in absolute terms, Albi's share of the total French market declined during the 1960s. Its products tended to fall behind too from the standpoint of technical excellence and design. And of course the plant was not getting any younger.

It seems to have become clear in 1971 that unless important changes were accepted, the future of the enterprise could only be one of irreversible, even if slow and undramatic, decline. A new plant, incorporating the most advanced technology seemed an inescapable requirement. Second, and something likely to be more objectionable to the grass-roots membership, modern management methods and professional managers would have to be brought in. Moreover, because of the relatively large numbers of new managers needed, most would have to be recruited from outside. That would mean scrapping the policy of internal promotion. In the absence of any very strong egalitarian philosophy in the outside world it was almost certain to mean the end of the old wages and salaries differential limits as well.

It was on the basis of an analysis on these lines that a package of proposals was eventually drawn up. One further point needs to be mentioned. The grass-roots members were to be asked not only to accept the package – they were also to be asked to put their hands in their pockets to help finance it. At that time the membership's standard contribution to the co-op's capital needs was 4 per cent of gross earnings. It was estimated that this figure would have to be raised to 10 per cent to finance the new plant.

In the end the grass-roots membership was offered a bargain: if members agreed to swallow the medicine of the new management methods (and the new managers) and if they agreed to increase their capital contributions from 4 per cent to 10 per cent, then loan money would be made available to finance the balance of the cost of the new plant. To their extraordinary credit the workers eventually accepted it in 1972 and a programme was adopted to 'assure the perpetuity of the co-op' ('d'assurer la perénnité de la Co-operative'). It is easy to believe that the shop floor found the transition to modern management systems – and the arrival of a bunch of quick-talking young managers (the French called them Les Cadres) – even more painful than the sharp increase in capital contribution. Under the old régime only three people, including the chairman and managing director (Le Président Directeur General), could properly have been called cadres; once the changes were complete this number had increased to eighteen. There was, too, a corresponding recruitment of additional secretaries and other white-collar staff. Relationships between the newcomers and the old hands were evidently far from easy to begin with. More than once they came to the verge of a strike. Gradually, however, some sort of equilibrium was achieved. Meanwhile construction of a most advanced plant, costing more than Frs 40m (£5m), just outside Albi was finally completed. By 1976 it was making more or less its full projected contribution to total output. In that year, after a net loss of just over Frs 3.5m in 1975, the co-op became profitable again. Moreover, there was sufficent confidence in the future for the capital contribution of worker–members to be reduced – not to the earlier 4 per cent figure of gross wages but to 6 per cent. Those crucial decisions of 1972 were beginning to pay off.

It is impossible to emphasize too strongly that those 1972 decisions – 'd'assurer la perénnité de la Co-operative' – were taken not by absentee capitalist shareholders, nor by office-bound bureaucrats in Paris, but by the co-op's elected board of administration (Conseil d'Administration), of which since the late 1930s, not less than two-thirds had come from worker members. In practice, however, the decision could not have been approved without the support of the majority of the co-op's members as a whole, and at Albi, though not by any means in all the old French industrial co-ops, membership of the general assembly is virtually automatic after an initial qualifying period.

In other words, the responsibility for taking those decisions at Albi rested with precisely those people whose futures were mainly affected by them. Indeed, the whole affair provides an extraordinarily good paradigm for the kind of decisions which should plainly be taken by the workforce under any arrangement of ultimate workers' responsibility and control. The distinction between these and day-to-day management decisions is underlined – with exceptional clarity in this case – by the happy chance that one of those basic policy decisions was precisely that day-to-day management should be greatly strengthened.

Yet both in themselves and in the character of their making the Albi workforce's decisions in 1972 suggest confirmation of a much more fundamental point. Of course, there is no way of proving that it was precisely because they enjoyed ultimate responsibility and control that the Albi workers reached decisions which involved short-term sacrifices in exchange for long-term benefits. Perhaps, who knows, a powerless Albi workforce would have acquiesced in these same decisions if they had been handed down by a capitalist board of directors or by Paris officials – we cannot tell. But there are so many examples of the opposite happening that it seems plausible to suggest that there may be a genuine link here: between ultimate workforce decision-making power and enlightened decisions and follow-up behaviour. It is on the basis of this sort of evidence that the experience of the old French co-ops points, at least tentatively, in an optimistic direction.

We shall look more directly at the decision-making structure at VOA, and in the other French co-ops, towards the end of this section. But three final points are worth adding about the Albi glassworks. The first is structural.

As we saw much earlier, because the views of the socialist centralists – and working-class supremacists – prevailed when the glassworks was originally set up at Albi, a majority of its board of administration was originally appointed by central working-class bodies in Paris. We also saw that these arrangements eventually became unacceptable to the Albi workforce who acquired control in the late 1930s. Here we may simply speculate whether, had working-class bureaucrats retained the decisive voice, those crucial decisions of 1972 would have been accepted by the workers.

The second point concerns the future of the Albi glassworks should the socialist-communist alliance come to power in France and introduce their 'common programme'. The two largest producers of glass bottles in France, Boussois Souchon Neuvecelles (BSN) and Saint Gobain, are both on the prospective public ownership list. On the other hand VOA feels (perhaps wrongly!) that it could scarcely survive as an independent producer if its two main competitors were nationalized. There is thus the intriguing prospect that VOA will join with those two capitalist undertakings and oppose public ownership in the name of the workers' freedom. One cannot help feeling that this opposition would have much more chance of success if all three, and not only VOA, were workers' co-ops.

The final point is more than unequivocally optimistic. Many of the young cadres recruited since 1972 seem to have become progressively more attached to the working within a co-op setting. It begins to look as if they might be prepared to work a good deal harder in a co-op than for a capitalist employer or the state. That obviously bodes well for VOA. And if more people of their calibre can be attracted into the old French co-ops prospects for future growth might begin to look quite promising,

Standing back from the particular case of VOA, what general lessons do the achievements and experience of the 'big five' suggest? The first and most important is that co-ops need not be restricted to the most dwarfish scale or to the lowest levels of technology and of capital intensiveness. A co-op need not be confined either to small artisan groups of 'cloth cap' builders or, still less, to part-time handicraft workers in raffia or papier mâché. Co-ops are not incompatible with at least good Second-Division manufacturing enterprises, using fairly advanced technology and operating on a reasonably large scale, even having started from the humblest origins. It is true that only a few have done so. On the other hand, it seems clear that the great majority of the French artisan co-ops simply have not *wanted* to develop thus. Where market conditions have allowed – and where the co-op members have wished it – growth has been possible. Again, and as was shown most strikingly by VOA, modern management systems and professional managers are needed to compete with industrial leaders.

However, this demonstration that 'cloth cap' enterprises can climb to positions of·industrial leadership is, in fact, of only limited contemporary relevance. For unless special 'midwifing' institutions are created, as at Mondragon, only small numbers of new co-ops are likely to be created and among them only very few indeed will grow into an Hirondelle or an AOIP. On the other hand, the success of the 'big five' does suggest that if a group of good, second-division private enterprises were transformed into co-ops, they would not necessarily be unable to compete with their capitalist and state-owned counterparts; they might even acquire an extra competitive edge.

There is a middle group of co-ops affiliated to the SCOP, which comes between the great majority of essentially artisan enterprises and the 'big five'. For convenient, if arbitrary definition I have chosen a turnover range from roughly Frs 4.5m (a little over £500,000) to Frs 55m (nearly £7m). There were almost exactly 100 French co-ops within this range in 1975. Their employment stretched from just below 50 to just over 500, and they accounted together for approximately 40 per cent of the total sales of the SCOP enterprises.

Roughly half of these middle-rank enterprises, including the largest – Constructions Modernes d'Armor (CMA), are engaged in building work; either they are general builders or specialists like the large heating and ventilation group Co-op Chauffage et Ventillation, or like

L'Electricité Lyons. They include half a dozen essentially middle-class co-ops which supply services like architecture and town planning, and they include the French equivalent of the 'Wedgwood Benn' job-saving co-op successors of failed capitalist enterprises.

Outside building, an illustrative sector of these middle-rank French co-ops is provided by six in newspapers and printing. By sales position in the SCOP 1975 sales league and approximate employment, they were as shown in Table 8.6.

TABLE 8.6   Middle-rank French co-ops

Name	Sales (Frs m)	Rank (approx)	Employment
Le Courier Picard	34·3	11	275
Yonne Republicaine	24·1	17	200
La Perseverance	8·5	53	125
Emancipatrice – Paris	7·3	63	50
Lithographie Parisienne	5·6	80	45
Gutenburg	5·3	84	50

Source: SCOP

Le Courier Picard and *Yonne Republicaine* are essentially provincial daily newspapers, the first at Amiens, the second at Auxerre. Both are also, by their origin, special cases. They were transformed into co-ops when France was liberated at the end of the war. From its 1975 sales figures *Le Courier Picard* is of a size roughly comparable with North of England Newspapers in Darlington, the latter achieving a turnover of just over £4m in 1976.

Le Courier Picard may indeed be of some interest to the British Newspaper industry because of the rather special arrangements which the powerful French print unions agreed to in its case in 1976. The paper had been faced with the tough problem of financing the high cost of new printing technology at a time when, because of astronomical wage costs, it had very little to deploy in the way of accumulated profits. In a complete break from the attitude adopted in negotiations with capitalist newspapers, the powerful print unions agreed in 1976 that *Le Courier Picard* might be permitted to reduce its wage bill. It was left to the co-op's membership to decided whether that should be done by cutting wage rates or numbers. It is intriguing to speculate whether the British National Graphical Association (NGA) would adopt a similar line if, for example, *The Times* was to convert itself into a co-op.

Those are obviously rather specialized questions. As for the SCOP printing sector as a whole, a study was commissioned in the early 1970s to produce measured comparisons between the performance of the SCOP printers and that of printing establishments in the private sector. It is the only systematic study of the comparative efficiency of SCOP enterprises which has been made; perhaps, inevitably, its results were inconclusive. In some respects the co-ops were performing better than their capitalist counterparts; in others less well. But perhaps the key point about the study is a negative one: it did *not* show that the printing co-ops were being generally outperformed by their rivals.

In the absence of any comprehensive studies, it seems plausible to imagine that what was found to be true of these printing co-ops would be true of the middle-rank enterprises more generally. Certainly, there is no inclination at the SCOP offices in Paris to make exaggerated claims on their behalf. If anything the informed view in Paris tends to emphasize one particular element, namely management, in which these middle-rank co-ops are frequently weaker than their rivals. It is stressed at the SCOP offices that success in a middle-rank co-op is nearly always correlated with strong management.

The two key figures at the SCOP headquarters in Paris, Antoine Antoni, the general secretary and François Espagne, the assistant secretary, are honest and confident enough to contrast the French co-ops unfavourably with the Mondragon ones – and management is one of the three main areas on which this unfavourable comparison almost invariably focuses. One is told about a traditional suspicion of professional management – clear enough in the experience of VOA; that that suspicion inhibits the demand for good management from the co-ops. On the side of supply, one is told that the old French co-ops still retain a basically negative image in the eyes of the dynamic young cadres – though it is conceded that that is perhaps starting to change.

A trickle of new recruits have been joining the ranks of the SCOP confederation, following capitalist failure, since the beginning of this century or even earlier. Indeed ACOME, one of the 'big five' joined the confederation in the 1930s (as we saw earlier), as the successor to a bankrupt capitalist undertaking. At SCOP headquarters one is told that there always have been and always will be new co-ops of this kind. The reason is that capitalist decisions to stop production – whether forced or voluntary – do not necessarily mean the enterprise is in an irretrievably hopeless position. Examples from the late 1960s include a shoe factory – the owners of which had simply been taking too much out of the business – and a printing works. The latter, sited near the Swiss border had, it seems, simply become too much of a 'hassle' for its Swiss owners. In both cases, with help from the SCOP, co-ops were established, though because of fierce new competition from Eastern Europe the shoe makers succumbed a number of years later.

Yet from the mid-1970s a dramatic change in the number of aspiring job-saving co-ops started to become apparent. Where there had been one or two in the space of five years, the number suddenly increased to roughly thirty a year. It is recognized at SCOP headquarters that in the majority of cases a capitalist closure, whether voluntary or involuntary, usually *does* mean that an enterprise cannot be revived. On the other hand, they are beginning to discover in Paris that in a significant number of cases, between a fifth and a quarter, the enterprise – or a large part of it – can be saved and can, in principle, be converted into a co-op with some chance of success.

An interesting mid-1970s example glanced at briefly much earlier in this book and which, as we also saw, was sadly forced out of business after an apparently promising start, was Co-op Sport-Vacances. It had to come into existence, in its co-operative form, following the closure by a German multi-national company, Bayer Chemicals of Munich, of a subsidiary outside Angoulême in south west France. In early 1977 it was being cautiously spoken of in Paris as one of the potential success stories among the latest batch of job-saving co-ops. The fact that it had failed by the end of that year strongly confirms the view that to bring off a successful conversion after a capitalist close down and then survive for any length of time is far from easy. Apart from anything else, survival is difficult because the successor co-op enterprise is essentially on its own. Unlike the position among the Mondragon co-ops, such an enterprise in France or Britain has no real access to supporting outside resources of either capital or management. If we also take into account the very tough market conditions of 1977, the failure of Co-op Sport-Vacances is no doubt fully explained. However, its brief history is still worth attention because it contains some intrinsically interesting features – and because most reasonable people would have supported the new co-op initiative when it was first launched. Of course in some sense, as it later turned out, they would have been wrong.

In its capitalist days the enterprise was called La Prairie. Its main products were small fibreglass boats (it was France's leading producer) and tents for camping (it ranked third among French manufacturers). Employment in the capitalist enterprise was in the 200 to 250 range. In April 1974 it was acquired from its previous German owners by Bayer Chemicals.

Bayer evidently lost no time sending a team to go through the books at La Prairie. They discovered that the enterprise, though profitable, was producing a return of no more than 6 per cent on its capital; that was not enough when compared with 18 per cent for the Bayer group as a whole. The management at La Prairie was invited to put up a programme which would increase returns to 18 per cent within a year.

After fairly exhaustive researches the answer came back that such an increase would be impossible in so short a time. Bayer again moved fast. In September 1974, less than six months after having acquired La Prairie, they announced the close down of the business on economic grounds.

Just as Bayer had moved fast, so did a determined group of La Prairie's former employees: Co-op Sport-Vacances was formally set up by a small group of twenty-five of them in April 1975. Rented premises were acquired and production started. The number of worker–members increased to eighty-five by the end of 1976. Moreover, the audited accounts for the first year of operations showed a very reasonable profit.

The driving forces came from Hellen Barreux, former commercial and sales director at La Prairie, a man in his middle thirties. This contribution was crucial. Through his contacts the co-op found orders to match its output; equally important, using skills developed in the trade union movement and as an active politician (he is a member of the small but important Radical Gauche Party in France), Barreux persuaded the others to pledge themselves financially as well as morally to the new venture. The twenty-five members were persuaded to borrow approximately £2,000 each in the form of seven-year loans from the French Credit Mutuel – money which formed the starting capital of the new venture. These borrowings were arranged entirely on the basis of personal guarantees. As seen elsewhere, capital involvement on the part of co-op worker–members can supply the enterprise with the most powerful kind of underpinning.

On the other hand, as we have also seen from the earlier example of the *Scottish Daily News*, this capital involvement by the workforce must not be thought of as a sufficient condition for the success of a job saving co-op or a co-op of any other kind. It must be conceded too that failures in this category – where workers' capital stakes have been involved – provide on the face of it some support for the traditional trade union argument that ordinary workers must not be exposed to the risk of losing their savings as well as their jobs when an enterprise fails. Yet, since without capital stakes the chances of failure will normally increase, it is hard to accept that argument. Perhaps the best answer is that the risks inherent in workers' capital stakes should only be accepted if they can be spread over a group of enterprises and not confined to isolated cases. As we shall see, that is what happens in the Mondragon group.

However, the institutions which would be needed to spread these risks seemed at least some way ahead in the France of the late 1970s. It seemed doubtful whether the individual SCOP enterprises, traditionally jealous of their independence, would themselves devise a set of mechanisms for spreading these risks effectively. It seemed improbable too that a French government of either Left or Right would take any initiative in this direction to help them. But unless and until some arrangements of that kind can be devised, the short history of Co-op Sport-Vacances is bound to be treated as more of a warning than an inspiration. And though the French success with job-saving co-ops was almost certainly greater in the middle and late 1970s than anything on the British side of the Channel, critics might still argue that the risks, as things stood, were too high to be tolerable.

So far nothing has been said about the formal structures of the old French industrial co-ops. In an earlier discussion it was pointed out that like those of the old UK 'cloth cap' co-ops these French structures inherited traditional arrangements from the Rochdale pioneers in one crucial respect — there was and is in the old French industrial co-ops no formal requirement that all co-op workers must be shareholder members of the enterprise and that only co-op workers may be. Since control is linked to shares and membership — not to work — the absence of this requirement means there is no formal protection against either of the dangers which the Webbs so insistently identified — that of the co-op being bought up by outsiders, and the danger that the initial co-op membership will come to behave like capitalists and employ non-members to do the work.

It is true that the French co-op law* allows non-workers to be co-op members and that it does not insist that all workers must be members. On the other hand, it does include strong safeguards against one of the two dangers identified by the Webbs. For it is laid down that, however the co-op membership is composed, not less than two-thirds of its board of administration must be workers. It is also laid down that in the event of liquidation any surplus funds may not be shared out among members but must be passed on to some other co-op enterprise. In this way, and unlike the position of Britain, the French co-op law effectively blocks the possibility of outside capitalist take-over.

There is another key provision in the French co-op law which mitigates against, even if it does not eliminate, the second danger: of a privileged group of members running the enterprise for its own benefit and employing non-members to do the actual hard work. The provision relates to profit distribution. It lays down that the workforce as a whole (whether members or not) must receive at least as large a percentage of profits as that allocated to members in respect of their shares. In this way

---

* A new law, likely to increase the percentage of worker–members completed its passage through the French Parliament on 1 July 1978.

a privileged group of worker–members is prevented from creaming off all the profits for itself (though such a group could always fix relative wage rates in a way which meant that non-member workers were exploited).

These are the most relevant provisions of the French co-op law. In practice outsider members had ceased to be an issue by the mid-1970s. On the other hand, there was and is considerable discussion about the problem of non-member workers. For the co-ops as a whole, non-members accounted for as much as two-thirds of the total labour force in 1975. In some sectors, and partly because of the uneven rhythms of the work – in building for example – the percentage of non-members was often even higher: sometimes 90 per cent. Although the profit shares of these non-members were safeguarded under the law, it was widely argued in Paris that the SCOP enterprises would be strengthened if the proportion of non-members could be reduced. One of the possible changes in co-op law hinted at by Giscard d'Estaing in his ICA address in September 1976 might well increase the proportion of members in the workforce of the old French co-ops.

In that it ensures a majority of workers on the Conseils d'Administration of the co-ops, and in that non-member workers are given some protection against exploitation, French co-op law is widely recognized as superior to its UK counterpart. On the other hand, the view at SCOP headquarters is that French law is in turn inferior to Spanish. Antoine Antoni was quite unequivocal about this when I raised the matter in 1976. 'As a veteran on the republican side in the Civil War, I hate to concede this,' he told me, 'but there is no question that Franco's co-op law is greatly superior to any in Europe.'

What the French have in mind when they commend the Spanish co-op law is, in the first place, precisely the set of points which we have been considering. Spanish co-op law effectively insists – as the French and the British laws do not – that a co-op's membership and the co-op's workforce are the same body. As well as ensuring against that kind of backsliding which so pre-occupied the Webbs, this also encourages optimum workforce motivation.

However, the French commend the Spanish co-op law on other grounds. They point out that an institution like the Mondragon co-op workers' bank (the Caja Laboral Popular) could not be set up under French law. They argue that the Basque industrial co-ops have thus had relatively easy access to capital – in contrast to what happened in France. Third, they commend those provisions of the Spanish law which lay down that significant proportions of any surplus must be allocated both to collective enterprise reserves and to projects for the benefit of the local community in which the co-op is established.

It may be a mistake to make too much of these legal points, for they may deflect attention away from the co-op enterprises themselves and from the internal dynamics of their success and failure. All the same there is clearly no case for maintaining an old set of laws when there are demonstrably superior alternatives. That applies particularly in Britain's case. But it is also easy to understand the feeling at SCOP headquarters that the co-op laws in France are markedly inferior to those in Spain.

This brief survey of the old French industrial co-ops has identified four main sub-groups within the SCOP:

1 Several hundred small or very small 'artisan' co-ops – many of them small builders.

2 A handful of enterprises which, starting very much from working class origins have achieved leading positions in their respective sectors.

3 Roughly 100 co-ops of intermediate size, with employment in the fifty to 500 range; in terms of economic performance there seems to be little to choose between these co-ops and similar capitalist enterprises.

4 A significant number of recently formed job-saving co-ops set up in the wake of capitalist closures.

The first of these groups falls to some extent outside the main focus of this book, though they and their achievement are not to be dismissed for that reason. Indeed, they may well provide valuable alternative models for the small family business and, in the special context of the UK building industry, for the 'lump'. More generally there is plainly something positive about small-scale enterprises which have the great advantage of spreading wealth and of encouraging self-reliance and group solidarity.

In the case of the second and the third groups there is no harm in acknowledging that there is some force in the predictable reaction of the critical sceptic who asks two questions. Why, if co-op structures enjoy real advantages, have more of these enterprises not emerged as leaders in their branches of industry? And why have co-ops in the third group failed to produce a significantly superior performance compared with their capitalist counterparts?

A small, but only small part, of the answers to these questions became apparent in the discussion of the formal legal structures. French co-op law, though better than British is flawed. As a result the improved motivation which should flow from the best possible co-op structures has only partly been achieved. Further, partly because French law does not permit them to mobilize local savings for development, the French co-ops have never really enjoyed adequate access to capital.

The main part of the answer is rather different. It is no accident that the word 'ouvriers' figures as prominently as it does in the title of the French industrial co-ops.* Historically, and still essentially in the late 1970s, they are working men's – working-class – enterprises. For most of their history they have been wary of professional middle-class management. Equally, with only a few exceptions, dynamic young executives have been reluctant to apply for jobs in the co-ops. As a result it is hardly surprising that French co-op management has tended to be less strong than that of similar capitalist ventures. If we add that many, perhaps most, of the small and middle-rank co-ops have simply not wanted to expand, then the small number of large co-ops should occasion no surprise. In a sense the fundamental point was made by Alfred Marshall a century ago: what we have seen is not a fair test. For this has not been a contest between like and like; it has been a contest between working men's enterprises and enterprises which have been in a position to exploit a complete range of resources.

Having dealt with the sceptics, how far can we take any positive assessment of this French experience? In the first place we can, I think, finally dispose of the Webb's position. The French experience shows that there is nothing in a co-operative structure which rules out the possibility of success. Co-ops in manufacturing industry are by no means doomed to failure as the Webbs asserted.

In fact, the evidence points a good deal beyond this negative conclusion. If I have read it correctly, we are entitled to suggest that if the French co-ops could reach a position to compete on even terms with their rivals – and if they could correct their faulty structures – then great things might happen. For there is real, if largely anecdotal, evidence from places like Albi that the shop floor can behave with extraordinarily enlightened self-interest. If shop-floor attitudes are enlightened, if historically weak management can be made good and adequate access to capital secured, these enterprises might well surprise the sceptics.

---

* The new Co-op law allows the less politically charged word 'travaileurs' to be substituted for 'ouvriers' in a co-op's title.

9
Political co-ops in Italy

The photograph of a benevolent, even cheery looking Joseph Stalin beamed out from the works' dining-room window when I visited the Co-operativa Lavoratori Fonderia Officina Cure at Scandicci, an overspill suburb of Florence, in March 1978. The foundry must by then have been one of Europe's longest surviving post-war job-saving co-ops, for it had resumed life in co-operative form in February 1955. Then it was one of a relatively few, but by the late 1970s it was one of a growing number of job-saving co-ops affiliated to Italy's Lega Nazionale delle Co-operative e Mutue (the Lega), the one communist-controlled among the country's three co-operative groupings. Yet the foundry's manifest capacity to survive was less interesting than the very different question to which that Stalin 'pin-up' gave rise. Are Italy's communist-controlled Lega co-ops genuinely independent and democratic enterprises? Or are they the enterprise creatures of the Italian Communist Party (PCI) controlled by the Party at the centre in much the same way as Russia's so-called co-operative farms are controlled from Moscow?

It was not possible, in early 1978, to give a categorical answer. However, since it is the most important one raised by the Italian co-operative movement as a whole, we shall have to come back to it at the end of this chapter. What is incontestable, on the other hand, is that the Italian co-ops have long differed from their counterparts in other Western European countries in being divided into three separate political groupings: the broadly communist Lega; the broadly catholic (or Christian Democrat) Confederazione Co-operative Italiane (the Confederation); and the republican and social democrat Associazione Generale dell Co-operative Italiane (the Association). Moreover, despite real statistical obscurities and confusions, there was no doubt in the late 1970s that among the Production and Labour Co-ops (Co-operative Produzione e Lavoro) – what we would call workers' co-ops – those affiliated to the Lega accounted for the largest volume of employment.

There is no doubt either that if the Lega enterprises are accepted as sufficiently genuine, Italy has more co-ops employing more people than any other European country – and, very likely, than the whole of the rest of Western Europe. Each of the three groupings includes other sectors – agricultural, housing, retail trade, credit and so on – as well as workers' co-ops, but the great size of the Italian movement, compared to the position elsewhere in Western Europe, relates to the sector of workers' co-ops alone. The best estimates – explained later – for the statistics of these in Italy in 1977 were, I believe, as those in Table 9.1.

TABLE 9.1   Italian workers' co-ops, 1977

	Lega affiliated	Confederation affiliated	Association affiliated	Total
Active enterprises	1,425	1,000	250	2,675
Nos employed	110,000	32,500	5,000	147,500

Source: Sig. Fabio Carpanelli in *Co-operation et Production*, ICA, October 1977.

However, before any false conclusions are drawn from these estimates, one point of fundamental importance for any understanding of the Italian workers' co-ops needs to be emphasized. More than half of this total employment was provided in 1977, as for all or most of the co-ops' history, by building and civil engineering enterprises. In this respect the position of the Italian movement is a more pronounced case of the French experience. The estimates also indicate that the average size of these Italian enterprises, like their counterparts in France, is quite small – roughly fifty-five employees.

In round figures the three groups together have roughly five times the number of enterprises and roughly five times the total employment levels of the corresponding figures in France – traditionally regarded as the country in Western Europe where co-ops have achieved the greatest success. There is a separate question, which I will ignore, namely why the traditional view has been implicitly dismissive of the Italian achievement. The immediate and obvious questions are why and how have these Italian workers' co-ops succeeded in multiplying to an extent which far outstrips anything which the French have achieved.

The short answer has, I think two parts. First, from the late nineteenth century to the early 1920s and then again from 1945 onwards – the position during the intervening Fascist period is more obscure – all Italian co-ops, and the country's workers' co-ops (if anything more than any other variety), have enjoyed substantial tax and other advantages from the state. Second, it seems a fair guess that at least since the early 1950s, when the separation off from the Lega of the majority of republican and social democrat inclined co-ops gave the movement its three-fold division, these enterprises have been helped rather than hindered by the party-political backing which they have received and which has ensured the continuity of the tax and other privileges they enjoy. It also seems clear that the Lega co-ops have benefited — especially during the 1970s — from their links with the increasingly influential and action-oriented PCI.

However, in order fully to understand the position of the Italian workers' co-ops in the 1970s we have to go back a long way — to the astonishing growth of these enterprises in the period of roughly forty years down to the early 1920s. For the records suggest that in 1921 there may have been as many as 2,900 active workers' co-ops. Moreover, contemporary observers were in no doubt that the co-ops in Italy's Produzione e Lavoro sector — and particularly the latter (which may be thought of roughly as navvying co-ops) — were a phenomenon without parallel in Europe. What happened during the thirty or so years of the Fascist régime tends to be rather obscured in official Italian publications, which invite us to believe that on the assumption of power by the fascists most of these co-operative enterprises simply closed down.* Many did so, Yet common sense as well as contemporary evidence — for example the then director of the Lega's industrial co-ops decided to remain in his post — suggests that very large numbers felt it better to put their political principles on one side and accept the new fascist-controlled co-operative syndicate which Mussolini had established as early as 1921. Of course it must be doubtful whether by the end of the Second World War more than a minority were still operational or could show an uninterrupted record of work during the Fascist period. Equally, it would be wrong to belittle the effort of enterprise reconstruction after 1945. All the same it seems plausible to assume that there was enough continuity to provide a substantial base from which co-op redevelopment could start after the war. If that is true, any explanation of the scale of Italian workers' co-ops in the late 1970s must begin before the fascists came to power.

The earliest recorded Italian co-operatives date from the 1850s. There was a consumers' operation started rather on Rochdale lines though without, it is said, even indirect Rochdale influence, by a General Association of Turin Workers (Associazione Generale degli Operati di Torino). More surprisingly, there was also a glassworks co-operative in the Savona Province at Altare. The starting date given for both is 1854.

However, as in the UK and France, so in Italy, it was the 1880s which saw the first substantial development of workers' co-ops. The first Italian co-operative congress took place in 1886 and the first co-operative

---

* An important new text, *Il Movimento Co-operativo in Italia 1926–1962, Scritti e Documenti* a cura di W. Briganti, Editrice Cooperativa-Roma, Edizioni APE — Bologna, appeared in April 1978 when this book was already in production.

federation was formed in the following year as the Federazione delle Co-operative Italiane; by a change of name it became the Lega in 1893. We have no firm data which would establish what percentage of the Lega's enterprise membership was accounted for by co-ops in the Produzione e Lavoro sector, but all the available studies suggest the figure was much higher in Italy than it ever was in France or the UK, and that these workers' co-ops probably constituted one-third of the total. Equally, there is no firm data to tell us what proportion of the co-ops up and down the country chose to affiliate with the Lega, but an estimate from the early 1920s suggests that roughly 50 per cent normally did so. On the basis of these two assumptions we can plot the growth of Italy's Produzione e Lavoro co-ops from a series of Lega affiliation figures published in a Fabian Society report in 1925 and given in Table 9.2.

TABLE 9.2   Lega affiliations

	Lega affiliations	of which P e L	P e L total
1896	68	23	46
1897	229	76	152
1916	2,189	730	1,460
1920	3,840	1,280	2,560
1921	4,302	1,433	2,866

Source: E. A. Lloyd, *The Co-operative Movement in Italy with special reference to Agriculture, Labour and Production* for the Fabian Society, Allen & Unwin, London, 1925.

It would be absurd to pretend that these figures give anything more than a very rough guide. There is also the point that, at any rate in the 1970s, Italian co-operative statistics had a reputation for being, if anything, more unreliable than those from elsewhere. Despite these qualifications, however, neither the reality of the growth of these enterprises, nor its substantial scale in the years before, during and immediately after the First World War, is seriously in doubt. It is unambiguously attested by Mr Lloyd's study. It is also vouched for in a more comprehensive work which must be considered something of a collectors' piece in co-operative literature, *Studies in European Co-operation* by C. F. Strickland of the Indian Civil Service, which was published by the Superintendent of Government Printing, Lahore, 1922.

It is clear from these two studies, and more importantly from original Italian sources quoted extensively by Mr Lloyd, that it was the Lavoro rather than the Produzione co-ops which provided the main element in this growth. I have called them 'navvying' co-ops, more accurately they should probably be thought of as co-ops engaged chiefly in civil engineering, but also in building work – with the Produzione co-ops consisting of manufacturing enterprises. The Fabian report says that the earliest of the (Lavoro) co-ops 'was formed on the banks of the Po by groups of "braccianti" ' (manual labourers or navvies) and that by the outbreak of the First World War they 'had spread to all parts of the country' and were 'actively engaged in the carrying out of huge contracts for the construction of roads, bridges, harbours, drainage schemes and public works of all kinds.' Figures quoted from an official Italian Ministry of Works report suggest that 15 per cent of these contracts for the entire country were being handled by Lavoro co-ops before the war, and that for particular areas the figures were very much higher: 85 per cent for Ravenna, 90 per cent for Ferrara, and in Emilia during the ten years before 1914 the co-operative labour societies had a virtual monopoly of these contracts. In 'red' Bologna, in late 1977, I was told by a high official of the Lega that the group's civil engineering and building co-ops had an 8 per cent share of the country's market and that the figure in the 'red belt' provinces of Emilia Romagna, Umbria and Toscana was much higher. He also explained, as we shall see later, that the Lega's market share was partly the result of the successful policy of amalgamating smaller building and civil engineering co-ops which it had been pursuing over the previous few years. But the point to emphasize here is that it was the growth of these Lavoro co-ops in the pre-First World War period which supplied the base and the tradition behind the strength of the Lega's position in the late 1970s and constituted in some sense the secret of its successful history.

Partly to illustrate the relative size and sophistication of some of the early Lega 'civil engineering' enterprises, it is worth mentioning that they were involved in railways as well as in the other headings enumerated in that Ministry of Works report. Mr Lloyd tells us that 'the traveller who goes from Reggio Emilia to Ciano does so on a railway constructed, owned and managed entirely by co-operative societies.' Other evidence suggests that at one time or another co-ops were responsible for the entire railway system of the province of Emilia Romagna. When I was in Bologna in late 1977 my attention was drawn to an unusual Lega co-op, the Co-operativa Lavori Ferroviari (CLF) – one engaged in railway maintenance. However, I was unable to establish whether it was directly linked with the railway co-operatives mentioned by Mr Lloyd. So far as I know, co-op involvement in railways is unique to the Italian experience. It seems to contradict the conventional wisdom that railways have to be run as unitary systems.

However, the most important question about this early development of the Lega co-ops is how and why it came about. Legal advantages have already been mentioned and were clearly important. Co-ops were first recognized properly under a law of 1883 which, among other things, granted them exemption from stamp duty for their first ten years. More significant, anyway from the viewpoint of the Lavoro co-ops, was further legislation, introduced in 1889, which allowed them to contract directly – and not through private contractors as intermediaries – with the state and provincial authorities. A fairly low limit was initially put on the maximum value of such contracts, but it was later removed. It could, of course, reasonably be argued that such provisions merely allowed the co-ops to compete on even terms with private enterprise. But perhaps the really key points are that the 1889 legislation also permitted the public authorities to grant the co-ops exemption from the requirement of putting up bonds and to sign contracts with them without recourse to competitive tender. This was the legislative framework which made possible the enormous growth of the co-ops in the period up to the early 1920s.

It is true that rather similar advantages were enjoyed during this period by the corresponding building and civil engineering co-ops in France. Yet the contemporary growth of such French enterprises, though considerable, was very much less than those of the Italian Lega. To explain this difference we have, I think, to refer to traditional or cultural factors. Independent artisans (artigiani), particularly in the building trades, had been very much a feature of Italian life for at least 100 years before the first co-ops were founded, and they are still very much in evidence in the late 1970s. We may think of these Italian co-ops as voluntary groupings of artigiani and braccianti.

Contemporary evidence about the performance of these Italian Lavoro co-ops is conflicting. On the negative side there was criticism that their prices were often higher than those charged by private enterprise – though a similar but opposite criticism was also made against their capitalist competitors. There was also much criticism, conceded to be just by the provincial and central organizations (and very much repeated in the world of the 1970s), of bogus co-operatives formed with the sole object of benefiting from the various legal advantages. On the other hand, an official enquiry in 1907 reported that 'there exist societies that are doing good work. They serve as an insurance against strikes.' Another favourable point was brought out by the Italian government's budget committee in 1909: 'whereas in contracts with co-operative societies the department has had occasion to comment of the rarity of disputes, the private contractors have shown a regrettable facility ... in creating disagreements.'

What seems certain is that those – and there were clearly not a few – who believed that the official policy of favouring the co-ops would prove totally disastrous, were confounded. One such was an economist called Boccardo. Mr Lloyd tells us that he foretold the 'absolute failure' of the policy:

> to believe that the working classes, with the elements of which they are composed, not only in Italy but throughout the world, are capable of carrying out great public works, demanding the continuous and intelligent action of a single powerful directive force is but an illusion of Utopia.

It is perhaps fair to concede that had the Lavoro co-ops consisted entirely of braccianti Sig. Boccardo's view might well have proved correct. However, Mr Lloyd goes on to point out that the works successfully undertaken had been carried out under 'the devoted guidance of technicians and professionals who have, in many cases, sacrificed brilliant prospects of personal advancement in order to stand by the workers, inspired by the ideal of mutual assistance'. In other words, these extraordinary Italian Lavoro co-ops, unlike the majority of their UK and French 'cloth cap' counterparts, so far from feeling uneasy recruiting professional management, succeeded in attracting some very high-level talents. Of the financial sacrifice involved for these people we shall find some apparent evidence in the 1970s.

Until 1919 the Lega was the single national organization of the Italian co-ops. It was not during this early period affiliated to any political party and embraced co-ops of any ideology or none. Its founders in the 1880s and 1890s had been basically liberals and republicans, but increasingly, in the years before and during the First World War, activists of a more socialist persuasion became influential. And this process was accelerated as Italian politics became more polarized in the last year of the war, following the Bolshevik Revolution in Russia. It is against this background that the establishment of the separate Catholic co-op grouping in 1919, the Confederazione Co-operative Italiane, should be understood. This was followed soon after, at the Lega's 1920 congress, by a resolution which created formal links between the Lega and the Italian Socialist Party. It is worth remembering that the Italian communists were still in that year members of that Socialist Party; they only separated off in 1921 following the widespread workers' occupation of Italian factories. In any event, between a quarter and a third of the member co-ops seem to have transferred their affiliation to the Confederazione in the few months after the Lega's formal links with the Italian socialists had been forged.

As it was, however, only four more years of independent existence remained to the Lega before it was officially dissolved by a decree of

Mussolini in 1925. On the other hand, though the Lega itself was no more, a large proportion of its member enterprises carried on. From a post-Second World War study by the ICA we learn in fact that slightly more than half the number of the old Lega co-ops were still in business in 1938.

Before I deal briefly with the formal re-establishment of the old Italian co-op organizations in 1945 and the first post-war generation, it may be helpful to take a quick glance at the position in 1977 and early 1978. Quite suddenly, from about the beginning of 1977, the co-ops became the focus of almost unprecedented attention. At a political level the leaders of the three groupings – the Lega, the Confederation and the Association – were received by the Prime Minister, Sig Andreotti, an event virtually without precedent in living history. Even the country's three trade union federations (which as late as 1976 had considered it beneath their dignity to reply to a letter from the co-ops), began to pay attention. Then, in January 1978, the Italian weekly, *Il Mondo*, devoted a fourteen-page report basically to the Lega co-ops but referring to the other two groupings as well. The article spoke of the Lega co-op's 'constant and silent growth' ('crescita costante e silenziosa') since 1896, interrupted only by the Fascist years. It then went on to suggest, if somewhat paradoxically, that the Lega had lately become seized by the conviction that it must break out from its 'historic lethargy' ('latargo storico').

It is true that there were special as well as general reasons for the unaccustomed coverage devoted by the Italian Press to the affairs of the Lega and its co-ops in late 1977 and early 1978. For reasons which we shall look at briefly later on its President, Sig Vincenzo Galetti, had been forced to resign and was replaced by a new chief executive on 28 December 1977. But the Galetti affair was only highlighted in the Italian Press because the co-ops had already become news, for two main reasons. First, they had been officially approached by the Italian government in 1977 to discuss the possibility that some of the loss-making Italian state-owned enterprises might be converted into co-ops – an approach which can only have enhanced their prestige and which they saw, not unreasonably, as some sort of endorsement of their competence. Secondly, all three groupings – the Lega most of all – had been involved (especially in the years following the oil price rise of 1973), in rescue operations to set up job-saving co-ops when capitalist enterprises went into liquidation. The Lega in fact claimed early in 1978 to have saved a total of something like 10,000 jobs – and to have converted roughly 100 enterprises – over the previous four years. In short, whatever may have happened between 1945 and the early 1970s, it was fairly clear in 1977 and early 1978 that the Italian workers' co-ops had 'arrived'.

If we now turn back to the years between 1945 and the early 1970s it seems probable that after the reconstruction effort and by comparison with the pre-1921 period, these were indeed times of relative 'lethargy'. There may, just possibly, have been 'constant' growth, but it was at best slow as well as 'silent'. Such is the character and quality of the available data that an enormous research effort would be required to establish whether there was any significant growth at all; I suspect that there was not very much. These were the years of the 'Italian Miracle' when private capitalism was riding high. In such an environment it seems unlikely, even when full account is taken of the availability of government credits, that large numbers of working people would have decided to set up new co-operative enterprises.

On the other hand, no 'lethargy' was shown in the post-war re-establishment of the co-op organizations or in the subsequent exercise of reconstruction. The Confederation was reconstituted on 15 May 1945 as an 'association of voluntary economic solidarity as the basis for co-operative life'. It is true that there is no reference to the Confederation's Catholic loyalties. Yet, or so it must be supposed, it was for reasons of this kind that while socialist and communist representatives were included in the first post-war Italian governments, the two co-op groupings, which became separate after the First World War, decided to pursue independent ways after the Second.

The re-constitution of the Lega was not far behind that of the Confederation. A Lega congress was summoned to meet in Rome in early September 1945. An ICA publication, *International Co-operation 1937–39*, says that at the congress 'concerned socialists, communists, and republicans, joined together to resuscitate the Lega.' A total of 4,722 co-op societies are reported to have been represented. It is a reasonable guess that up to one-third were in the category Produzione e Lavoro. In any event the representation figures appear to confirm that there was substantial continuity with the past.

Apart from their successes of re-establishment and reconstruction, the co-ops may reasonably claim important political achievements in the immediate post-war world of 1945. The first and the key to what happened later, was the inclusion in the new Italian republic's constitution of an article (No. 45) which effectively guarantees official support for co-operative endeavour: 'The state will assist by the most suitable means the development of co-operative organisations, founded on the principle of mutuality and will supervise their activities.' Formal legislation in the spirit of this article was passed in 1947; under it the co-ops were to enjoy all or most of the privileges they had won in the pre-1914 period, together with some new ones. As well as the ten years exemption from stamp duty, interest on members' capital was exempt from tax. They were also to be eligible for special low-interest loans and to enjoy their old exemptions in the matter of bonds and tender procedures. Moreover, the provincial and local authorities were permitted to grant special treatment to the co-ops. It is true that, in the exercise of its supervisory functions, the government imposed various restrictions. The maximum amount of members' capital was limited. It was laid down too that 50 per cent of any co-op's profits must either be distributed to members or held on their account for insurance and welfare purposes. In the event of dissolution the co-ops were not permitted to distribute any net assets to their members – any that there were would have to be devoted to social projects. And there were various other restrictions. For example a co-op was not normally allowed to have a membership of below twenty-five, though in special circumstances the minimum was nine.

These restrictions may have been important at least in theory, but the general effect of the 1947 legislation is not in doubt: the advantages which the co-ops had won before 1914 were confirmed to them and, if anything, extended. The importance of these advantages is underlined by the fact – admitted by the co-ops' central organizations in the 1970s, as it had been half a century before – that they led to an immense mushrooming of more or less bogus and unaffiliated co-operative ventures. I shall refer to this point again later on, but for the moment it is sufficient to use it as evidence of the real benefits which co-ops enjoy under Italian law – and to report that in early 1978 the three central groupings were discussing with government how the abuse of the law could be checked.

There is one further historical point. In 1952 a minority of the co-ops affiliated to the Lega seceded and formed the Associazione Generale delle Co-operative Italiane. The motive behind the split, which was led by a political lawyer, Sig. Amando Rossini, were unambiguously political. Evidently, despite its formal link with the Socialist Party in 1920, the Lega had moved progressively closer to the PCI in the years after 1945. The co-ops which seceded were of republican and social democrat persuasion and Sig. Rossini clearly felt that these two parties, as well as the PCI (and the socialists), should have their own organization. Still it is fair to point out that some social democrat and republican co-ops chose not to leave at that time. Moreover, it would be wrong to imply that the Lega, despite its close ties with the PCI and its communist leadership, became monolithically communist. The actual composition of its membership is probably best reflected by what had become by the late 1970s the customary distribution of seats on its ten-man Presidential Council: PCI six, socialists three, social democrats and republicans together one.

In some respects, because of common characteristics and experience, it seemed reasonable in the late 1970s to treat the workers' co-ops of the three separate Italian groupings as a single species. They were operating under the same laws and shared the same basic structures. Building and civil engineering enterprises accounted in all three cases for the greatest part of employment. They came as one body to their discussions with the Italian government and they shared a common interest in the amendment and improvement of the legal régime under which they operated. To a greater or lesser extent they had all − though the Lega more so than the other two − been involved in exercises to salvage jobs by converting failed or ailing capitalist enterprises into co-ops. Because of the obvious social and economic importance of such rescue operations − at least where these could be justified by the prospects of the converted co-op − they had received a substantial measure of government 'recognition' and, for the Italian public, they had all in some sense 'arrived'. They had 'arrived' too in the sense that more of their countrymen were beginning to look to the co-ops as providers of possible enterprise models.

If we ignore the differences of political leadership and outlook − and the real effects that these may have on the way the co-ops actually work − the model and structure which they offered in the late 1970s was basically the same. Sovereign power rested with a general meeting of members. Most workers − rarely less than 60 per cent in an active co-op − were normally members. Only a handful of non-workers, if any, normally enjoyed membership. The members in general meeting elected what was essentially a policy-making board. The board in turn appointed the management, an appointment which might or might not have to be ratified by the general meeting. In other words these Italian workers co-ops were using, in the late 1970s, what was becoming the classic co-operative control structure.

Despite these and other similarities, major differences were also exhibited both as between the three groupings and as between individual co-ops. The inter-grouping differences will become apparent in a moment. Perhaps the most significant difference as between individual co-ops, anyway in the late 1970s, was their varying policies on capital subscriptions as one of the prices of membership. In many of the Lega co-ops, as would be expected from a grouping with a basically collectivist ideology, these capital subscriptions were quite nominal − say the equivalent of £5. But in other Lega co-ops, as well as in many of those affiliated to the Association and to the Confederation, significant sums were sometimes insisted upon. An example inside the Lega is provided by the co-operative Florence foundry mentioned at the start of this chapter. New members joining the co-op in 1978 were required to subscribe a sum equivalent to about three months' starting salary: Lire 1m. (roughly £600). On the other hand, since these membership subscriptions (unlike those in the Mondragon co-ops), may only be credited with interest under Italian law – and not with individual profit shares – it is arguable that the differences in the subscription sums laid down by the different co-ops are not really of fundamental importance.

Because there were the smallest number of them in the late 1970s, the workers' co-ops affiliated to the Association can be dealt with first, but although their numbers were quite small they proved astonishingly difficult to pin down. An enquiry into the position, as did other enquiries for firm data about the Italian co-ops, illustrated for me rather vividly the problem of the realities behind the official statistics.

To begin with an official review by the Italian Labour Ministry, published in April 1977 to mark a national co-operative conference, records a total of 8,572 co-ops in the category Produzione e Lavoro. However, since less than half of these reappear in the broken down totals for the three co-operative groupings, we have to start from the position that there were more unaffiliated workers' co-ops in Italy, bogus or otherwise, than affiliated ones in 1977; but our statistical troubles are not over. The same publication's figures show 652 'produzione e lavoro' co-ops affiliated to the Association. On the other hand, since the Association eventually conceded that the total labour force of its 'active' workers' co-ops was no more than 5,000 – and since each co-op must normally have a minimum of twenty-five members – it seemed impossible to reconcile the numbers employed with the number of enterprises. However, Association officials finally admitted that not more than 250 of their affiliated enterprises were actually operating in early 1978. That is the source and explanation of the figure in Table 9.1.

Rather more than half of the active workers' co-ops were civil engineering and building operations, including their largest single enterprise which was employing between 400 and 500 people. There were also a fair number of building material co-ops (particularly in marble and other stone cutting) and printing and footwear production co-ops. A number of industrial service enterprises, particularly a group of office and factory cleaners, were included; but no complete and up-to-date breakdown was available from the Association in early 1978.

There was, however, some evidence from the Association's President,

Sig. Ragliani (who is also a Republican Senator in the Italian Parliament), of active policies and of involvement in job-saving operations. A consortium of building co-ops was being formed. One of the Association's credit banks had recently acquired control of another in the Ravenna region: a marble-cutting operation outside Pisa had been successfully converted into a co-op. Admittedly, compared with the scale of contemporary Lega initiatives, none of the Association's moves. Sig. Ragliani conceded, had been more than modest. But he insisted that because of real ideological differences the Association was right to retain its independence; he doubted the Lega's claim – and indeed the PCI's – to have been genuinely converted to 'pluralism'; he believed that it remained committed to collectivism and 'syndicalism'; and he believed that the Lega operated through directions and instructions from the centre. By contrast, the Association's co-ops enjoyed a real independence from the centre and would not rejoin the Lega at the cost of giving it up.

The essential points about the Association's workers' co-ops in early 1978 seemed to me to be two contrasting ones. On the one hand there was the reality of some 200 small and barely medium-sized enterprises, the bulk of them building operations employing no more than twenty-five people. Of course, this is not to denigrate small co-operative builders. As the French experience showed, this may well be the best way of ensuring that small building works are efficiently done. Yet in contrast to the Association's scale there was the evidence both of government recognition and of more active policies and initiatives. Clearly, if the Association is to have any significant impact outside the world of small building over the next decade, it is the latter, the new active policies and initiatives which will have to be pushed. In particular, or so I would imagine, the Association will need to achieve a sharp increase in the number of successful rescue operations and conversions.

There are rather similar difficulties about basic data on the co-ops affiliated to the Confederation. The Labour Ministry's 1977 publication recorded a total of 1,681 and when I visited the group's headquarters at the end of that year I was told, not unreasonably, that the figure had since increased to 1,703. I was even given a breakdown by subsectors: which is given here in Table 9.3.

TABLE 9.3   Co-ops affiliated to the Confederation

Building and civil engineering	901
Manufacture	310
Services	362
Artisan co-ops	130
Total	1,703

However, Sig. Bruno Catalano, the President of the Confederation's Produzione e Lavoro co-ops, later revealed that not more than 1,000 were in fact active. He claimed that total employment amounted to 45,000. This figure was strongly contradicted by other sources, notably the Lega, which put it at no more than 20,000. In Table 9.1 at the start of the chapter I have simply split the difference existing between the two claims.

Here again, as with the Association, the main reality is a group of small and barely medium-sized building enterprises with the largest also employing 400–500 people. Of course, there are many more of these operations affiliated to the Confederation, and their average size is distinctly larger: perhaps a total of 600 with an average employment of up to forty-five. However, I would doubt whether these differences were of much significance as Sig. Catalano emphasized to me that the co-ops themselves wished to remain independent (and small?) and not to amalgamate. Once again I must make explicit the disclaimer that there is anything to be ashamed of in this situation. Indeed many will see it as a reflection of true co-operative virtue. But the point for the 1980s is the same as in the case of the Association: unless new initiatives are undertaken the impact of the Confederation's workers' co-ops is likely to remain restricted to the world of the small builder.

To be fair, Sig. Catalano seemed to be aware of this. A man of apparent energy and drive, he foresaw in particular that 'conversions' rather than 'new start-ups' would account for 70 per cent of the Confederation's new workers' co-ops over the years ahead. Early in 1978, or so he told me, he had in fact been involved in the conversion of a fairly substantial textile enterprise in Milan which, in its capitalist days, had employed more than 1,000 people. At the time he was speaking, March 1978 – which was still very early days for the newly converted co-op – it had absorbed roughly 450 employees, making it already the largest manufacturing co-op in the Confederation group. He was cautiously optimistic about its future, and he argued that were it not for the hostility of the trade unions the Confederation's conversion record from 1974 onwards would have been as strong as the Lega's. As it was he had received more than 100 rescue and conversion appeals. Other factors too, but chiefly the unions, had blocked success in all but two cases. If this account is broadly accurate and if potentially rescuable enterprises continue to present themselves, then it seems clear that the Confederation will have to persuade the unions not to frustrate its initiatives if it is looking for a substantial role in the next decade.

Without wishing to belittle the future impact of either the Confederation's or the Association's workers' co-op efforts, it seemed probable in early 1978 that the main potential lay with the Lega. To begin with, its workers' co-ops already accounted for a far greater volume of employment than the other two groupings put together. Its employment figures, used in Table 9.1, are taken from an article by Sig. Fabio Carpanilli, the President of its workers' co-op section, published in the ICA bulletin *Co-operation de Production* and dated October 1977. On the other hand, I have reduced the figure for the number of building enterprises given in that article by 250 to 352. Otherwise these data cannot be reconciled with the claim, made repeatedly by the Lega in late 1977 and early 1978, that employment in its building and civil engineering co-ops averaged, as a result of amalgamations, 185. With this adjustment the figures are as shown in Table 9.4.

TABLE 9.4   Lega workers' co-ops 1977

	No. of enterprises	Employment
Building and civil engineering	352	59,500
Manufacturing	315	20,800
Services	758	31,000
Totals	1,425	111,300

It is not only the Lega's overall numbers which suggest that we should look to it for the main development potential of the Italian workers' co-ops. Particularly in building and civil engineering, but to an important extent in the building materials and building plant sectors where it is also strong, its enterprises are significantly larger than those of the other two groupings. Moreover, from the mid 1970s onwards the Lega co-ops began to demonstrate their ability to secure contracts overseas. Equally important, as we have already seen, it started to pursue a vigorous and fairly successful policy of rescue operations and conversions from the time of the 1973 oil price rises, and the resulting period of difficulty for the Italian economy. Third, at its end-1977 congress the Lega committed itself to an ambitious programme of expansion and development. It is worth looking a little more closely at each of these points in turn.

The largest Lega enterprise is Co-op Muratori Cementisti (CMC), (The Bricklayers' and Cement Workers' Co-op), a civil engineering and building concern with its headquarters in Ravenna. With a 1977 workforce of over 3,000 CMC almost certainly ranked as the third largest co-op in Western Europe – after Mondragon's ULGOR and AOIP in France. By the same yardstick another civil engineering and building enterprise, Co-op Edilter, based on Bologna was probably the second largest Lega business – with a labour force of roughly 1,400. The Lega further claimed that another ten of its building and civil engineering enterprises were employing an average of 680 people.

These substantial Lega enterprises result in large measure from a policy of promoting amalgamations since 1973. I noted earlier the average figure of a workforce of 185 claimed by the Lega for its building and civil engineering enterprises in 1977; the corresponding figure four years earlier is given as 55.

It is true that the Lega's manufacturing enterprises are generally much smaller in employment terms – averaging not more than sixty to seventy 'occupati' – than its building and civil engineering co-ops. On the other hand they do include a handful of good medium-sized (as well as large numbers of barely medium-sized) enterprises: for example, a foundry in Modena with a 700-odd workforce and a building plant manufacturing co-op employing over 400. But the main points about the Lega's manufacturing sector seems to me to be first its relative concentration in building materials and building plant production and that, secondly, if the policy of rescue operations is successfully maintained, then we must expect that Lega manufacturing will grow disproportionately fast in the 1980s. For it already accounted for a high proportion of the roughly 10,000 jobs and roughly 100 enterprises which the Lega claimed, in early 1978, that it had saved through rescue operations and conversions over the previous four years.

The high apparent success rate of these Lega rescue and conversion operations (very much greater than anything achieved elsewhere in Western Europe) deserves to be separately studied. Common sense suggests, however, that two factors have been of special importance: access to cheap credits under the privileges enjoyed by all Italian co-ops; and the congruence of the Lega's social and political objectives with those of Italy's main communist-controlled trade union federation. Evidently its rescue operations have normally been immune to the trade union hostility which, it is claimed, has thwarted the Confederation's efforts.

Local authorities have also sometimes helped. A case in point (though from the 1950s not the 1970s) is that Florence foundry. The then Christian Democrat Mayor, Sig. Lapira, was apparently instrumental in persuading the local authority to take over the foundry premises and re-let to the co-op for a nominal rent. Similar cases are quoted from the 1970s. Of course, it is true that a successful conversion does not ensure long-term survival; a co-op can also go bankrupt. There were in fact two Lega bankruptcies in 1977: a glassworks and a small building co-op. On the other hand the procedures for dealing with a co-op bankruptcy differ in at least one important respect from those which apply in the private sector. It is not the courts but the Labour Ministry which appoints the liquidator. Moreover, his powers of discretion are wider than those of a court appointee. He is in a position to take steps which may allow the co-op to revive, and there have certainly been examples of this in the 1970s, as in previous decades.

Just as the apparent success of its rescue operations suggests considerable vigour and dynamism on the part of the Lega leadership, so does the move into export markets by consortia of its building and civil engineering enterprises. According to Sig. Carpanelli, its export contract order book jumped from nothing in 1975 to £80m in 1976 and £150m in 1977. The most important contracts were secured in Third World countries with socialist-inclined ideologies: Algeria, Mozambique, Somalia, Tanzania. The Lega, through its former National President, Vincenzo Galetti, signed fairly comprehensive agreements with the governments of these countries in 1976 and 1977, but it has also been prepared to work in overseas environments which are ideologically less sympathetic: its co-ops formed part of a consortium, alongside private and state owned Italian enterprises, which was building the new Iranian port of Bandarabas in the late 1970s.

Final evidence that the Lega is not daunted by tough and ambitious new challenges is provided by its three-year expansion and development plan (1978-80). The most formidable objective is the creation of 12,000 new jobs, a high proportion of them in the Mezzogiorno south of Rome. Total investment is put at Lire 370,000m (or somewhat more than £220m). The projected budget indicates that 40 per cent of this sum is to be sought from new capital subscriptions by Lega members (10 per cent) and from the co-ops' own cash flow (30 per cent). According to Sig. Carpanelli only half of the balance will be sought in the form of cheap subsidized credits, with the rest obtained from the banks and leasing companies at commercial rates.

In sum the Lega is, in the first place, a substantial group of co-operatively structured and communist-led enterprises, employing – if service co-ops are included – well over 100,000 people. Geographically they were still at the end of the 1970s – as their pre-1920 forebears had been – heavily concentrated in northern and central Italy: perhaps as much as 80 per cent of their employment was accounted for by the three 'red belt' provinces of Emilia Romagna, Umbria and Toscana. Industrially they were still heavily concentrated in the civil engineering and building sectors in line once again with their early history. In manufacturing their main strength lay in the related areas of building materials and building plant.

These Lega co-ops, like the other Italian groupings and as their predecessors had done, enjoyed in the late 1970s favourable access to cheap government credits and other privileges compared to their private enterprise competitors. These latter were again not new. What was new, probably from about 1973 onwards, was the renaissance of the Lega's leadership. Something of the same kind was happening in the Confederation and the Association, but the scale and scope of the Lega's 'awakening', capped by its ambitious three-year plan, was such as to make it much more important than those of the other two.

Two general points about the Lega in the late 1970s are worth emphasizing. The first is that workers' co-ops, if they are to move successfully into sophisticated and highly technical export markets, must have solved the old 'cloth cap' co-ops' problem of attracting and accepting professional management. It is true, as noted earlier, that there is evidence of this problem having been partially solved before the First World War. However, I suspect that in a majority of the Lega's co-ops the acceptance and recruitment of professional management is a more recent phenomenon. The second point is related. Whatever else the Lega achieved by amalgamating small building and civil engineering co-ops in the 1970s, the result was clearly such that these enterprises finally transcended their 'cloth cap' or braccianti origins.

It seems clear that much of the credit for the Lega's awakening and for its dynamic new policies must go to Vicenzo Galetti. He took the job of National President in 1973, moving to the Lega's headquarters in Rome from Bologna, where he had been the PCI's provincial secretary for the previous seven years. His early experience had been as the leader of a manual workers' union; it does not appear that he had ever worked in a co-operative.

At first sight it must seem odd that after what can only be accounted a most successful four years, Sig. Galetti was forced to resign at the Lega's congress at the end of 1977. He was only fifty-two years old, and, like the great majority of senior Lega officials and co-op managers, he was apparently content to accept a fairly modest rate for the job (roughly Lire 820,000 of £500 per month including salary and allowances) – significantly less than three times the normal lowest industrial wages. Sig. Galetti himself, in an interview with *Il Mondo* in January 1978, suggested that his mistake had been to underestimate the hostile reactions which his dynamic policies would provoke among those opposed to them. But he did not indicate whether these opponents should be looked for inside or outside the Lega.

The specific reason for his forced resignation seems to have been that he had taken an improper initiative in seeking to purchase for the Lega a medium-sized Italian steel stocking company, Duina. Formally his first mistake was to attempt to buy it at all – behaving as if the Lega was some kind of holding company rather than the federal organization, structurally controlled from the bottom upwards, of a group of independent co-ops. His second mistake was to launch the initiative without proper consultations. From discussion in Rome in early 1978, it seemed clear that it was not only reactions outside the Lega which forced his resignation. What he had done, I was told, was also unacceptable to the bulk of the Lega's membership.

The details of the affair fall outside the scope of this book and chapter, but the central issue it raises is crucially relevant in any assessment of the reality of the Lega co-ops' independent and democratic existence. We are back to the question posed at the start of this chapter. Are these Lega co-ops genuinely independent and democratic enterprises? Or are they the creatures of the PCI controlled from the centre? Is the central headquarters free to act without reference to the member co-ops – as Sig. Galetti apparently attempted to do in the Duina affair – or is it rather the servant of the member co-ops?

There were plenty of professional PCI watchers in Rome early in 1978 who were anxious to explain Sig. Galetti's forced resignation as an elaborate piece of stage management. They saw it as designed to demonstrate the Lega's commitment to democratic principles at a time when the spotlight was very much turned on to the reality of the PCI's position on precisely the same issues. They argued that the Party and the Lega were still basically 'democratic centralist' organizations, by conviction as well as by habit, and they suggested that beguiling talk of conversions to pluralism was simply a charade.

However, there were also those in Rome in early 1978 prepared to express their belief that the PCI and other Italian communist organizations like the Lega had made genuine adjustments in their positions in a more democratic direction and that change for the better would continue. There is no satisfactory method, as I suggested at the beginning of this chapter, of adjudicating between these two assessments. So the real character of the Lega's co-ops at the end of the 1970s will have to be left with a question mark as systematically ambiguous. We can only wait and see.

There is a second fundamental question about the Italian workers' co-ops which we shall also have to leave unsettled. Let us grant that all three groups, and the Lega in particular, can point to some fine social and economic achievements, in their early history, in the reconstruction phase after 1945, and then from the mid-1970s onwards. The question then is this: how far can their success be explained by tax advantages ana otner privileges and, more generally, would the Italian economic and social system have worked better if these advantages had never been granted to the co-ops? In this case again I can see no reliable method of answering the question.

10
The Mondragon group

Reasonable people who have come this far may still remain sceptical on balance. They may accept that the record of democratic and co-operative enterprises is not nearly as dismal as has been generally supposed. They may accept too that such enterprises have to contend with special handicaps, some self-inflicted, some imposed by the environment. They may even concede that there have been some modest successes and that, more important, there *is* evidence that enterprise structures of this kind can lead to important changes of attitude by shop floor and management alike and to improved vertical team-work. Yet they may still remain unconvinced. I suspect they would feel uneasy and apologetic about advocating such structures to groups of hard-nosed businessmen or workers; though progressive in a general way it would probably seem to them vaguely cranky and far-fetched − like advocating a massive increase in the number of clean living vegetarians on the boards of the nationalized industries.

However, the experience of the Mondragon co-operatives in the Basque provinces of Spain provides grounds for an altogether more optimistic assessment. There can be no doubt that here is an enormous success story. In the space of a generation − or only twenty-one years if the later of the two starting dates is taken − the Mondragon co-operatives have developed from nothing into a many-sided operation which in 1976 employed more than 15,000 people. In the same year the group included housing co-ops, a chain of consumer stores, co-operative farming enterprises, a self-managed insurance and social welfare system and an educational establishment which is everything from a local technical college to a university for advanced engineering − and which contains within itself a co-operative industrial enterprise for its students. Moreover, the whole group is presided over and protected − a mean English translation of a French scholar's* lyrical 'coiffée et corseté' − by the only successful and democratically-structured workers' bank in

---

* Henri Desroches in Quintin Garcia, *Les Cooperatives industrielles de Mondragon*, Les Editions Ouvrières, Editions Economie et Humanisme, Paris, 1970, p. 8.

history: the celebrated Caja Laboral Popular – the 'bank of the people's labour'.

What is more, and especially as co-operative enterprises go, the Mondragon group includes relatively large-scale and high-technology operations. ULGOR, the largest single industrial unit employing nearly 3,500 people in 1976, had been Spain's leading producer of refrigerators and other domestic appliances since the late 1960s. (Its name is an acronym of names of its five founders: Usatorre, Larranaga, Gorronogoita, Ormaechea and Ortubay,) Danobat, one of more than a dozen capital goods producers in the group, had probably become, by that same year, Spain's foremost producer of machine tools. Of course, these are not examples of the highest levels of contemporary technology; there are no computer manufacturers in the Mondragon group, nor any builders of nuclear power stations. But equally, we are not dealing with elementary production – textiles or boot and shoe manufacture – still less with artisan or craft workshop operations. Nor are the units of a minuscule scale: the 'average' industrial co-op in the group employed over 200 people in 1976. Finally, the Mondragon co-ops are not something which, having 'arrived', are standing still. A high level inter-co-operative research and development centre was nearing completion in Mondragon at the end of 1977. Four new enterprises started production that year and it was planned that the rate of new enterprise starts would not fall below roughly that figure for the foreseeable future.

These co-operative enterprises had spread out from the town of Mondragon by the mid-1970s into each of Spain's four Basque provinces of Vizcaya, Guipuzcoa, Alava and Navarra; the Basque area is roughly half as large as Wales. However, the greatest concentration of enterprises is in Guipuzcoa – containing well over half the industrial co-ops in 1977. The nerve centre as well as the origin of the whole group is the town of Mondragon.

If you look for Mondragon on a large scale map – and you will not find it on a small one – you will be struck first by the unpromisingly mountainous character of its geography. That impression is confirmed if one picks up a bus in San Sebastian or Bilbao – there is no railway connection – and travel the 50 or 60 km which separate Mondragon from the Biscay coast. One is driven over high passes on serpentine roads through magnificent mountain scenery. Grand for a hiking holiday, one might think, but hardly an area which industrial geographers, planning academics (or bureaucrats) would recommend as a site for modern industrial development.

Yet, though a look at the physical map — and the scenery — would leave you with the impression that this is an area, like Switzerland, with plenty of geography and not much history, that would be a very partial view; a population map would do much to correct it. For Guipuzcoa, smallest of the four Basque provinces and the one in which Mondragon is situated, is densely populated: 240 per sq km at the time of Spain's 1960 census and unquestionably higher today.

A geology map further corrects first impressions, showing the iron deposits of neighbouring Vizcaya and, to the west, the country's most important coal workings, in the Asturias region and around the town of Oveido. Steel-making and metal industries based on these two raw materials had already, before the Spanish Civil War, turned Guipuzcoa and Vizcaya into two of the most industrially advanced provinces of Spain. The view from the bus might evoke images of Switzerland, but a closer parallel comes from nearer home; the industrial valleys of Guipuzcoa can perhaps best be compared with South Wales.

History too supports this interpretation. Though large scale development took place in the nineteenth century, the iron- and steel-making traditions of Vizcaya and Guipuzcoa are ancient. Some of the iron mines around Bilbao are said to have been worked since pre-historic times. Moreover, Mondragon has been anything but a peripheral participation in this tradition. As unlikely a source as the fourteenth edition of the *Encyclopaedia Britannica* (1929) tells us that the 'swords of Mondragon were renowned before those of Toledo'. Quintin Garcia* amplifies this account by reporting that the fame of Mondragon's forges dates from the Middle Ages; ships' anchors and chains were manufactured there from mediaeval times — as well as the swords and lances in demand for Don Quixote and Sancho Panza.

Moving closer to our own day, alongside this ancient metal-working tradition of Mondragon there clearly developed a strong political and social awareness among its working people. In the early years of this century an important capitalist enterprise, the Union Carrajera established itself in the town. Initially it appears to have been a lock-making concern but it has long since diversified production to cover a wide range of steel products. Quintin Garcia reports a prolonged strike of the company's workforce in 1916. The strikers held out for three months before being brought to their knees and back to work by hunger.

The political militance of Mondragon's working people was reflected again during the Asturias Rebellion in 1934 and in the subsequent Spanish Civil War. When the Asturias miners raised the flag of workers'

---

* In *ibid.*, p. 36.

Revolution at Oviedo in October 1934, the only armed contingent which marched to their support from outside the region came from Mondragon. In Mondragon itself, during those few revolutionary October days, a Conservative Deputy to the Madrid Cortes (the Spanish Parliament) – a Sr Orega Elosegui – was shot dead. When it came to the Spanish Civil War three Mondragon battalions fought on the republican side: one socialist, one nationalist and one made up of less directly affiliated 'volunteers'.

The Basques generally, and the Basque church, were solidly against Franco in the Civil War; between October 1936 and June 1937, as the independent Basque Republic, they fought in alliance with the official republican government of Spain. And that introduces the third key element, Basque Nationalism – and the strong identification with it of the Basque priests – in the relevant Mondragon background. There are some grounds for believing that partly because of its rather central placing in the Spanish Basque country – roughly equi-distant from the three traditional main towns of Vitoria, Bilbao and San Sebastian – Mondragon may have always enjoyed a special position in Basque nationalist thought. What is certain, however, is that Mondragon's Basque clergy were most strongly identified with the nationalist cause. Hugh Thomas* recounts that one, the Arch-Priest Josquin Arin, a man 'deservedly famous locally for his piety', was among fourteen Basque priests shot by Franco's forces during the Civil War.

These factors – industrial and metal working skills, working-class awareness, Basque Nationalism and a Basque church strongly identified with it – are clearly important in explaining the origins of the Mondragon co-operatives. Adapting a point of Professor Henri Desroches† we might say the co-ops have not 'fallen from a clear sky'. Nor, as he goes on to point out, was it a miraculous event. The factors mentioned can indeed best be understood, according to Desroches, as *necessary* (though by no means *sufficient*) conditions to explain the origin of what came later.

Basque Nationalism should mainly be thought of as providing a potential driving force and source of extra motivation in the Mondragon context. Some would argue, however, that more subtle national characteristics are also relevant: traditions of democratic local autonomy in the Basque mountain villages, sturdy yeomen values and a tradition which respects hard work, and, possibly, customs of 'solidarity' in informal drinking clubs. They might posit the high value placed in

---

* Hugh Thomas, *The Spanish Civil War*, Eyre & Spottiswoode, London, 1961, p. 484.

† In Garcia, *op. cit.*, p. 13.

Basque culture on thrift; and they might well want to emphasize that the very special character of the Basque language makes for a very special and especially solid variety of local nationalism. Perhaps none of these should be excluded from any full discussion of the Mondragon background. I shall mention some later on but I am in no position to assess what weight, if any, they should be given.

To complete this sketch of the general Mondragon background, it is worth mentioning what is missing from the context — as well as what it contains. Professor Desroches rightly emphasizes the absence of any local co-operative tradition. Raymond Carr has shown there was nothing much of that anywhere in Spain.* More surprising (and disappointing for some) is the apparent absence of any strong links between Mondragon and the Spanish anarchist movement. The trade union position, before the Civil War was rather more complex. There were the specifically Basque trade unions, federated as the Eusko Langileen Alkartasuna — Solidaridad de Trabajadores Vascos (ELA-STV) — which incidentally emerged victorious in the first trade union elections in the Basque provinces early in 1978. But for the rest it was the conventionally socialist Union General de Trabajadores (UGT), rather than the anarchist Confederacion Nacional del Trabajo (CNT) which was strong among Mondragon's working people up to the defeat of the Basques in the Civil War; but the CNT was unambiguously libertarian; the UGT solidly bureaucratic.

The Spanish Civil War lasted into 1939, but Bilbao, the final Basque outpost against Franco's armies, had fallen in June 1937 and Mondragon seems to have been overrun some months earlier. The ensuing years were ones of almost unrelieved wretchedness: the Basque language was officially forbidden; Franco's troops and paramilitary police, the Guardia Civil, evidently behaved like an army of occupation; the people, by all accounts, were deeply demoralized and cowed.

In this unpromising situation a young Basque priest, Fr Jose Maria Arizmendi† arrived to work in Mondragon in February 1941. Not yet twenty-six (he was born in April 1915) he had fought in the war. At one stage, after being captured by Franco's troops, he had been under sentence of death. However, he had managed to avoid execution and before he was ordained he had studied theology at the seminary in Vitoria.

Fr Arizmendi's bishop had given him a special task — a special area of concern — in Mondragon. He was to concentrate on the social task of the church and concern himself especially with young working people. 'My

---

* Raymond Carr, *Spain 1808–1939*, Oxford University Press, 1966, p. 463.
† His full name was Arizmendiarrieta.

concrete mission', he later wrote, 'was to be the counsellor and adviser of your working people.'

Unusually for a priest in the early 1940s, Fr Arizmendi quickly perceived that the necessary priority for Mondragon's young people was technical education. Primary schooling was available, but above that level an apprentice school at the Union Cerrajera provided all that the town had to offer. Moreover, the numbers of places in the school were restricted to the company's own modest requirements. And its courses were not designed to turn out people above the level of skilled journeymen.

Lecturing at the Union Cerrajera's apprentice school was among Fr Arizmendi's duties. His lectures dealt with 'religious and human values', yet the young priest's preoccupations seem to have centred at least as much on more quantifiable matters He was deeply dissatisfied with the small and − in his view − quite inadequate number of places at the school. He pressed the company to agree to its expansion and undertook, with the help of church organizations and parents, to raise the necessary extra cash. The company refused.

Fr Arizmendi then set about achieving his ends in a different way: he would promote a new and separate technical school. Support from the community was mobilized by techniques which were both ingenious and daring. Ballot-box type objects, 'urns', were placed at street corners; members of the community were invited to drop pieces of paper inside indicating whether they would support a new technical school with cash or in kind. It is said that 600 positive responses were found when the 'urns' were emptied. Since Mondragon's population was then about 8,000 the response represented support from roughly 25 per cent of the town's families.

In any case, though both the local authority and the Union Cerrajera chose *not* to contribute, the support promised in the 'urns' was judged sufficient to go ahead. A small new school, with an initial enrolment of twenty students, was opened in October 1943. Equally important, the involvement of the local community was strongly maintained. Those who contributed elected the school's management committee. Moreover, because of recurrent costs, fund raising was also continued. The students themselves, we are told, played a large part in organizing the activities which brought in the money. Their link with the local community was thus put on a more or less permanent basis − and they had gained some first experience of organizing themselves and others to get things done.

The problem of too few apprenticeship places had been partially eased by Fr Arizmendi's initiative, but there was also the problem of progressing beyond courses at the apprentice level. The new school was able to initiate intermediate courses for junior technician and foremen-type posts on its own, but students with the potential to go even further were anxious to have the opportunity to do so. They persuaded Fr Arizmendi to approach the school of technical engineering in Zaragoza. In 1947 it was agreed that a small group, while working for their living in the normal way in Mondragon, would press on with their studies at night for the appropriate Zaragoza examinations. So it was that eleven Mondragon students successfully passed the Zaragoza engineering examinations in 1952. The group included five young men who were, a few years later, to be the founders of ULGOR.

As well as being the indirect ancestor of all the later co-operatives, the apprentice school which first opened its doors in October 1943 is the direct forebear of a magnificent educational operation – the Escuela Profesional Politecnica – with places for over 2,000, and with courses running from sub-engineering to degree level, in Mondragon today. That, together with its key role in the group as a whole, will be described later. It is enough to record here that the original school was first recognized by the Spanish authorities in 1947 and has been receiving some state financial assistance since then; that in 1948 its governing body was reconstituted more formally as the League of Education and Culture (later itself to become a co-operative of the second degree); and that the extensive modern premises in which it is now based, about a mile from the centre of Mondragon, were completed in 1967.

So far I have deliberately emphasized the technical and practical character of the new educational initiatives launched by Fr Arizmendi. And that is where he put the emphasis on the only occasion that I met him, four years before his death, in 1972. He seems to have been impatient of any theory divorced from practice. It was from practice, he told me then, that new theories and structures must come – not the other way round. He was proud that the Professional and Polytechnic School was much more notable for its co-operative practice at that time than for the teaching of co-op principles.

Thus it is easy to believe that the ideological content of his own teaching in the school, and of his own wider contacts, formal and informal, with the student body, was pragmatic rather than dogmatic and the antithesis of anything doctrinaire. Quite apart from his own preferences and temperament we also know that he had to take the utmost care, particularly in his early years at Mondragon, to avoid falling into either of two opposite and equally lethal traps: that of being stigmatized by the people as a collaborator with the hated Franco régime; or the trap of being accused of subversion and being thrown into prison or worse. In the circumstances, perhaps the only safe policy was to confine himself to stressing the importance of work and technical skill in the first place, and recalling the more progressive social teaching of the Catholic church, such as it was, in the second. That at any rate was what one of ULGOR's founders remembered, many years later, from his earliest contacts with Arizmendi.

What struck me most, when I was lucky enough to meet him, was his commitment to the values of freedom as well as to the importance of work and of technical skill. His emphatic pre-occupation with the second had seemed to me to align him rather with Mao Tse Tung. I can still remember the amused delight in his eyes when I suggested the parallel. He opened a locked drawer at the bottom of his desk and proudly produced for my inspection a copy of the Spanish translation of the *Little Red Book*. On the other hand, I was then all the more surprised when he repudiated Mao's reliance on compulsory productive work. The context, I hasten to add, was not labour camps, but the inclusion in the curriculum of schools and colleges of sessions of compulsory productive work. Fr Arizmendi had just described – and described with obvious satisfaction – how students at the professional and polytechnic school were able to cover their required contribution to school fees by taking part in productive work for the market – but he insisted that they must be free *not* to do that if they so wished.

Yet, whatever the precise content of Fr Arizmendi's teaching, there can be no doubt about its impact. The students who graduated in engineering at Zaragoza in 1952 had been technically well prepared for their profession. Furthermore, five of the eleven had also been so affected by the non-technical parts of this remarkable education that they were shortly to launch, admittedly after a false start or two, an enterprise of an entirely new kind. Clearly they could not have done so if either ingredient in their education, the technical or the non-technical, had been missing. By their own account what they emerged feeling most strongly was that existing enterprise structures had to be changed.

It would be hard to deny that the peculiar and peculiarly repressive conditions which prevailed in Mondragon after the Civil War contributed to the possibility of this outcome. There is evidence that Fr Arizmendi himself would not have been posted there by his bishop if the circumstances had been more normal; his own preference while in the Vitoria seminary had apparently been for the life of a scholar and theologian. More important than that, it is hard to believe that if Franco's authorities had allowed popular opinion to express itself in more normal ways – through politics and trade unions – the community could have been mobilized by anyone, Fr Arizmendi or anyone else, to direct its energies into as unorthodox an expression of reconstruction and development as Catholic technical education. Yet that is what happened – and it is as certain as anything can be that had it been otherwise, there would have been no ULGOR, no Caja Laboral Popular (CLP), and no group of prosperous and dynamic co-operative enterprises centred on Mondragon today.

ULGOR, the first and largest of today's Basque industrial co-ops, started to manufacture in Mondragon and in its own premises in 1956. Before the five founders set themselves up in new premises in Mondragon in 1956, they operated briefly in Vitoria during the year before. The initial move to Vitoria, where they had bought a bankrupt business, is explained by the fact that the official permissions and licences were much easier to obtain when an old business was acquired than when a new one was started from scratch.

Between 1952 and 1955 all five except Larranaga had worked for the Union Cerrajera – in which they came to hold senior management posts. Motivated in large measure by the social teaching of Arizmendi, after graduation, their first intention had been to see whether they could work successfully for changes inside that traditional capitalist company. It was only when they had satisfied themselves that progress inside the Union Cerrajera was impossible that they decided to launch a new venture on their own.

A small part of the starting capital needed to acquire the Vitoria operation and then to set up in Mondragon came from the savings of the five founders. The remainder was raised from the Mondragon community and in particular through friends and contacts in age-group drinking clubs – 'chiquitoes' – which are a strong feature of Basque cultural life. These drinking clubs are quite small – with not more than ten to twenty members – and they characteristically encourage lasting relationships of high trust and solidarity between fellow members. Their normal premises consist of a rented kitchen and dining-room. Apart from more formal gatherings at regular intervals, members are free to make use of these premises and to consume stocks of food and drink whenever they wish. All takes place on a basis of mutual trust; whatever is consumed is simply signed for. Of course it would be absurd to imply that these convivial clubs were of equivalent importance in the origin of the co-ops as, say, the links which had been established between the technical school and the community. Yet they can, I think, be seen as a symbol of that mutual Basque solidarity which has been a key element in the success of the co-ops from the start.

The detailed workings of the chiquitoes need not concern us, though they look like most agreeable and worth-while institutions which might well deserve to be copied on their own account. The point is that a large proportion of the necessary starting capital (Pesetas 4m according to one authority, Pesetas 11m according to another) was raised with their help. Contributions were received from roughly 100 people – it was an astonishing fund raising achievement. We must imagine that the long association of the Mondragon community with the Professional and Polytechnic School, as well as drinking club solidarity, and the personal respect which the founders and fund raisers enjoyed, were important factors behind the success. No security beyond the personal commitment of ULGOR's founders was offered; in an important sense there was nothing else which could have been offered. Contributors were entitled to be sure that they would get their money back if the enterprise prospered, but they must have realized that even on the most optimistic assumptions good results might well take some time to achieve.

For the short period at Vitoria, and then for its first three years at Mondragon, ULGOR operated without a formal constitution but as an informally democratic entérprise. Its co-operative constitution was adopted only in 1959. By then it must have begun to appear probable that the venture would succeed. Its labour force, Garcia records, had already grown to 143 by the end of 1958 compared with only twenty-four in 1956. Meanwhile what had started with the manufacture of oil stoves had been greatly strengthened in 1958 by the addition of an important new product: butane gas had reached Mondragon for the first time; the production of gas cookers was begun.

Besides ULGOR five more of the Mondragon group date from the years before the establishment of the Caja Laboral Popular in 1959. It was in this period too that ULGOR effectively absorbed two previously capitalist foundries in the nearby village of Escoriaza. In 1963 they were subsequently separated off from ULGOR, as part of a general policy of splitting it down, and became Ederlan. One important motive for their absorption was to assure ULGOR of a source of supply for some of its main inputs, but what was most extraordinary in all this was the entrepreneurial vigour which ULGOR's young leaders were beginning to demonstrate.

The same vigour is shown by another early move. The first of the present chain of co-operative consumer stores, later amalgamated with others to form the sub-group EROSKI, dates from this pre-CLP period and was established in Mondragon itself. We must assume too that the five other pre-1959 industrial enterprises were largely encouraged into existence by ULGOR's example, for totally spontaneous generation does not seem plausible and their sudden appearance is otherwise incomprehensible. With their main current products and their geographical location, these 'early five' industrial co-ops were: Funcor at Elorrio making foundry products; Tolsan at Amorebieta producing forgings; Arrasate at Mondragon making machine tools; Constructiones San Jose at Hernani producing waste-grinding machines; Talleres Ochandiano at Ochandiano producing food handling equipment.

However, the outstanding example of entrepreneurial thrust and farsightedness was the setting up in 1959 of the CLP. Formally its creation was a joint effort, in which ULGOR Funcor, Arrasate and the newly established Mondragon co-op store, all participated. But it is reasonable to assume that the main drive came through ULGOR. The prime mover behind the scenes, who set off the whole initiative and overcame considerable reluctance on the part of ULGOR's leaders to take the step, was none other than Fr Arizmendi. One of ULGOR's founders has described their initial reaction to Fr Arizmendi, when he put forward the proposal, thus: 'We told him, yesterday we were craftsmen, foremen, and engineers. Today we are trying to learn how to be managers and executives. Tomorrow you want us to become bankers. That is impossible.'

However, Fr Arizmendi was evidently a master of persuasion and of research. He it was who found out that a banking-type operation could be set up as a credit co-operative under Spanish law. He also discovered that, if registered as a 'workers' credit co-operative, such a bank could pay an extra 1 per cent over the going legal maximum on its interest rates. The upshot was that after a somewhat informal start in Mondragon in 1958 – using temporary accommodation at the school and at the Catholic Action centre and relying on ULGOR's founders to do the necessary paper work unpaid – the CLP was recognized by a notice in Spain's official gazette in July 1959 and subsequently registered. In the same year two branches were set up – in Mondragon and in Elorrio in the neighbouring province of Vizcaya. The concurrent opening of branches in two provinces was decided upon as a precaution against the possibility that one or other of the two provincial administrations might turn against the initiative.

So by 1959 or at least by the beginning of 1960, the systematic mobilization of local savings behind the development of the Mondragon co-op group was under way. Providing that the initiative proved a success, ULGOR's founders had in effect solved one of the most acute problems of co-operative history: reliable access to adequate capital. Moreover, they had done so without in any way impairing the group's independence.

The establishment of the bank also solved two other specific problems.

First, it enabled the position of ULGOR's original outside lenders to be regularized. Second, it provided a central social insurance service for the worker members of the various co-ops. Under Spanish law members of co-operatives are rightly treated as self-employed. They are thus not eligible to participate in the national insurance scheme. A section of the bank, which was later to become a separate organism with the name of Lagun Aro, took on social insurance responsibility for the group as a whole.

However, what had been established was from the start and by design an institution which was to play a much bigger role than that of providing adequate capital funds, crucial as that was, and a centralized social insurance service. One of the most powerful arguments which Arizmendi had used in urging that the bank be set up was that the 'isolation' of individual co-ops entailed the most formidable risks to which their worker–members should not be exposed. Another had been that the potential for co-operative enterprise would never be adequately developed if the task of encouraging and midwifing new initiatives was left to the individual enterprises themselves. Isolation could only be overcome if there was an institution with an explicit inter co-op co-ordinating role, and the full development potential could only be exploited if responsibility for promoting it was given to the co-ordinating body. It made obvious sense for these two responsibilities to be taken on by the new bank. That is, of course, what happened.

The detailed arrangements of the CLP and its record will be reviewed in a later section. Here we may simply note that by 1960 all the principal elements of the Mondragon group were in place. Including ULGOR, there were half a dozen industrial co-ops employing nearly 400 people. There was the Professional and Polytechnic School – to ensure, among other things, that the group's needs for skilled manpower were met; and there was the bank, which, as well as performing its straightforward capital mobilization and social insurance functions, was charged both with overall co-ordination and promotion.

I suspect, however, that the key to what subsequently happened lay as much in the men, and the confidence which they felt and inspired, as in the institutions they had created. Apart from Arizmendi – whose prestige in Mondragon and the neighbourhood must have been a major factor – the two key figures who emerged were almost certainly Jose Maria Ormaechea and Alfonso Gorronogoita; it is no accident that one became the bank's chief executive, the other its elected President. They still held those offices eighteen years later.

Two more industrial co-ops were started before 1961, the year when the promotional activity of the CLP first seems to have borne fruit to a significant extent. They were Dormico-op at Elgueta manufacturing furniture and Vividendas y Contratas in San Sebastian involved in house building (the only building enterprise in the entire group).

Some idea of the subsequent pace of expansion can be derived from the number of new starts for industrial co-ops over the next sixteen years to 1976. Excluding housing co-ops, agricultural co-ops, consumer stores, and schools and including only the most immediately productive enterprises, the number of industrial co-ops started each year is as follows: 1961, four; 1962, six; 1963, eleven; 1964, three; 1965, four; 1966, four; 1967, four; 1968, one; 1969, three; 1970, none; 1971, two; 1972, one; 1973, three; 1974, seven; 1975, one; 1976, two.

Thus fifty-six new industrial co-ops came into existence within the Mondragon group between 1961 and 1976, together with five agricultural co-ops. From the industrial total it is perhaps correct to exclude two as special cases: Aleco-op, the students' co-operative enterprise at the Professional and Polytechnic School (started in 1966) and Auzo-Lagun, a co-operative of cleaning and catering women who work on a part-time basis (like their sisters in 'Little Women' in Sunderland) started in 1969. Excluding these and adding the eight pre-1961 industrial co-ops we get the figure of sixty-two industrial enterprises at the end of 1976.*

We can examine the industrial enterprise growth in a different way by listing the number of fully fledged industrial co-ops in existence in each year: 1960, eight; 1961, twelve; 1962, eighteen; 1963, twenty-nine; 1964, thirty-two; 1965, thirty-six; 1966, forty; 1967, forty-three; 1968, forty-four; 1969, forty-six; 1970, forty-six; 1971, forty-eight; 1972, forty-nine; 1973, fifty-two; 1974, fifty-nine; 1975, sixty; 1976, sixty-two.

Both sets of figures indicate a reduction in the rate of new industrial co-op creation after 1964. For the earlier period we have an average of five new industrial enterprise starts annually; the corresponding figure for the later period is just over two. This difference becomes only slightly less sharp if we exclude ULGOR's offspring.

Discussion at Mondragon suggests that the group was progressively more affected by external market conditions from 1967. That is certainly the published view of Inaki Gorrono in the most recent detailed study† of the Mondragon experience. It may well be that external conditions, by

---

* The only further qualification is that four of the new industrial creations between 1961 and 1976 – Ederlan and Copreci (both started 1963), Fagor Electronica (1966) and Fagor Industrial (1973) – had been parts of ULGOR from which they were hived off.

† *Experiencia Co-operativa en el Pais Vasco*, Bilbao, 1975, p.117.

making market entry more difficult, were a big factor in the slower growth rate of new co-ops. If, however, employment (i.e. new jobs created) is taken as a criterion, rather than simply the birth rate of new enterprises, the growth record is much more straightforward (see graph, Figure 1. p. 179).

The graph makes clear that there was no significant change in industrial job expansion in the Mondragon group as a whole between the earlier and the later periods. Given the key responsibility of the CLP for development and expansion, together with its limited resources at any one time, there is always likely to be a trade-off between the expansion of existing enterprises and the creation of new ones. Gorrono's study seems to confirm this (p. 129). He points out that employment at ULGOR alone increased by nearly 900 jobs – from 1,228 employees to 2,100 – during 1969. It may be no accident that the three years 1968–70 show the lowest average new enterprise birth rate since the CLP was set up. Its professionals may well have been too pre-occupied with ULGOR's expansion to have had much time for promoting new enterprises.

Yet that is detail; so is the small year to year variation in the group's employment expansion. Percentage growth rates are in any case liable to be misleading in the early stages of development – as anyone who has had to describe the growth of industries like Malawi's cement industry will know. However, what must be given its full weight is the achievement of expanding the group's industrial employment by an average of roughly 800 jobs a year and for a total of over 13,000 jobs between 1960 and 1976. Something of the *quality* of these new jobs will be seen in the sectoral composition of the industrial co-ops in 1976. Here we need to emphasize a quantitative point: that the total of new jobs *created* was at least 90 per cent of the group's overall job expansion. The number represented by jobs in capitalist enterprises which were converted into co-ops is less than 1,000. Thus, whatever else is true about the Mondragon experience, it is an extraordinary record of new job creation. The Mondragon record certainly seems to compare favourably with the achievement of the Ulster authorities; in the thirty-odd years since the war only 70,000 new jobs have been successfully created in the entire province.

As will be seen later, the success of the CLP in mobilizing local savings for industrial job creation has been an important factor, but so too has been the policy of very high profit plough-back (normally 90 per cent) which the co-ops have imposed upon themselves and their equally crucial insistence on capital contributions from all new member–workers. A further significant factor has been the

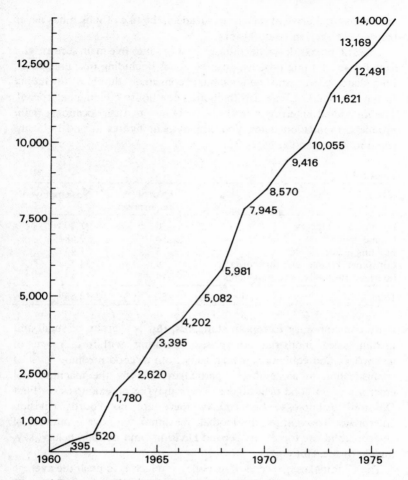

Figure 1 Expansion of industrial employment 1960–76

Sources: 1960–5 F. Aldabaldetrecu and J. Gray.
         1966–75 Caja Laboral Popular Annual Report 1975.
         1976–   Caja Laboral Popular: Verbal estimate.
Note: According to figures supplied by the CLP itself employment in the
        industrial co-ops alone amounted to 13,892 at the end of 1976 –
        excluding the four most recently launched industrial enterprises. If we
        add the employment in the CLP itself, in the five agricultural co-ops, in
        the consumer stores and Lagun Aro the total number of jobs in the group
        as a whole must have been about 15,000 by the end of 1976.

entrepreneurial drive of the group's leaders, the like of which has never before been seen in co-op history.

The CLP breaks down the industrial co-ops into five main sectors, viz: foundry and forging products; capital goods (including machine tools); immediate goods and components; consumer durables (including furniture); building materials (including one house building enterprise). The individual enterprises in these sectors, with their locations, main products, foundation dates, and employment figures at end-1976 are given in an appendix, pages 261–3.

TABLE 10.1

Sector	No. of enterprises	Nos employed
Foundries and forges	6	1,809
Capital goods	14	2,684
Building materials, etc.	5	1,237
Consumer durables and furniture	9	4,324
Intermediate goods and components	23	3,483
Total	57	13,537

By contemporary European standards, this is a group of small and medium-sized industrial enterprises operating within a range of technology and equipment which runs from a 'good medium' level of sophistication to something – particularly among the machine tool enterprises – a good deal higher. There may be no examples of 'First Division' technology, but equally there are no Fourth Division enterprises. To continue the football metaphor we have a number of enterprises at the top of the Second Division; and nothing below, say, middle of the Third.

The CLP makes no secret of its policy – which is to push the average level of technology continuously upwards. Seven of the new industrial enterprises started in 1973 and 1974 involved a total investment of just under £4.5m and the new jobs created totalled almost exactly 300. In other words, the average capital cost of each extra job in those new enterprises was approximately £15,000. According to the CLP, the new jobs in the enterprises established after 1974 were even more expensive – and averaged well over £20,000. The group thus has had an outstanding success in job creation. But is it profitable? Is it competitive inside and outside Spain? Has it really succeeded in creating wealth as well as jobs?

The best evidence for the competitive strength of the group inside Spain is its success in the markets for domestic appliances and machine tools. By the late 1960s ULGOR had become Spain's leading producer of an important range of consumer durables: refrigerators, washing machines, cookers. By the mid-1970s Danobat had become the country's single most important producer of machine tools. These positions could not have been achieved by operations which were less than fully competitive in the Spanish market.

The group's export effort is of more recent origin for it did not start seriously before the end of the 1960s. Between 1969 and 1975 export sales as a proportion of the group's total sales ranged from just below 10 per cent to nearly 15 per cent as Table 10.2 illustrates.

TABLE 10.2

	Export sales	Total sales (Pesetas m.)
1969	503	6,386
1970	753	7,102
1971	1,060	8,164
1972	1,343	10,377
1973	1,565	12,625
1974	2,435	16,068
1975	2,344	19,319

Source: CLP

The group's leaders recognized in 1976 – and indeed earlier – that the days of the heavily protected Spanish market were almost certainly numbered, and that more effort and resources would have to be diverted to exports. However, already in the middle 1970s they could point to some quite striking individual achievements in the export field: Danobat's foreign sales exceeded 20 per cent of its total sales in 1975; ULGOR, during the first half of the 1970s, was successful in winning export contracts to build complete domestic appliance manufacturing units in Tunisia, the USSR and Mexico.

Inaki Gorrono has studied the varying record of profitability of the Mondragon industrial enterprises over the five years 1968–73. For the group as a whole he compared net profits with four key variables: with the group's internally owned capital, with its long-term capital, with its total liabilities and with its total sales. His average figures for profits as a percentage of key variables 1968 to 1973 are as follow: *internally owned capital: 17.65; long-term capital: 13.16; total liabilities: 7.53; total sales: 7.31. The year to year figures showed considerable variation around these averages. According to Gorrono's study the highest and lowest figures for profits as a percentage of key variables 1968–73 were:

---

* The sum of members' individual capital stakes in the enterprise and its collectively owned funds; the Mondragon equivalent of 'Shareholders' funds'.

internally owned capital: 8.1 and 25.9; long-term capital: 6.1 and 18.3; total liabilities: 3.7 and 10.7; total sales: 3.7 and 10.1.

Gorrono's year to year figures do not imply any general trend towards either greater or less profitability on the part of the group as a whole. If success should be measured by these percentages then the group's best year was 1973, its worst 1971. The same is broadly true of all the main sub-sectors. This is shown clearly by the results for these two years as reflected in the figures given in Table 10.3 for profits as a percentage of internally owned capital.

TABLE 10.3   Profits as a percentage of internally owned capital (by sub-sectors)

	1971	1973
Foundries and forges	13·4	29·5
Capital goods	5·4	28·6
Intermediate goods	15·4	25·4
Consumer durables	1·7	21·6
Building materials	13·0	29·5

It may be plausible to explain the very low 1971 figure for the consumer durables sub-sector as partly the consequence of the immense expansion – a labour force increase from 1,228 to 2,100 – undertaken by ULGOR in 1969, but the relatively low profits in all the other main sub-sectors in the same year show that market factors were also at work.

There is one other point of detail which seems worth extracting from Gorrono's results. The sub-sector foundries and forges is shown as having actually made a loss in 1968. The market situation is the explanation he offers, but perhaps the important point is that this negative result serves as a reminder that the Mondragon co-ops are not immune from loss-making. As it turned out, however, the recovery was quite sharp. The sub-sector's losses were 4.7 per cent of its internally owned capital in 1968; in 1969 profits showed a return of 16.1 per cent.

What is the intelligent layman to make of this profit record? The answer seems to be that for enterprises of this size and character – up to the end of 1973 before Spain's rate of inflation began to accelerate – these profit results are at least respectable and 'in line' with similar capitalist experience elsewhere. A more precise judgment would only be possible after a very detailed and professional examination of the Mondragon books and of their accounting conventions. On the other hand, it is worth emphasizing at this stage, for subsequent amplification, that the average profit figures imply, under Mondragon's system of worker–ownership, a by no means insignificant profit share for the individual worker–owners. How these profit shares might compare with wages for the average person will be examined later.

Given that profit levels depend rather heavily on accounting conventions, some alternative measure of the economic performance of these industrial co-ops – and of their ability to create wealth – seem to be called for. Figures are available for sales per head covering the group as a whole from 1968 to 1975. They are as shown in Table 10.4.

TABLE 10.4   Group sales per head (in Pesetas 000s)

1968	697	1972	1,045
1969	827	1973	1,173
1970	827	1974	1,284
1971	867	1975	1,467

Sources: 1968–73 Inaki Gorrono; 1974, CLP, 1975.

The weakness of sales per head as an indicator of economic performance is that these figures vary from industry to industry in line with the ratio of contribution of bought-in supplies to the final enterprise product. This particular distortion is eliminated if we substitute value added per head for sales. A series of figures for value added per head, broken down into the five main Mondragon industrial subsectors, is available for 1971 to 1975 in Table 10.5.

TABLE 10.5   Value added per head for main Mondragon industrial subsectors (in Pesetas 000s)

	1971	1972	1973	1974	1975
Foundries and forges	318	376	454	646	658
Capital goods	243	344	436	549	592
Intermediate goods	226	299	355	420	434
Consumer durables	224	335	407	467	528
Building materials	290	336	448	470	585
Average (weighted)	247	334	412	496	543

Source: CLP

In fact, whether we take the figures for sales or for value added per head, the professional judgment is that the performance which they reflect is a good deal better than respectable. Of course, comparisons of these sort of figures as between one country and another must always be treated with caution – if only because of distortions which result from exchange rates and rates of inflation. All the same, it seems safe to conclude that a group of companies, with the same mix of industries in Britain which achieved corresponding results, would have at least matched average performance – and would very likely have done better. Thus it seems safe to claim that the Mondragon industrial co-ops pass the 'acid' tests of economic performance – and of wealth creation – with a score which is at least equal to bogey for the course.

There is one further economic performance which needs measuring and, so far as possible, judging: that of the bank itself. Physically the CLP's growth is most easily shown by the increase in branch offices, viz: 1960, two; 1961, two; 1962, four; 1963, six; 1964, eleven; 1965, twenty-one; 1966, twenty-six; 1967, thirty; 1968, forty-one; 1969, forty-seven; 1970, fifty-four; 1971, fifty-four; 1972, fifty-four; 1973, sixty; 1974, sixty-two; 1975, sixty-five.

There have been similarly rapid increases in the numbers of savings accounts, in the figure of total savings it has attracted and in its own internally owned capital, as is shown in Table 10.6.

TABLE 10.6   Mondragon: Savings

	No. of savings accounts (Pesetas m.)	Savings total	CLP's own capital
1966	21,653	659·7	60·5
1967	29,577	1,015·7	73·1
1968	43,979	1,449·9	151·3
1969	64,116	2,359·2	236·9
1970	87,807	3,204·2	311·9
1971	˙108,502	4,669·3	415·8
1972	126,929	6,355·6	572·2
1973	148,331	8,389·6	778·0
1974	169,000 (Est)	11,351·2	1,069·3
1975	190,000	14,699·0	1,519·5

Source: Nos of accounts 1966–73, Inaki Gorrono. All other CLP.

This is an impressive growth record. Those responsible for pulling in the savings could scarcely be other than very pleased with more than a twenty-fold increase in a decade – whatever the comparative performance of their competitors. In fact a mid-1970s control study by CLP staff showed that this 'workers' bank outperformed all its conventional savings bank rivals in the ten years to 1975.

The achievement is, on the face of it, all the more impressive in view of the fact that the CLP is the first institution of its kind in the Basque country, in Spain, and indeed, so far as I know, in the world. Common sense suggests that people are likely to be especially cautious when deciding where to place their savings. Quite apart from anything else, the CLP has succeeded beyond all reasonable expectation in overcoming a natural 'conservative' resistance.

The upshot, according to the bank itself, is that from the early 1970s onwards the expansion and development of the Mondragon group was not constrained by a lack of capital resources. Instead market factors, manpower resources and general policy considerations, became the main determinants of the group's growth rate, and in mid-1976 the bank was unable to foresee when future plans might again become limited by a shortage of cash.

The bank's success as a mobilizer of local savings and capital cannot, naturally, be divorced from its success as a lender and thus from the success of its biggest debtors, the industrial co-ops. Had the bank experienced a run of bad debts in its lending to the co-ops, old and new, it is a certainty that it would have forfeited the confidence of the local saving public and its fund-raising capacity would have been seriously undermined, if not destroyed. As it is, bad debts had been negligible up to 1977. By a mixture of extraordinarily thorough preparation before an investment is made, and the most systematic back-up and performance monitoring after it, bad investments had been kept down to virtually zero; that, of course, is a very large element in the secret of the group's success, and will be analysed later.

What needs to be emphasized here is the CLP's success in the more traditional banking task of mobilizing the savings of the public. Britain has no banking institutions the main aim of which is to raise ordinary people's local savings and then invest them in local productive industry (whether private, state-owned or co-operative); the conventional wisdom has been that that cannot or should not be done. The CLP's record shows that that conventional wisdom can be wrong.

Looking back, for a moment, on the economic record of these industrial co-ops and their bank, various points stand out. Measured by the yardstick of 'profit' the record has been at least respectable. By the alternative measures of sales or value added per head, it looks distinctly good. Measured either by the criteria of worth-while jobs – or by savings mobilization – it is outstanding.

Moving from the economic record to the co-operative forms and structures of the Mondragon group, it is necessary first to distinguish, as they do, between the 'co-operatives at the base' and the 'second degree' co-operatives. The second degree co-ops are, in effect, the institutions shared by members of the group as a whole: the CLP, the Escuela Profesional Politecnica, and the welfare insurance organization, Lagun Aro. Before describing these second order arrangements I will look at the form and structures of the 'co-operatives at the base'. These are all the co-ops which are not second degree co-ops: at the end of 1976, sixty-two industrial and five agricultural co-ops, a chain of consumer stores, fifteen schools organized as co-ops, housing co-ops and one co-operative sporting club. However, it is the constitution of the industrial and agricultural co-ops and of the the consumer store chain that will be examined. The schools, housing co-ops and clubs, though immensely interesting, fall outside the scope of this study.

The first formal co-op constitution was adopted by ULGOR in 1959, after an initial three years of operating on an *ad hoc* basis as an informally democratic enterprise. Again, as he did for the creation of the bank, Fr Arizmendi pressed hard for this position to be regularized and it was he, inevitably, who produced the first draft of ULGOR's model statutes.

The founders of ULGOR have frequently emphasized that their adoption of a co-operative constitution was not because of any conscious ideological bond with the Rochdale pioneers or with other co-operative forebears − it was a characteristically pragmatic choice. Various possibilities were considered and a co-operative form under the Spanish co-operative law was found to come closest to the enterprise structure which they had independently decided would suit them best.

It is characteristic of the same pragmatism that neither the original ULGOR constitution nor the 'fair copies' of it which were adopted, with variations of detail, by the other 'co-operatives at the base', have been static. For example, the first ULGOR model provided for weighted voting in the sovereign assembly of all the enterprise's worker−members; and this was the general rule throughout the group until 1974 when a system of one man one vote was introduced. Constitutions had also to be modified to take account of the setting up of the CLP and to formalize its monitoring and co-ordinating role. And they have had to be adapted periodically to take account of changes in the country's co-operative law and for other reasons. This process of modification, of adjustment to changes and of searching for improved structures, is almost certain to go on.

In spite of this constant adjustment, and variations at least of detail between enterprises, the constitutions in 1976 of the 'co-operatives at the base' showed sufficient similarity to be thought of as one basic constitution. The chief features of that constitution are contained in a 'contract of association' with the CLP by which all enterprises which wish to join or remain in the group must abide.

The document which sets out ULGOR's current statutes (Estatutos Sociales) contains sixty-two Articles divided into nine chapters. Its internal rules (Reglamento de Regimen   Interior) are even longer, running to 144 Articles. There is an added complication in ULGOR's case: since 1966 it has formed, with five other industrial co-ops, a federal sub-grouping, ULARCO, within the Mondragon group. I will ignore the

ULARCO complication and treat ULGOR's arrangements as typical.

There are eight key and distinct groups of provisions which together form the foundations of the co-operatives' structure and policies:

1 Provisions designed to ensure full bottom-upwards and democratic self-government.

2 Provisions to promote efficient management.

3 Provisions to promote management–shop floor solidarity, communication between the two, and intra-enterprise solidarity more generally.

4 Provisions which require the contribution of capital stakes by all worker–members, which distinguish the collective indivisible elements in enterprise ownership from those credited to individual worker–member accounts, which limit the return on capital, and which regulate the distribution of profits (or losses).

5 Provisions designed to protect job security and to impose a régime of work behaviour and discipline appropriate to a co-operative structure.

6 Provisions designed to promote inter-co-op solidarity and to ensure optimum group co-ordination.

7 Provisions designed to promote solidarity both with the local community and with non-co-op workers and enterprises in the neighbourhood.

8 Provisions designed to ensure that the co-op does not become inward-looking but pursues 'open door' policies of maximum job creation.

The democratic, self-governing and bottom-upwards character of the Mondragon 'base' co-op is ensured by provisions and by articles which define who are to be its members (socios). Subject to a short probationary period, ULGOR's relevant statute (Article 11) says simply the co-op's members will be its 'workers, manual administrative and technical of both sexes'. Article 12 lays down that membership is not transferable and later articles provide that members will have equal voting rights according to the formula 'one man one vote'. Thus self-government is ensured, because membership and voting power cannot pass outside the group, and democracy is ensured because all members are equal when it comes to a vote.

The body with ultimate control over, and responsibility for, the co-op is the General Assembly of all members (the Junta General de Socios). This body elects the leadership – thus power should flow upwards from the bottom. The institutional form of the co-op's leadership is a governing but non-executive board, the Junta Rectora, which is described as the leadership organ (organo directivo). There is, however, no question that the management is constitutionally subordinate to the Junta Rectora, one of the tasks of which is to appoint the chief executive or general manager.

The Junta Rectora at ULGOR includes a president, two officers and nine other members. It must meet at least monthly. Those elected to it serve a four year term – thus to a large extent ensuring continuity of leadership and insulating it in some measure from the risk of volatile opinion in the General Assembly. But there is a partial retirement and thus a partial election every two years although re-election is permitted. Broadly, the Junta Rectora may be thought of as a governing, policy-making, but non-executive board, which is answerable and responsible to the general meeting. Its relationship with the latter differs in no obvious way from that of a capitalist board which is formally elected by, and responsible to a general meeting of shareholders.

The management (La Gerencia) and its management roles are fairly sharply distinguished from the Junta Rectora and its roles in the ULGOR statutes. Not only is it the co-op's executive but its executive duties are defined as covering the co-op as a *productive unit*. Article 49 says it may consist of one person or be a collegiate body. The same Article lays down that though the manager (or managers) cannot be members of the Junta Rectora, they may attend its meetings and speak but not vote. In another key provision La Gerencia, in its turn, is in some measure insulated from the possible hazards of ultimate bottom-upwards control. The manager or managers must be appointed for a minimum of four years; and such appointments cannot be terminated unless one of a number of specified serious conditions is satisfied.

This is a highly sophisticated attempt to reconcile the need for genuinely democratic structures with the need for efficient management and management continuity. Basically, it is achieved by separating management from ultimate enterprise leadership and government. One obvious theoretical danger is that La Gerencia and the Junta Rectora might fall out. Another is that either or both might drift away from the general membership in the Junta General de Socios. The attendance of management at meetings of the Junta Rectora is obviously some kind of safeguard against the first danger. There are, however, other safeguards and more general provisions to promote enterprise solidarity and optimum communication.

The provision for management attendance at the Junta Rectora's meetings is symmetrically balanced by the provision that a representative of the latter may attend management meetings. Yet the danger that the two bodies may drift apart (or even go 'scooting off' in opposite directions) is further guarded against by a statutory 'consultative' body which links the two. This is the Council of Direction (Consejo de Direccion) on which senior management and senior members of the Junta Rectora come together. It is described as having a 'consultative and assessment' role *vis-à-vis* management and the Junta Rectora. The moral seems to be that if management and leadership are separate there must be a third institutional mechanism which brings them together, otherwise communication between the two is liable to break down, or even worse things may happen.

Communication between the grass-roots membership, the Junta Rectora and La Gerencia is provided for by yet another institution: the Social Council (Consejo Social). Members of this body are elected by the separate divisions of the co-op acting as constituencies. The Consejo Social may be seen as performing functions similar to those of a shop-stewards' committee; it has special responsibilities in areas like health, safety, working conditions and payments systems while funds allocated by the co-op to the local community are also channelled through it. The Social Council encourages communication in both directions, from the bottom upwards and from the top downwards, but its existence is also an acknowledgment that even in a genuinely democratic enterprise the interests of the rank and file may require special representation. Of course, it must be possible since trade unions became formally legalized in Spain in 1977 that there may be pressures for some of the Social Council's functions to be performed under trade union auspices.

Obviously both the Council of Direction and the Social Council have generalized roles of promoting internal enterprise solidarity, but the most unusual, famous, and controversial arrangement used by the co-ops to promote that goal is rather different: it is their 3:1 maximum differential between the highest and lowest rates of pay before tax. As a general rule that maximum ratio is applied without qualification. Co-ops may, however, approve increases of up to 50 per cent in the very top salaries which they pay (taking the differential maximum to 4.5:1) if they feel it is justified by extra work and responsibilities.

Mondragon's leaders will concede that there is nothing sacrosanct about any particular differential ratio, whether 3:1, 4.5:1 or any other, but they will argue that an important principle is involved. That is, in effect, the need to strike some balance between the demands of enterprise solidarity and the constraints of the market. The former will tend to narrow the differential maximum, the latter to open it.

Given the co-ops' policy that lower pay rates must be in line with those prevailing in the neighbourhood, the ratios adopted mean in effect that those on the higher rates are getting significantly less than they would in non-co-operative enterprises. That is clearly a factor which tends to promote internal enterprise solidarity. Whether these particular differential figures could be applied successfully in, say, France or Britain is something else. It may be worth emphasizing that Spanish income tax is quite light so that post-tax differentials are close to pre-tax ones in Spain. A post-tax differential maximum of 4.5 in Britain would probably involve sacrifices for only a very few in British industry.

I have lumped together in one group the whole bundle of co-op statutes which deal with capital, ownership, profits and related matters. The details are complex. Their rationale can perhaps best be understood as an attempt to harmonize various sets and pairs of interests: of the individual worker–member and the co-op as a whole of capital and labour; of the co-op and the local community in which it works; of those who already work in the co-operatives and of that potentially unlimited number still outside who, according to Mondragon philosophy, must be given the chance of eventual membership by an unremitting 'open door' policy of job expansion. Taken together these arrangements are an extraordinarily subtle and imaginative exercise in social engineering which make all other attempts at industrial structure building − whether by the Webbs or Ernest Bader or the Rochdale pioneers − look like the artefacts of Stone Age workshops.

To begin with, a reconciliation between the individual worker–member's interest and those of the co-op as a whole is initiated by dividing what is, in effect, the Mondragon 'equity' into two parts: an indivisible part which is collectively owned; and the balance which is credited to individual member's capital accounts. As a social and economic enterprise with an indefinite life, the co-op's interest is to be financially strong and thus the indivisible parts of its capital should be prudently large. On the other hand this collectively owned element must not be enlarged beyond the point at which the interests of the individual members − and thus their incentive to identify with it − start to be seriously undermined. A balance needs to be struck. There must be substantial individual 'ownership' − otherwise the interests of individual worker–members will not be securely linked to those of the co-op. Moreover, this individual 'ownership' must, at the outset, be purchased, not acquired as a gift, otherwise there will be no psychological feeling of responsible ownership (otherwise, too, the open-door policy of job expansion will be undermined). Yet, on the other hand, there must be substantial and fully protected collective ownership. For, if not, the ability of the co-op to survive and progress will be weakened. How is this balance to be struck?

When a new co-op starts, or when a new member is admitted into an existing co-op, the answer is quite simple. The balance struck is 80:20, on the side of individual ownership. The capital sums differ in the two situations. In 1976 members of a new co-op starting from scratch were normally required to put up capital contributions (Aportaciones en concepto de capital) roughly equivalent to £2,000; while the figure for joining an existing enterprise was approximately half that; in each case 20 per cent of this capital contribution would immediately be appropriated to collective funds.

When profits or losses are earned by a co-op the balance in which they are distributed between collective and individual accounts is more complex. Broadly, the position with profits is that not more than 70 per cent can be credited to individual accounts, while in the case of losses not *less* than 70 per cent must be debited to these same individual accounts. Broadly, again, if profits are low the percentage credit to individual accounts may be as high as 70 per cent, while if they are high it will be lower. The fine details will be discussed later on, but here it is worth emphasizing that the initial capital contributions are significant sums. They are significant from the individual's viewpoint; they represent a minimum of several months' wages – and it is thus plausible to assume that they encourage responsibility and positive attitudes to productivity. However, they are significant also from the viewpoint of the open-door policy. Not less than £20m has been raised by the co-ops and devoted to job creation in this way.

There is, however, one further important set of provisions which affect the balance of interest between individual members and the co-op. Money may not normally be withdrawn from individual capital accounts except in the case of retirement, death or on extreme compassionate grounds. It is true that if both the co-op and the individual's account succeed in meeting a stiff set of financial conditions (the achievement of which effectively ensures that there are no financial constraints on the co-op's possibilities of job expansion and thus that the open-door policy is not undermined) limited drawings may be made. However, in practice these conditions have rarely if ever been met. On the other hand, these 'blocked' capital accounts can be, and are, used as collateral against which personal loans can be raised.

What happens to an individual capital account when a worker–member chooses to leave? The answer is that the Junta Rectora is free to decide in those circumstances that up to 30 per cent of the individual account may be forfeited and credited to collective funds. That will not happen, however, if the resignation was caused by events beyond the individual's control – if, for example, family ties force a move to a different part of Spain. In such cases the full capital account will be paid out.

What we have here is a finely tuned reconciliation between the interests of the individual worker–member and the collective interests of the co-op. In a sense, the balance may be said to be struck on the side of the worker–member: up to 80 per cent of the original capital stake is personally retained and up to 70 per cent of net profits may be credited to individual accounts. On the other hand, the balance is tilted back in the opposite direction and the collective interest protected mainly in two ways: first by the provisions under which, as profits increase, a larger percentage of them is credited to collective funds; second, by the provisions which restrict withdrawals from individual capital accounts.

The reconciliation of capital and labour is achieved rather differently. In the first place it is achieved, simply and brilliantly by merging the two. All worker–members must make capital contributions, and thus become capital owners. No non-worker members are allowed to do so, thus no outsiders may become owners. The ancient conflict between one set of people who supply labour and another who supply capital is removed at a stroke.

Notwithstanding, there is still the possibility of conflict between the two different pulls exerted on a single group of capital and labour suppliers, the pull exerted on them *qua* capital suppliers and the separate pull exerted on them *qua* labour suppliers. More precisely a balance has to be struck between their interests as suppliers of capital and their interests as suppliers of labour. In this the Mondragon co-ops have partially followed an old co-operative principle: capital is entitled to a fixed rate of interest and nothing more.

Not more than a total of 6 per cent of direct interest may be paid annually on individual worker–members' capital accounts. These payments are, of course, treated as a cost – to be deducted before any net profit, or loss, is struck. Notionally the 6 per cent figure is made up of two elements; a 4.5 per cent element of basic interest (or money rent); and 1.5 per cent element regarded as compensation for risk of loss.

But these interest payments are not quite the whole story of how the member is rewarded *qua* a supplier of capital. To begin with, periodic revaluations of the co-ops' assets are provided for – so that adjustments can be made to take account of falling money values. When the assets are revalued, individual capital accounts may be revalued correspondingly. It should go without saying that the revaluation exercises are tightly controlled by the CLP and can only take place in accordance with asset-value index figures which the CLP compiles and circulates.

Second, the capital accounts of the individual worker–members play some part in determining individual profit (or loss) shares when these are calculated at the end of an accounting period. Once the total amount to be distributed in credits (or debits) has been calculated, the figure is divided in proportion to the sum of the individual's work income and of his capital account interest income over the relevant accounting period – and not just in proportion to the former. At least in successful co-ops, therefore, the profit (or loss) shares of long serving member–workers – who have larger accumulated capital accounts – will tend to be boosted compared with the shares of more recent arrivals. This sum – of work income and interest income – is used again in its own right when profits exceed a specified high level.

The formula which covers profit distribution when profits are high must next be briefly explained. It is only applicable when net profits exceed 50 per cent of the sum of members' work income and interest income during the accounting period. When that happens, instead of the normal 30 per cent minimum net profit allocation to collective reserve funds and social projects the 'collective percentage' is determined in accordance with the following formula:

$$Cp = \frac{P}{P + I} \times 100$$

where Cp = the percentage of net profits to be allocated to collective funds.

P = net profits to be distributed.

I = the income of worker members: both work income
(including social security benefits) and interest income.

In effect the formula means that, once the 50 per cent condition has been met, the percentage of net profits allocated collectively will be the same as the percentage which net profits themselves represent on a base of net profits plus all workers' income. Quentin Garcia supplies a valuable concrete example of the application of this formula to ULGOR's 1967 results. The key figures, in millions of Pesetas, were as follows:

Net profits		101
Work income	67	
Interest income	15	
Total income		82

Thus in ULGOR's case in 1967:

$$Cp = \frac{101}{101 + 82} \times 100 = 55 \text{ per cent}$$

In this case, therefore, 55 per cent of ULGOR's net profits (or Pesetas 55.55m) were allocated collectively and 45 per cent (or Pesetas 45.45m) to individual member–workers' accounts. It is easy to see that the higher the level of profits, when this formula applies, the higher also will be the proportion of net profits allocated to collective funds.

The inclusion of interest income as well as work income in this key formula reflects partly pragmatic, partly theoretical considerations. There is the common-sense requirement that those with longer service and thus normally larger accumulated capital accounts should not be penalized compared with relative newcomers; but there is also a theoretical consideration. The first chapter of ULGOR's statutes which is headed 'Fundamental Guidelines' (Normas Fundamentales) talks about the need for a 'just reward' for capital, and states that this is to be found in balancing the amount of compensation paid for sacrifices past and present. The theoretical justification is that capital is seen as 'accumulated work' rather than as some foreign or hostile element.

When we move to the co-ops' need to take account of the interests of the local community, it is easy to see that this requirement is particularly strong given their great dependence on local savings. The whole history of the Mondragon group is founded on the strongest possible links with local people. Of course, simply by the successful provision of employment and training, the co-ops have conferred immense benefits on their neighbourhoods; and it is hard to challenge the view that even without any special provisions a genuine mutuality of interest and benefit already exists. However, there are also special provisions. Not less that 10 per cent of each co-op's net profits must (by Spanish law) normally be allocated to educational, social and cultural projects in the local community. It is strictly laid down that these projects will in all normal circumstances exclude any which are for the direct and exclusive benefit of the co-op's own members (a 'co-op only' sports centre would not, for example, qualify). The 10 per cent rule may only be modified if money has had to be paid out to deal with involuntary stoppages of work (part of the whole set of arrangements covering job security, which will be looked at subsequently).

Finally a balance between the interests of all the co-op's members taken together and those of all relevant outsiders (i.e. prospective or possible new members) is reached by the co-op's formal commitment to the 'open door' policy of job expansion. That policy, strongly buttressed by the controls on capital withdrawals, appears to constitute one of the few major ideological commitments of the Mondragon group. As in the case of the old London Corresponding Society – and of other pioneering organizations of British working people after the French Revolution –

one of the key rules of the co-ops' is 'that their membership should be unlimited'.

The co-ops have been known to suggest that an important factor which may affect their comparative profit levels *vis-à-vis* their capitalist counterparts is what amounts to something very close to an employment guarantee. It is claimed that there has not in fact been a single case of involuntary redundancy during the group's history. The section of ULGOR's internal rules which covers inescapable stoppages may illustrate the way in which the employment guarantee operates.

It is provided, in the first place, that if there is an inescapable stoppage in ULGOR itself, the affected worker–members may be directed to alternative employment in one of the other five co-ops which make up the federated sub-group of ULARCO. Once the possibilities of redeployment within ULARCO have been exhausted, ULGOR's rules provide how those actually to be laid off with be selected: first, those whose work is directly affected; second, if lay-offs have to be extended beyond that, according to the time-honoured trade union principle of 'last in – first out'. Aside from the facility for redeployment within ULARCO there is, of course, nothing unusual compared with capitalist practice so far.

However, where any worker–members are laid off ULGOR's rules provide that they receive 80 per cent of their normal work income until their direct and active employment resumes. This, of course, is the provision which differentiates Mondragon from normal capitalist practice (public or private). It constitutes an earnings and thus, indirectly at least, an employment guarantee.

With characteristic attention to detail, ULGOR's rules also lay down how the cost of meeting this guarantee will be met. If moneys are available, pending investments which have not yet been made, in the funds allocated for community projects, then the incomes of those laid off will be maintained by debiting the following accounts in the following proportions: 25 per cent community projects fund; 25 per cent collectively owned funds; 50 per cent individual capital accounts of all worker–members. Where no community project moneys are available, the costs will be debited 50:50 to collective funds and personal accounts.

Since job security, at least in today's mixed economy countries, is one of the key concerns of working people and trade unions, it is worth emphasizing both how successful the Mondragon group has been and the quite evident importance which they attach to it. In a sense, perhaps, it is because of this guarantee, and the fact that it has never been dishonoured, that the group has been able to impose a pretty tough régime of labour and work discipline. The most eye-catching feature of the disciplinary code is that the initiators of strikes which arise from causes inside the co-op face the most condign punishment. Nor is that the only feature with which those brought up on traditional trade union freedoms might find it hard to come to terms.

ULGOR's rule about strikes for reasons internal to the enterprise begins by stating flatly that they are 'in contradiction with the co-operative arrangements which have been accepted'. It then goes on to prescribe that anyone instigating or supporting such a strike will be immediately brought before the Junta Rectora for punishment. In the case of strike supporters, it continues, the penalty will be proportionate to their degree of responsibility for it; for the strike's instigators the rule demands that the penalty be expulsion.

No attempt is made to conceal that there has been at least one strike at ULGOR for reasons internal to the enterprise. (It is arguable that there have been two, depending on one's definitions and judgments of fact.) The stoppage occurred in 1974 and lasted less than one week. The main cause seems to have been dissatisfaction with a new set of job classifications which the management were seeking to introduce. These had evidently provoked considerable shop-floor resentment notwithstanding the fact that the existing classifications of the entire workforce had been officially protected. However, the key point is that, by a decision of the Junta Rectora, the punishment of expulsion was imposed on seventeen ringleaders and lesser penalties on 397 other worker–members. These punishments were appealed against before the full ULGOR assembly (Junta General de Socios), but the assembly ratified them.

As for strikes for reasons external to the co-op, ULGOR's rule lays down that the Junta Rectora will deal with these on the merits of each case. There has certainly been at least one strike in sympathy with Basque Nationalist demands. The framers of this rule, in the conditions of Franco's Spain, may well also have had in mind the possibility of strikes in sympathy with general working-class and trade union objectives on a national basis.

Strikes aside, work discipline appears to be closely regulated by ULGOR's internal rules. Three levels of errors or misdemeanours are classified: light, grave and very grave (faltas leves, graves and muy graves). Some examples of each are:

'light'   — more than five unjustified cases of unpunctuality in six months;
                  — unjustifiably missing more than two hours' work in one month;

'grave'
- more than ten unjustified unpunctuality cases in six months;
- unjustifiably missing more than eight hours' work in one month;
- the display of public or violent incompatibility in a way which interferes with collaborative team work;

'very grave'
- more than twenty cases of unjustified unpunctuality over a six month period;
- unjustifiably missing more than twenty hours' work in one month
- theft from either a fellow member or from the co-op;
- refusing to accept punishment for a grave misdemeanour;

Some examples of the corresponding penalties are:

'light'
- written warning;
- suspension from employment and forfeiting of income for up to two days;

'grave'
- suspension from employment and the forfeiting of income for up to fifteen days.

'very grave'
- suspension from employment and the forfeiting of income for up to sixty days;
- disqualification from that part of any year-end profit share associated with work income.

Leaving aside the question of how acceptable or otherwise discipline codes similar to ULGOR's would be to a free trade union movement in a mixed economy, what stands out in all this is, I think, a combination of professionalism and tough-mindedness. The professionalism is shown in particular by the attention to detail. The tough-mindedness is the direct antithesis of what ordinary people tend to expect from co-operative ventures. This is how far the Mondragon group is from basing its discipline on an 'idealistic' but sloppy assumption that all worker—members will 'naturally' behave well.

One of the great comparative advantages which, according to traditional theory, a co-op sector should enjoy *vis-à-vis* its capitalist competitors, private and public, is the advantage of inter-enterprise support and assistance, inter-co-operative solidarity. The fact that there have been precious few concrete examples of anything of the kind in industrial co-op history, does not necessarily mean that these advantages are not available. The Mondragon experience apart, the industrial co-ops of Western Europe over the last century have been too dwarfish – and too scattered – for there to be really significant possibilities in this direction.

There can be no doubt that the Mondragon group attaches considerable importance to 'solidarity' between the 'base' co-ops as well as to the effective co-ordination of the group's activities. The second, spearheaded as it is by the bank, is easy to grasp and describe even if, as we shall see there is a tricky and sensitive set of balances to be struck there too. The first, mutual support of the 'base' co-ops one with another, is perhaps more elusive, at least in its concrete manifestations.

The injunction to the 'base' co-ops to practise policies of solidarity is spelled out in a long, extended clause (4.4) of their Contract of Association with the CLP thus:

> In order to ensure the strongest possible support for all institutions
> and to optimise the business efficiency of the group as a whole, the
> Associated Co-operative will respect the principle of intergroup
> loyalty and mutual assistance when formulating future plans
> concerning production, selection of personnel, the establishment of
> business links between co-operatives, where to place orders, and other
> facets of their business by which co-operatives associated with the
> Caja Laboral could be made to benefit, without affecting the interests
> or autonomy of the co-operative itself.

On the other hand, no hard data are available about the extent to which any of this happens. Of course, it is almost certainly correct to make some negative and neutral assumptions: that there is no 'poaching' of superior labour and management as between one base co-op and another (because of the generally applied differential limits the scope for this may anyway be rather reduced); that other things being equal, one 'base' co-op will order its supplies from another; and that two 'base' co-ops will avoid manufacturing the same product in competition. However, what we do not know is how far, if at all, one 'base' co-op will actually initiate positive policies which support another, or offer aid and succour if a neighbouring co-op is hard pressed. It is true, in relation to employment protection, that these things do happen within the federated sub-group of ULARCO. The CLP itself is also very much a source of help to 'base' co-ops in trouble, but it is not clear how much support the average 'base' co-op is likely to give to its neighbour, nor how far inter-co-op solidarity has been an important factor in the success of the Mondragon experience.

Even so, there can be no doubt about the CLP's very real part in the co-ordination of the group as whole, or of its immense and beneficial importance to the entire group. Its supporting professional back-up and general planning functions will be looked into in the section on the bank itself. What we are simply concerned with here is the set of relationships which link it with the 'base' co-ops.

In its treatment of these relationships the provisions of the Contract of Association are quite spare. Basically, three points are covered:

1 the exchange of information;
2 directly financial relationship;
3 auditing.

The Contract of Association is careful to provide that the information flow will be a two-way affair. While the 'base' co-op undertakes to supply the CLP with its annual balance sheet and proposed budget, and to provide monthly data on actual performance, the bank undertakes to send periodic reports down the line to the base co-op. These will cover the progress of the bank's own budget as well as 'other information of an economic and technical nature'.

The mutuality of the relationship also features in the provisions for the financial dealings between the base co-op and the CLP. On the one side the associated 'base' co-op will have access to the resources of the CLP for 'its own financing under all agreed credit terms'; on the other side the 'base' co-op commits itself to deposit any surplus cash with the bank. Finally, in the matter of auditing, the Contract of Association lays down that the CLP will, as a free service, produce a comprehensive audit of the 'base' co-op's affairs every four years. It can, of course, be asked by the 'base' co-op for a more frequent audit; but the service will then normally have to be paid for.

These essentials which govern the relationship between the CLP and the 'base' co-ops seem deliberately to have been confined to a formal minimum. There seems also to have been a deliberate attempt to achieve a balanced relationship. Certainly, the bank is very conscious of the need to preserve as genuine as possible an independence for the 'base' co-ops. By confining itself to questions of audit, information flow and finance, the Contract of Association leaves the emphasis by implication on the side of enterprise independence. However, a visit to the bank suggests that in practice the banks co-ordinating function goes a good deal further. The information gathered from the independent co-ops is used, for example, as the starting point for plans covering the group as a whole. The elaboration of rolling five year plans has become established as one of the bank's most important functions. Though the information comes from the independent 'base' enterprises, the bank's role in group planning evidently goes beyond a scissors-and-paste assembly of individual enterprise budgets.

More generally it is clear that if full advantage is to be taken of inter-enterprise co-operation, the bank's role as group co-ordinator must be an active one. In particular it is difficult to see how the individual enterprises could go on indefinitely maintaining their employment guarantee policies unless there were concurrent policies at the centre to ensure the overall employment levels of the group.

Though it may be impossible to quantify the benefits it is obvious that the bank's co-ordinating function – as well as its fund raising and its provision of professional support – has been a crucial ingredient in the group's success. Yet it is easy to understand, as the bank itself clearly does, that any policy of central co-ordination in the Mondragon group must seek to preserve as far as possible the independence of the 'base' co-ops.

Under Spain's current co-operative law (which is more highly regarded than its Franco-régime origins would lead one to expect), all co-ops must contribute at least 10 per cent of their net profits to educational and social projects within their geographical communities. Because of how they started – and of their continuous emphasis on the need for all-round solidarity – it seems likely that the Mondragon enterprises would in any case have imposed this sort of obligation on themselves. As it is the Contract of Association simply repeats this provision of Spanish law.

On the other hand, a highly distinctive policy of the Mondragon group is that the co-ops must keep their total wages, salary and other personnel costs in line with those prevailing in their neighbourhood. The general principle is set out in the Contract of Association thus: 'The total annual "*anticipos*" [wages salaries and other personnel costs] cannot be in excess of the personnel costs which obtain on average in the associated co-op's zone of operation ...'.

However, in order not to impose excessive paper work, the Contract goes on to explain that this result can be achieved if the 'base' co-op fixes its relevant rates somewhere between 90 per cent and 110 per cent of the rates which the bank uses for its own staff and which are circulated. In practice, since the bank uses prevailing non co-op rates for lower paid posts as the reference point for its calculations, and since the 3:1 differential limit is applied, to follow the bank's figures means that the lower paid receive slightly more than the locally prevailing rates, those higher up the scale significantly less. Between these two extremes the rates for the intermediate grades can be calculated by simple arithmetic. For example ULGOR's internal rules distinguish six separate grades and lay down payments on the 1:3 scale as follows: operative and auxiliary posts 1.0–1.4; professional and responsible posts 1.4–1.5; subordinate executives 1.5–1.8; intermediate executives 1.9–2.1; important executives 2.2–2.4; high executives 2.5–3.0.

The logic of the differential maximum has already been discussed; the logic of this policy of alignment with zonal wage rates is rather different. The idea seems to be to avoid friction or the creation of unnecessary divergence of interest with other, non-co-operative enterprises in the region. There is in effect a conscious effort to create some basis for solidarity with non-co-operative working people and with non-co-operative enterprise leadership in the 'zone of operation'.

The details of these various arrangements, policies and provisions around which the Mondragon group of co-ops has come to be structured may seen complex; in many respects they are. Moreover the details have an importance on their own account. It would be absurd to argue that they do not matter. For in some ways it is precisely in their imaginative attention to detail that the originality of the Mondragon group, in comparison with other co-operative experiments, consists.

Having said that, it seems reasonable to suggest that two key ideas pervade these structures: balance and solidarity. Looked at as an exercise in creating balances, the features of these structures which stand out most clearly are:

1 The balance between capital and labour.
2 The balance, within the enterprise, between the individual's interest and the interest of the enterprise as a whole.
3 The balance between democratic control and efficient management.
4 The balance between the interests of the enterprise and the interests of the local community (or region) within which it works.
5 The balance between individual responsibility (capital stakes, tough disciplinary provisions) and collective responsibility (e.g. for employment protection).
6 The balance between the independence of the individual base enterprises and the strong central co-ordination by the bank of the group's operations as a whole.

Alternatively we can put the emphasis on the idea of solidarity and see the key structural features as those which encourage:

1 Solidarity between capital and labour.
2 Solidarity between shop floor and management.
3 Solidarity between the enterprise and the local community.
4 Solidarity between the base enterprises and the bank at the centre.

It is, I think, in these terms of solidarity and balance, rather than in terms of more traditional co-operative categories, that the Mondragon structures can best be understood.

A word needs to be said about some of the group's service co-ops other than the bank. If we ignore the lower level schools and the housing co-ops (which are scarcely relevant in a debate about alternative industrial structures) there are four which require some attention: Eroski, the consumer store chain; Lagun Aro the social insurance organization; Centro de Investigaciones Technologicas, the group's research and development centre; Escuela Profesional Politecnica, the group's main source of skilled manpower.

The first consumer store associated with the group was founded in 1959. Others followed. Ten years later in 1969 all were formed into a single enterprise, Eroski. Total turnover in that year was worth just under £1.5m. By 1976, the figure was over £10m from thirty branch stores which together employed around 300 people.

The size of this operation, in relation to the industrial co-ops, neatly reverses the position in Britain and elsewhere in Western Europe where the consumer stores have dwarfed the directly productive enterprises. And the Eroski stores differ from their UK counterparts in a further way. As in the industrial co-ops a capital stake is required of all employees; and the employee force participates alongside Eroski's consumer members in the group's profits and final control.

Lagun Aro, the group's social insurance organization, was initially a branch of the CLP, but was separately organized as a 'second degree co-operative' from the mid-1970s. Like other second degree co-ops associated with the Mondragon group it has two categories of membership – the other co-ops as institutional members, and its own employees as individual members. Control is shared between the institutional and individual members.

A full range of sickness and industrial injury benefits is provided by Lagun Aro, as well as family allowance type payments, pensions and various other benefits. The need for it to exist at all is explained partly by the fact that the Mondragon workers, as officially self-employed, are not allowed to belong to the state's main social security system. Meanwhile the body with which they must be registered, the Association of the Self-employed (La Mutualidad de Autonomos) is thought to provide inadequate service. Lagun Aro may be seen in part to supplement that.

Its pension rates, 100 per cent of pre-retirement salary, looked in 1977 decidedly generous and were much higher than anything offered by the state, but its rules also reflect a hard-nosed concern to protect the system against possible abuse – for example by insisting that sickness benefit will not normally be paid until after the first three days off work. For the rest Lagun Aro claims that its administrative costs are low. As in the other second degree co-ops – the Polytechnic, the bank and the

Development Centre – its own full-time staff must make the normal capital contribution on entry. These capital accounts are then credited each year with the average of the individual profit shares distributed by the 'base' co-ops.

Work on the group's technological research centre Inkerlan was only begun in the mid-1970s and had not been fully completed by the end of 1977. But the case for such a unit was clear enough. In the early 1970s the group had come to believe that it must reduce its dependence on outside technology – which it had mainly relied upon since the foundation of ULGOR. At the end of 1977 the staff of the centre was just over forty, with roughly half of that number full-time. The basic economic policy is to charge the 'base' co-ops for work done; and thus to be self-financing.

If the Inkerlan is the newest of the group's 'second degree' institutions, the Escuela Profesional Politecnica is the oldest. By 1976 it had grown from the twenty-odd student body enrolled in 1943 to over 2,000. Apart from its organization as a second degree co-op it is unusual, among institutions of this kind, in including a range of courses which stretch from craft apprentice level to university level degrees in engineering.

It is even more unusual in having promoted a productive enterprise – Alecoop – in which its students may work and be paid. Alecoop, which produces components of various kinds, had a labour force of 587 at the end of 1976, of whom the great majority were students. Their daily programme normally includes five hours of directly productive work and five hours of study. What they can earn is a good deal more than what they need to pay in fees.

The Professional School and Polytechnic is clearly a most attractive, worth-while and liberal institution; liberal in enabling its students to combine paid work with study, but equally liberal in not forcing them to do so. It is liberal again in its acceptance of non-co-op enterprises as institutional members and in its willingness to take their employees into the student body. It deserves to be studied in its own right by anyone who is concerned about the inadequacy of technical education establishments elsewhere. Its main relevance here, however, is as a source of skilled manpower to the industrial co-ops. Its programmes and courses can be tailored when required to the changing skilled needs of the 'base' co-ops. Its has enabled the group to become largely self-sufficient in supplying its own skilled manpower; just as the bank has enabled the group to become self-sufficient in meeting its capital requirements. These two together are an immense source of strength for the group.

As well as the 'base' co-ops and the co-ops of second degree the Mondragon group has included since 1965 a sub-federation or complex: ULARCO. In 1976 ULARCO covered six 'base' co-ops including ULGOR the largest enterprise in the whole group. When the complex was formed in 1965 only ULGOR and three others were included. The two subsequent recruits were both formerly divisions of ULGOR. ULARCO members with their joining dates, main products and workforce numbers at the end of 1976 are given in Table 10.7.

TABLE 10.7   ULARCO members

Name	Joining date	Main products	Workforce end 1976
ULGOR	1965	domestic appliances	3,462
Arrasate	1965	machine tools	469
Ederlan	1965	foundry products	614
Copreci	1965	components	831
Fagor Electrotecnica	1966	electrical components	615
Fagor Industrial	1973	mechanical components	266
Total workforce			6,257

The workforce figures show that ULARCO accounted for more than 40 per cent of the industrial employment of the Mondragon group at the end of 1976. Considered as one unit it was also the largest single industrial co-operative enterprise in the Western world, being comfortably larger than France's telephone equipment co-op, AOIP, employing some 4,500. Moreover, as Inaki Gorrono emphasizes, the output of the five smaller ULARCO enterprises strongly support that of ULGOR.

From the start ULGOR was a substantial buyer of Copreci and Ederlan's outputs. And a visit to the main ULGOR works will confirm that Arrasate is one of its most important suppliers of heavy machinery and equipment. In short the ULARCO complex represents the kind of vertical integration which is increasingly familiar in the capitalist world.

The degree of integration within ULARCO has evidently increased. For the purpose of calculating individual shares of profit at the end of each year the results of the member enterprises were partially pooled at the start; by 1976 they had become completely pooled. By the early 1970s such key matters as finance, personnel, work organization and planning studies were being handled mainly at the level of ULARCO. None of this integration could have taken place without democratic consent; the majority of individual worker–members must have approved the integration moves.

ULARCO can best be seen as a mechanism which seeks to combine the advantages of any available economies of scale while preserving the separate identity of its constituent enterprises. The general feeling at Mondragon in 1976 was that the experiment had proved on balance a success. The encouragement of 'other ULARCOs' became an important policy of the CLP.

None of this means, of course, that ULARCO has fully solved the familiar industrial dilemma of small scale versus large scale. It is recognized at Mondragon that ULGOR remains too large. Since a workforce of around 500 is considered about the limit within which a co-op can maintain satisfactory internal cohesion, it is obvious that ULGOR's size is far from satisfactory in theoretical terms. On the other hand, while it continues to achieve excellent economic results, common sense decrees that it should be left alone.

Despite the qualification about ULGOR's size, the ULARCO complex clearly represents a useful model of how to set about combining the advantages of small and large. The small independent co-ops, without renouncing their independence, agree to operate for some purposes as a federated enterprise. It seems plausible to imagine that other enterprises in the Mondragon group will see the logic of trying the same kind of thing.

The structural set up at the bank is the same as for the other second degree co-ops. There are two categories of members – individual and institutional and final control rests with a combination of the two voting in the General Assembly. The staff constitute the individual membership. The 'base' co-ops, through elected representatives, account for the institutional membership. The two membership categories have 50 per cent each of the General Assembly's votes. It is the assembly in turn which elects the Junta Rectora – which then appoints the executive management. In these latter respects, as in the more detailed structural arrangements, the set up at the CLP does not significantly differ from that of a 'base' co-op.

Since the separating off of Lagun Aro, the bank has contained, below the level of a unified top echelon, just two divisions: its economic division (division economica) and what it calls its entrepreneurial division (division empresarial). The economic division is effectively the savings bank. Its main job is to attract local savings through a network of branch offices and as we saw earlier it has succeeded astonishingly well; so much so that from the early 1970s shortage of capital imposed no constraints on the Mondragon group.

The banking division is much larger than the 'empresarial' division, as is shown by staff figures in September 1976.

TABLE 10.8   CLP staff

Unified top echelon	12
Other common services	53
Banking division	467
'Empresarial' division	95
Total	627

Source: CLP

The bulk of the banking staff (344) were working in the sixty-two branch offices scattered over Spain's four Basque provinces. The remaining 123 were employed at head office in Mondragon.

It makes sense to highlight the success of the banking division. No similar institution anywhere in the world has succeeded, so far as I know, in attracting small savings and in putting them primarily to work in the promotion of local industry. Once these points have been given due weight, there is nothing further which really needs to be said about the banking division. What we have here is an efficient local (or regional) savings bank operation – rather like the savings attraction side of a successful regional building society. The assessment of the whole thing at CLP headquarters is almost bland. The operation of a successful savings bank is really very easy, I was told.

Of course, that is not the whole story. The attraction of local savings when the bank first started depended on the strong links established with the local community from shortly after the arrival of Fr Arizmendi in the 1940s. Once established it was a necessary condition of continued success in attracting savings that only successful ventures should be supported and that bad debts should be minimized. That side of the business has, of course, become one of the primary tasks of the 'empresarial' division.

The main tasks of the 'empresarial' division are to provide back-up management and professional services for all the enterprises in the group and to play a major role in the promotion of new co-ops. It is also responsible for much of the work which enables the CLP's leadership to plan and co-ordinate the activities of the group as a whole, and that is clearly work of great importance. However, the division's own essential roles are the provision of professional and management advice and the midwifing of new ventures. The breakdown of its staff in mid-1976 makes this clear: promotion, 9; engineering, 4; town planning, 5; direction, 6; personnel, 5; research, 4; industrial building, 9;

accountancy, 9; housing (architects, etc.), 16; agriculture, 3; education, 3; other, 22; total, 95.

Unlike the banking (economica) division of the CLP, the 'empresarial' division is not directly 100 per cent self-financing. Some of the services which it supplies to the 'base' co-ops are fully charged so as to recover all costs. Others, such as the four-yearly audit, it is obliged to undertake for all the 'base' co-ops, are not charged. Others again are charged at prices which will partially recover costs. Because it sees the division's role as being concerned essentially with the protection of existing investments and the promotion of new enterprises, the CLP does not impose any narrow requirement of absolute financial self-sufficiency in the division. However, it does lay down two controls: first, the division must recover at least 60 per cent of its costs; second, its net (unrecovered) expenditure must not exceed 0.20 per cent of the CLP's total balance sheet liabilities. The division's projected budget for 1977 was as follows: total expenditure, Pesetas 144m; recovered, Pesetas 93m; net, Pesetas, 51m.

It is the proud boast of the 'empresarial' division that with the single exception of one short-lived foray into a co-operative fishing boat project, it has never backed a loser and has suffered not one single bad debt. For many this is the most astonishing in the whole array of achievements which have come out of the Mondragon experience. In fact a large number of bankers and businessmen find it too astonishing to believe – saying that they could not conceivably accept such a claim unless it could be verified by their own accountants. Is the claim in fact true? And, if it is, what are the secrets behind it? Since the promotion of new ventures is notoriously a business of greater risk than the support of established ones, we will look first at the division's midwifing procedures.

To begin with, the division insists that the first initiating step, which may or may not eventually lead to the establishment of a new co-op, must come not from itself at the top but from the bottom. It must come from a group of ordinary working prople who have decided they would like to work together in a co-operative set up if possible. Over the mid-1970s approaches of this kind were apparently coming forward to the CLP 'empresarial' division at a rate of about ten a year.

Once a group has come forward a series of preparatory conditions must be satisfied before detailed work on the possibility of a new co-op will be undertaken. A potential manager must be found, conceivably from within the group, preferably at any rate by the group; only as a last resort will the 'empresarial' division come forward with management suggestions – and even then the group will have to choose between alternatives.

Equally important is the fact that during this preparatory phase all the requirements of Mondragon co-operative working, as set out in the contract of association, must be fully explained to the initiating group and understood and accepted. In particular the capital contribution requirement must be fully spelled out plus the fact that the group's members will have to be responsible for finding this money. Groups may never get beyond this stage; but assuming they do so, the question of what is to be manufactured will clearly have to be raised. By 1976 the empresarial division had come to prefer that it should normally itself be the main source of product suggestions. (Previously it had thought it better that the initiative in this area too should come from the prospective working group.)

Given provisional agreement on a manager, and on a product or products, and given that the group has understood – and not been deterred by – all the conditions of association, then a second phase of much more detailed study and work gets under way. For this second phase the prospective manager will be brought into the 'empresarial' division and work alongside the division's staff. In effect a detailed series of feasibility studies will be undertaken, and all aspects of the proposed activity will be minutely studied: the product, the market, the organization of work, etc., as well as the capital and recurrent cost implications of what is proposed. Within the division, a member of the 'empresarial' division's promotions staff, a 'godfather' as he is called, will be responsible for seeing this work through. The prospective manager will work as closely as possible with the 'godfather' and his salary will be met for the time being from the Bank's funds. On the other hand, assuming that the new co-op gets off the ground, these salary payments will be accounted for as a debt to the bank.

Through all this long process of study and work (which may involve, for example, visiting leading enterprises anywhere in Europe where the prospective product or products are manufactured), members of the group will be kept as closely in touch as possible with what is going on. In the nature of the situation they are free to abandon the project, either individually or collectively, at any stage before the final decisions are taken; it follows that if they remain during these long months of study–work their commitment to it is likely to grow.

Even assuming positive results from the feasibility studies, the group must still participate in the final decision to go ahead, and it will be a necessary condition of the project's implementation that they have found their capital contributions and decided to go ahead with it. It is difficult to see how a stronger advance commitment to the enterprise by the prospective workforce could possibly be achieved.

Though capital contributions from group members and a positive set of feasibility studies will be necessary, they are not the only conditions for implementation. The balance of the required capital budget will also have to be found. Under Spanish regulations a new co-op may normally qualify for up to 20 per cent of its total starting capital from state funds. (These are normally provided through the Fondo Nacional de Proteccion al Trabajo at a 3 per cent interest rate and a maximum repayment period of ten years.) After the state money and the group members' contributions have been put together, the balance of the capital will have to come from the CLP. Hence the CLP will also have to participate positively in the final decision. In effect both the group and the CLP will have a right of veto.

Once a decision to go ahead has finally been taken – and in roughly four cases out of ten which start this is said to happen – the last pre-production phase is mainly one for the specialist sections of the 'empresarial' division. A site is identified and, if not already in the CLP's bank of land, purchased; the premises are built and the machinery is bought and installed. Then, perhaps two years after the first arrival of the group at the Bank's front door, production gets under way.

But the midwifing role of the 'empresarial' division is still not yet quite completed. The new enterprise's 'godfather' will continue to be closely associated with it for at least a year from the day production begins. During that period he will normally attend all meetings of the Junta Rectora and will be available for consultation with the management.

It should also be made clear that a new co-op may well not be expected to start showing a profit for up to two years – or indeed, in the perspectives of 1976, for even longer. More precisely, and other things being equal, the preparatory feasibility studies may well be regarded as satisfactory if the cash flow projections can show that the enterprise will start making a profit after the end of its first two years, or perhaps even later. During the projected loss-making phase debt will simply be accumulated, with the Bank. On the other hand, during any initial period of projected losses, the capital contributions of the founder members will be protected from being written down – otherwise, or so the argument goes, founder members would suffer unreasonably compared with subsequent recruits.

Despite the thoroughness of these procedures, many businessmen and bankers in my experience remain incredulous about the promotional success record of the 'empresarial' division. What other factors, if any, are involved?

Part of the answer may perhaps lie in the rather specially favourable conditions of the protected Spanish market for industrial goods, particularly until towards the end of the 1960s. Committed men with first class professional advice and all the necessary equipment were perhaps more likely to succeed in these conditions than they might have in Britain or France at the end of the 1970s. Another special, objective factor is that as the Mondragon group expanded it became an important market for intermediate goods. It may be no accident that a fair proportion of the new enterprises of the 1960s is classified as intermediate goods' producers.

Yet the 'empresarial' division has not only proved successful as a midwife of new enterprises – with the exception of the fishing boat co-op, all its 'babies' have so far survived. Have there been any special factors to explain this second success?

The first point to emphasize is that when a 'godfather' finally takes leave of a new co-op, that does not mean that the 'empresarial' division ceases to be interested in its fortunes – quite the contrary. Under the Contract of Association the co-op must submit regular control figures to the bank. The operative point is that these figures come through *monthly* – not just annually. By comparing actual results with projected budgets on a monthly basis the 'empresarial' staff should be in a position to foresee any serious difficulties before they become unmanageably large. Early corrective action should therefore be possible.

Moreover, if serious difficulties do arise the co-op is free to call on the 'empresarial' division for special assistance and will normally do so. The point is made by the 'empresarial' division's staff that given the men's commitment to the co-op's success, and their very real capital stake interest in warding off disaster, the Junta Rectora will normally have no hesitation about asking for help in times of trouble. For, given a properly trained and positively motivated workforce, or so the argument goes, the only real problems which can arise are technical management ones – and thus the Junta Rectora will have no guilt feelings about asking for help to solve them. Technical management problems are, of course, precisely those which the 'empresarial' division has been created to overcome.

When the 'empresarial' division is called in to help by a 'base' co-op, the outcome may well include a package of measures. If the existing executive manager is at fault, then the Junta Rectora may decide to dismiss him – this has happened on more than one occasion; if the main problem is associated with the product, then the product, as well as the manager, might be changed or modified. There is at least one case in which a product was completely changed.

In many cases, whatever the precise nature of the problem, additional finance will be needed before the co-op can be expected to resume profitable trading. In principle, provided that the men remain committed, and provided that the 'empresarial' division is satisfied with the proposed solution, its staff will recommend to the Bank that additional loans be extended. A new financial package will be arranged.

It does sometimes happen – and in the early struggling days of the first co-ops it evidently happened more often – that the worker–members of the co-op will make some direct contribution, in the shape of wages foregone, to the financial recovery of an enterprise. Unpaid extra hours may be worked in the evenings or at weekends; another possibility is opened up by the standard co-op practice of paying annual wages (anticipos) in fourteen monthly instalments, with one extra 'monthly' payment in the summer, the second at Christmas; it has been known for one of these payments to be waived; a third alternative is that previously projected and 'normal' increases in the co-op's rates of 'anticipos' may be postponed. Finally, under the terms of the Contract of Association, the men may have to accept that the lion's share of any losses are debited to their personal accounts.

Just as the worker–members of the co-op may accept some financial sacrifice as part of a recovery package, so may the CLP itself. Aside from that fishing boat venture, there have been no bad debts. On the other hand, the CLP *has* agreed to postpone interest payments which would otherwise have fallen due; on at least one occasion it has even agreed to a temporary lowering of interest rates on outstanding loans.

Though quantified data are not available, it seems clear that it is the combination of commitment plus the acceptance of some sacrifice on the member's side, with back-up professional support plus the possibility of new loans from the CLP, which is at the heart of any explanation of the almost total absence of failure among the Mondragon co-ops. Both elements seem crucial. The Bank's 'empresarial' division staff ensure the availability of management and professional expertise to find theoretical solutions to the co-ops' problems, the Bank's money means that time can be bought to see these through. On the other side the interest and commitment of the men – and their consequent readiness to make some sacrifices if necessary – mean that when a solution has been found on paper it will actually be implemented.

It could still be argued that the true reason for the absence of failure is that the CLP has simply not allowed any of the industrial co-ops to go bankrupt. Moreover, it might be further suggested that this is a misguided policy; that its real costs have been excessive and that the CLP profits would have been much higher if it had permitted some bankruptcies – and restricted its support to the most profitable co-ops only. There are two main answers to that. The first is that the CLP has in fact been highly profitable and has outperformed its local savings banks competitors by this and other yardsticks. The second is that the CLP's members, both individual and institutional, attach an independent importance to the creation and subsequent preservation of worth-while industrial employment. In that respect their success has been almost without parallel.

In the face of the group's record of job creation and preservation and of the vital contribution to that of the CLP in general and the division in particular, it would be perverse to believe that the Mondragon group could have achieved its growth without the CLP. There have been a number of necessary conditions for the group's success, but the CLP, and perhaps its 'empesarial' division in particular, is certainly one of them.

The success of the Mondragon co-ops is so striking both in absolute terms and, more particularly, by comparison with any other industrial co-ops or democratic enterprises at any time since the Industrial Revolution, that a large body of opinion remains sceptical about its validity. We may agree that more detailed studies are desirable and that 'case history' research into a sample of the individual co-ops would be valuable. Yet it seems inherently improbable to presume that these investigations would confront us with a picture radically different from the one I have tried to sketch. It seems implausible to believe, for example, that the co-ops have benefited from secret subsidies from some fairy godmother source – the Spanish state, the Basque Nationalists or the Vatican. It seems wildly unlikely that 'laundered' cash has been surreptitiously introduced into the system and thus that the group's apparent success is a fraud.

Common sense suggests that structural and institutional factors have played their part in the achievement as well as environment ones (market conditions), culture (Basque traditions and attitudes) and extraordinary personalities (Fr Arizmendi). This supposition of the importance of structural and institutional factors is reinforced by the consideration that the Mondragon group *is* distinguished in a number of these ways from all the other democratic and co-operative ventures which we have looked at. Though we may not be able to put them in order of importance, we *are* able to identify these key distinguishing features. I would suggest there are at least eleven:

1 Ultimate control rests firmly and democratically with the General Assembly of the entire workforce. No outsiders may be members; and no workers may not be members. This is the condition which ensures, at the very least, shop floor consent.

2 Each worker–member must purchase a significant capital stake in the co-op. The value of the stake will rise or fall depending on the fortunes of the enterprise. This is the condition which, by creating a direct link between the interests of the members and the enterprise, ensures genuinely responsible behaviour and a positive attitude to productivity.

3 A significant proportion of the co-op's capital is and remains collectively owned and indivisible. This is the condition which makes possible the indefinite survival of the enterprise.

4 The first initiative for the setting up of a new co-op comes from a group of ordinary working people and it is a necessary condition that the group should share in a positive decision to launch it. This ensures psychological commitment from the start.

5 Wage and salary differentials are fixed to take account of the needs for enterprise solidarity as well as of market constraints. This is the condition which ensures vertical solidarity within the enterprise and thus facilitates vertical team-work.

6 The separate executive functions of management are clearly defined and management, though appointed by and answerable to the co-op's elected representatives, normally enjoys security of tenure for periods of four years. This .is the condition which makes possible efficient and professional management.

7 The isolated individual co-ops have continuous access to a full range of high-level professional advice. This is the condition which makes it possible for relatively small-scale and independent units to compete successfully in the market.

8 The co-ops have access to capital which is at least not inferior to that enjoyed by their capitalist competitors. This is a necessary condition for expansion; and it is also an essential requirement if a co-op which runs into difficulties is going to have a real chance of pulling itself out.

9 The co-ops, partly through their support for local social and educational projects, enjoy strong backing from the community. This is a condition which is likely to produce considerable benefits in terms of high local morale.

10 The co-ops have access to, and to some extent control over, a continuous supply of new skilled and high-level manpower. This condition obviously confers a great comparative advantage in a world of rapidly changing techniques. It has also resulted, indirectly, in keeping the average age of the Mondragon group workforce quite unusually low. (For example, the average age of those working in the Bank's Empresarial division was no more than twenty-eight years and four months in mid-1976.)

11 Though the independence of the individual co-ops is jealously guarded they are essentially integrated into a group. In this way they have overcome the weakness which must always attach to an isolated co-operative venture.

The main question which this account of the Mondragon experience raises is clear enough. What we want to know is to what extent it has been these structural and institutional arrangements and to what extent those other cultural and personal leadership factors which have been responsible for the success. We can get a little way – but not very far – towards a non-controversial answer to this question by distinguishing between the early, heroic, pioneering moves and what happened later, once the first batch of co-ops and the Bank were firmly established. Clearly if it had not been for Fr Arizmendi those early steps could never have been taken. Quite possibly too, had the Basque environment in the 1940s not been what it was, those initiatives would never have happened.

However, an analysis of the ingredients of Mondragon's origins seems in a sense less important than an analysis of the ingredients of its later success. For at least theoretically it should be possible, copying the Mondragon model, to build a similar set of enterprises with a similar set of structural arrangements elsewhere. The question then is would those enterprises, once built, succeed as the Mondragon group has succeeded? Or would they fail because some essential Basque ingredient was missing? Short of an actual experiment there is not, so far as I know, any scientific way of establishing the answer. On the other hand, the structures and institutions which have been evolved at Mondragon seem so well suited to the realities and the real problems of democratic and co-operative enterprises, that it would be odd if other 'Mondragons' were to end in total disaster.

But perhaps the real problem is that the attitudes and values of which the Mondragon co-ops are both cause and effect – of collective and individual self-reliance, of collective and individual responsibility and of hard work – are so out of tune with the predominant attitudes in the welfare state, trade union and class-struggle dominated societies of the Atlantic world, that a genuine experiment could never be launched. Perhaps it would be too strongly opposed by the bureaucratic socialists; perhaps it would be seen as too much of a threat by the trade unions. In the end it may be factors of this kind, rather than the non-replicability of Basque culture, which will determine whether 'other Mondragons' have any real chance of getting off the ground and of emulating the Mondragon success.

11
Experience elsewhere

To look, as I have done in some detail, at the experience of workers' co-ops in Britain, France, Italy and in the Basque provinces of Spain, should not be taken to imply that there are no similar enterprises elsewhere; nor do I wish to imply that the examination of experience in those countries selected has been comprehensive. The justification is that we have enough evidence from the cases studied in detail to form reasonably firm conclusions about the necessary, though not perhaps the sufficient, conditions for the success of enterprises of this kind.

There is a second contention which may reinforce the justification for this selective treatment. For a series of historical reasons it is precisely in those four countries of Western Europe – Britain, France, Italy and Spain – that the existing institutions of private and state capitalism seem least acceptable to ordinary workers and that those institutions seem to be performing least well. Thus the search for new and more acceptable enterprise forms is more obviously urgent in those countries than elsewhere.

By contrast the situation appears to be qualitatively different in the US where a tough-minded and confident, traditional capitalism does not seem seriously threatened by working-class hostility and which can presumably look after itself in the face of criticisms from intellectuals or academics – whether associated with the *Monthly Review Press* or not. Similarly, though for rather different reasons in each case, the institutional *status quo* of mixed capitalism looks reasonably firmly rooted in social acceptance in the two next largest market economies – in the Federal Republic of Germany and in Japan. Equally, at the other end of the size scale, existing arrangements enjoy an apparently adequate measure of popular support in the smaller and more socially cohesive countries of Scandinavia, Switzerland, Austria, Holland and Luxembourg. (Owing to its division into two linguistic communities, close historical ties with France and relatively early industrial revolution, Belgium may be a special case. However, an examination of whether shop-floor attitudes in Belgium are more like those in Holland or those in France, falls outside the scope of this book.)

Just as workers' co-ops, or similar enterprises exist in other member countries of the Organization for Economic Co-operation and Development (OECD), so Third World and communist bloc countries also contain examples. There is, of course, also the experience, in Yugoslavia, of roughly thirty years' duration by the late 1970s – which I have referred to earlier. That experience would require at least book-length treatment on its own. Leaving that aside, the point to emphasize here is that statistics published by the International Co-operative Alliance (ICA) suggest that in its category of 'workers' production and artisan co-ops', there are more enterprises in Third World and communist bloc countries than in the OECD area.

The justification for less detailed treatment of those cases is partly the very different environment and partly their doubtful credibility. Even staunch co-operators will privately admit that scepticism may be in order in relation to some of the enterprises registered as industrial co-ops from communist and Third World countries. Some phantom enterprises may be included – like those phantom members of constituency Labour Parties who seem to figure on the registers of Transport House, and even when not phantoms they may be enterprises which would not qualify as genuine industrial co-ops in the West.

Notwithstanding these various qualifications, it seems sensible to glance, if briefly, at some of the experience elsewhere. I happen to believe that, in so far as I know and understand it, this other experience tends to confirm rather than confound the main lessons that emerge from the more detailed case studies. However, readers may well not want to take that on trust and this chapter will look at some relevant experience – in the communist countries (aside from Yugoslavia), in the Third World, in Western Europe again and in the US and Canada.

Either for historical and political reasons, or simply because none exist, no workers' co-ops from the Soviet Union or the German Democratic Republic are affiliated to the ICA or figure in its statistics. On the other hand, roughly half the affiliated European enterprises appear to come from five communist and centrally planned countries, namely Poland, Hungary, Bulgaria, Czechoslovakia and Roumania (see Table 11.1).

Of the workers' co-ops in these communist countries those in Poland have attracted most attention in the West and I shall look at them separately. As for the other four countries, common sense suggests that the relatively more liberal the environment in which the co-ops operate, the more independent they are, and the more real is their commitment to co-operative and democratic rules. It follows, for example, that in the middle and later 1970s, the workers' co-ops in Hungary were more

TABLE 11.1   Workers' productive and artisan co-ops affiliated to ICA

	1970	1974
Poland	2,741	2,333
Hungary	1,107	1,095
Bulgaria	702	702
Czechoslovakia	601	495
Roumania	409	375
Sub-total	5,560	5,000
Europe total	10,390	10,593

Source: Statistics of Affiliated Organizations, Comparative Statements 1973–4, ICA, London, 1977.

likely to resemble the genuine article than those in, say, Bulgaria. Common sense in addition to the information available from Poland also enables a reasonably confident guess about the part which these enterprises play in the national economy. Characteristically, on the Polish evidence, their role is to fill some of the gaps in the supply of goods and services which the centrally controlled state enterprises are simply too large to satisfy. Typically, on this view, they are small and medium-sized enterprises with a low ratio of capital to labour.

Before looking at the Polish evidence in any detail a word of general caution must be introduced. As will be seen, I do not believe that the basic statistics of Polish workers' co-ops are likely to be significantly more unreliable than figures from anywhere else; neither do I believe that their democratic arrangements are mainly bogus – for example that their secret ballots are a sham and the votes rigged. I also believe, on the evidence to which I have had access, that by the late 1970s the Polish workers' co-ops had achieved a measure of financial independence and thus some protection from continuous government surveillance and interference. However, when all that has been said a cautionary qualification is still necessary. The Polish workers' co-ops exist in a state controlled by the Communist Party through a powerful central bureaucracy. They are tolerated by the Communist Party but are in some sense only permitted a measure of real independence on sufferance for their good behaviour. And the authorities can always show where the final power rests – for example, by clearly indicating that a particular individual would be unacceptable to them in a senior leadership position or, as has also happened, by insisting that two successful co-op metal working enterprises be transferred to the state in 'exchange' for a clutch of small ones making things like waistcoat buttons or haberdashery.

In other words none of what follows should be seen as suggesting that the Polish workers' co-ops live other than under the shadow of the communist state. The Polish communists seemed, however, in the late 1970s to want to use their supreme and pervasive power with increasing discretion. So, like the country's Catholic church, the Polish workers' co-ops appeared in early 1978 to enjoy a limited measure of freedom; of course, like the Polish Catholics, they would have wished to enjoy a great deal more.

Polish co-ops of all kinds, agricultural, housing, consumers' and so on, as well as workers' co-ops, were the subject of a series of special studies in a Paris-based learned journal in 1975.* The basic statistics reproduced in those studies are in line with those of the ICA though not identical to them. Where they part company I shall follow the former. There are also some statistics of a later date acquired as a result of a visit to Poland in mid-1977 by my friend Lt-Col Alastair Campbell. I am grateful for his permission to draw on these.

These Paris studies confirm in broad outline the picture which emerges from ICA data of a real and substantial group of businesses significantly larger than any other similarly classified group elsewhere in Eastern Europe. There are more enterprises in the Polish group, and they are of significantly greater average size.

In 1974, according to the Paris data, 800,000 people were employed by the Polish workers' co-ops. In the country's manufacturing and service sectors together, these co-ops accounted in that year for one job in every eight. Moreover, by the mid-1970s average enterprise size was surprisingly large. The Paris data gives us an average employment figure of just over 330 per co-op − 800,000 people in 2,406 enterprises.† Campbell's figures indicate that by mid-1977 the average size was even larger: he reports that employment was then over 850,000 and that, as a result of the co-ops' continuing policy of amalgamations, the number of enterprises was only slightly more than 1,500. Thus by the late 1970s the average Polish workers' co-op was employing over 500 people.

However, the gratifying and startling picture presented by Campbell's figures needs to be qualified in three important ways which mean that we are not really entitled to think of the Polish economy as inhabited to a significant extent by enterprises which are, say, more like than unlike the Meriden Motorcycle co-op in the UK. First, some 150,000 of Polish co-op employment was accounted for in the mid-1970s by people working from their homes. Partly, no doubt, because of its large peasant and privately owned farming sector, there seems to be a special demand for work which can be undertaken at home, and on a flexi-time or part-time basis. The Polish workers' co-ops have apparently been rather successful

* *Archives Internationales de la Co-operation* no.38, 1975.
† Jean-Pierre Claveranne in *ibid.*, pp.22 and 23.

in meeting this demand. However admirable and imitable as these arrangements may be, this is clearly not the situation normally evoked by the picture of workers' industrial co-ops.

Another special sub-section is made up of enterprises which cater for disabled and handicapped people. They accounted for as many as one-quarter of all jobs provided by Polish co-ops in the mid-1970s. It was as if organizations like Remploy and others which offer protected employment in the UK, were structured as co-operative enterprises; quite possibly we have something to learn from the Poles in this case. But once again this is a special class of enterprise not normally structured on co-operative lines in other countries.

Third, the Polish co-ops' policy of amalgamations may result in a misleading picture for a quite different reason. A growing number of their jobs are in the service sector: garage and motor repair services, laundering, hairdressing, building repair and maintenance and so on. Characteristically, under the policy of amalgamations, all the co-op garages, or laundries, or builders in one town or region have been amalgamated into one single unit for organizational and accounting purposes. Yet this will clearly not, for the most part, have involved a physical coming together. The actual work places will typically remain scattered. There are doubtless good reasons for the policy, but the results must qualify our picture of the average Polish workers' co-op – employing over 500 people in 1977.

In the case of this last qualification there are no hard numbers to help quantify its importance. However, a reasonable guess is that not more than half – probably less – of the Labour force employed in Polish workers' co-ops in 1977 were normally fit people working full-time in manufacturing industry and in coherent units of more than 500. Even so the numbers would be large – almost certainly larger than those similarly employed in the whole of Western Europe and North America. It is to these Polish enterprises that we now turn.

In one of the Paris articles published in 1975, the Secretary General of the Polish workers' co-ops, Mr Bohdan Trampczynski,* distinguishes three main types of product in which Polish workers' co-op manufacture was of some importance:

1 Predominantly small articles which were not basic necessities: toys and dolls, folk art products, small objects of metal, leather or wood, paint brushes and other brushwear, etc.
2 Products which were supplied by large-scale state enterprises, but

---

* Bohdan Trampczynski, 'Participation de la co-operation industrielle au developpement socio-economique', in *ibid*., pp.33 and 36.

which needed to be offered in short runs of small batches: fashion goods (clothing, footwear or furniture) to satisfy changing individual and local tastes.

3 Products requiring very highly skilled manufacture: medical and laboratory apparatus, scientific instruments, measuring equipment and the like.

The same article supplies statistics of the percentage of the total Polish output of various products accounted for by the co-ops in 1974: clothing, 36.9%; footwear, 22.7%; other leather goods, 60%; medical laboratory equipment, 50%; hosiery, 20.2%; furniture, 20%; Christmas tree decorations, 78.5%; folk art products, 80%.

We can leave Christmas tree decorations, and folk art products aside; owing to fierce nationalism and strongly held religious beliefs, Polish demand may well be exceptional and untypical. For different reasons the importance of medical equipment may be a special case; perhaps it is connected with the co-ops' role in providing work for the physically handicapped and the disabled. The co-op suppliers of medical equipment may enjoy something of a special relationship with the market in this case. What remains is the importance of co-op production in three sectors – clothing, leather, furniture – which share the characteristics of requiring modest capital investment and of being exposed to relatively volatile changes in demand.

The Polish co-ops claim that in these areas, as elsewhere, they have to compete with both the state-owned and the residual private and single-family business sectors. They also claim that, while the co-ops received important government support in the early post-war years, they had become substantially self-financing by the end of the 1950s. They insist that there were no hidden subsidies from state funds which enabled them to survive and grow. Given the respect they have won from independent Western observers, it is probably right to accept these claims. On the other hand, in a country where consumer goods and services are in high demand and short supply, to compete successfully may not mean quite the same as it would in the West. There is also the point, conceded by Trampczynski in his article, that co-op wages are slightly below those in the state sector.

A better argument to support the claim of these co-ops to be genuinely efficient and competitive is provided, at first sight, by their success in export markets. According to their own statistics, whereas a mere 1.5 per cent of their output was exported in 1957, it had climbed to 12 per cent by 1975 when exports were valued at $200m. I see no sufficient reason to doubt these figures. However, we do not know what proportion of those exports consisted of semi-monopoly items – folk art products and Christmas tree decorations – supplied to meet the special demands, in the US, France, Britain and elsewhere, of the Poles of the post-war diaspora.

To some extent, therefore, judgment about the economic performance of these Polish workers' co-ops can be only provisionally favourable. On the other hand, both the French sources and Campbell suggest that we need have no serious reservations about accepting the reality of the democratic and co-operative structures which they have evolved. According to Campbell all (according to French sources 80 per cent) of those who work in them are members of these Polish co-ops. There seems to be no doubt that the membership elects the co-op's leadership by secret ballot on a one man one vote basis.

Most striking of all is the sophistication of the structures which have evolved – and the strong element of individual ownership which has been incorporated. Campbell has indeed argued forcefully that the Polish and the Mondragon models of workers' co-op are essentially the same. Some may hesitate to follow him quite that far, but there are important similarities.

To begin with, the elected leadership of the Polish workers' co-op hires and fires the management. Thus the function of management is quite clearly distinguished from the function of final control. The parallel with Mondragon is almost equally sharp when we move from management and control to ownership. As at Mondragon, so in the Polish co-ops, members – the entire workforce according to Campbell, 80 per cent on average according to the French source – must contribute a substantial capital stake: the figure is the equivalent of three months' salary. But there are provisions (as at Mondragon) for this capital sum to be deducted from wages, so no one is debarred from joining the co-ops through lack of savings.

The parallels with Mondragon in the financial arrangements adopted by the Poles go further. With regard to profit distribution there is the key provision that profits must be divided between individually and collectively owned funds. These proportions are not, it is true, identical. As we have seen, the share of profits which goes to collective funds in the Basque country is a variable and increases if the surplus rises above a pre-determined level. In the Polish co-ops the basic split, between individual and collectively owned profit shares, appears to be invariable: 50 per cent is credited to individual accounts; the balance goes to collective funds with a minimum of 10 per cent being deposited on an interest-bearing basis with the central co-op institutions for the development of the Polish workers' co-ops as a whole. Nevertheless, these differences of profit distribution arrangements between the Polish co-ops and those of Mondragon are clearly of minor account. The essential point is that each has developed an ownership and profit distribution structure which combines elements of both individual and collective ownership. As at Mondragon, so in Poland individual members may normally withdraw their capital stakes only when they leave the enterprise or in rather exceptional circumstances.

The Polish co-ops claim both that they have become financially strong (and largely self-financing) over the years and that this strength can be substantially attributed to the ownership and profit distribution arrangements. Again I cannot see sufficient reason to dispute these claims, and the parallel with experience at Mondragon appears to be rather striking.

Campbell argues that there is a further important parallel between the Polish and Mondragon co-ops. In effect he suggests that the federal body of these Polish co-ops, the Central Union founded in 1954, operates in very much the same way as the Caja Laboral Popular at Mondragon. Since not less than 10 per cent of enterprise profits must be deposited with it, it plays the part of a co-op central bank making loans to individual enterprises in support of their investment programmes. But, the Central Union, with the sectoral sub-federations into which the Polish workers' co-ops were regrouped in the 1970s, acts as a supplier of specialized management services and advice; the individual enterprises can and do take full advantage of these resources. It may be doubtful in the Polish case whether the links between individual units and the centre are as strong or as close as they are between the Mondragon enterprises and the Caja Laboral Popular. The Central Union was, after all, looking after some 1,500 enterprises in the late 1970s and covering the whole of Poland, whereas the CLP was responsible for no more than about seventy in a much smaller geographical area. All the same, Campbell seems to me to make an excellent case for the view that the parallels are strong. There is even a claim in the French sources that at least up to 1975 no Polish co-op which had applied for help to the Central Union had ever been let down; moreover, that there had been no casualties after a Central Union rescue operation had been mounted.

On the face of it, the achievement of these workers' co-ops in Poland is most remarkable. Setting out from the unpromising material and social conditions of post-war Poland, and with only a vestigial local tradition of 'cloth cap' and artisan co-ops to refer to, they succeeded in organizing themselves and then in building up a network of co-operative enterprises larger than anything of its kind anywhere else in the world. Moreover, on Campbell's evidence, they continued to grow and to create new employment right through the tough economic conditions of the mid-1970s. If their claims are to be believed, they did all or most of this, after some government help in the early stages, on the basis of their own resources.

It is tempting to suppose that these co-ops have somehow managed to elicit the support of nationalism and cultural pride for which their country has been famous for centuries. Perhaps too, given their relative independence from the Polish state, they have attracted their more enterprising, energetic and freedom-loving fellow countrymen. Without positing some ingredients of this sort their success seems almost baffling – even when full allowance is made for the sophistication and balance of their structures. For without some of those qualities it is hard to understand why, despite their relatively lower rates of pay, labour turnover in the co-ops is apparently quite modest.

The Polish workers' co-ops, so far at least as I understand the position, are rather a special case in Eastern Europe, in terms of quantity and, I suspect, in terms of quality. If, however, it is right to anticipate a gradual liberalization – and a growing assertion of national identities – in this whole area of Eastern Europe over the next generation then, I suppose, it may be reasonable to anticipate that the workers' co-ops in all these countries may also become gradually more important.

There is one final, if somewhat romantic and visionary, point which suggests itself. Let us suppose that over the next generation there is indeed a gradual development of the workers' co-ops of Eastern Europe. Let us suppose too that there is a parallel and more or less synchronized development of workers' co-ops in those countries of Western Europe – France, Spain, Italy and the UK – where they already have some sort of foothold. We might then foresee that links between similar enterprises, in Eastern Europe and in Western Europe, might come to form the first part of a bridge between the very different social, political and economic systems of the two areas. Co-op enthusiasts might indeed want to argue that such a bridge already exists in embryo in the shape of the industrial committee of the ICA, and they might point to the fact that among its senior elected officers are a Frenchman, an Italian and a Pole.

Before considering the Third World, we might note a certain congruence between the characteristic rhetoric of Third World political leaders and the moral values of non-exploitative group self-help which lie behind at least the 'high-minded' tradition of workers' co-ops elsewhere. There is an obvious affinity between the values of Kenneth Kaunda's 'Zambian humanism' – and of Julius Nyerere's intellectually much sharper mix of 'socialism and self reliance' – and those of the Christian Socialists in the last century, and perhaps, say, of Mahatma Ghandi. More generally and more recently anyone who spent time in the Third World in the 1960s or early 1970s will confirm that hardly a week passed without some new appeal from the political leadership for greater co-operative efforts towards the goals of national and community development. In short, and at least in the post-colonial period of generalized hostility to private capitalism, the political climate in developing countries has been apparently favourable to co-operative endeavour.

At a local and enterprise (or enterprise-cluster) level there have, it is true, been isolated examples of success on the part of workers' co-ops, or similarly structured operations in the Third World's post-colonial period. I know of the odd example at first hand, but the main story is rather different and it is in two parts. If we exclude the Chinese experience (which is still the subject of highly conflicting interpretation) part one of the story of workers' co-ops in the Third World is the record of general disaster where, as in Algeria after the departure of the 'pieds noirs', governments have backed these enterprises on any substantial scale. Part two of the story would be a discussion of why, despite their commitment to a highly congruent set of values, most Third World governments have not, in fact, given significant backing to enterprises of this type. That discussion could, of course, be extended far beyond the limits of this book, but it is not difficult to guess what a Marxist contribution to it would be; nor is it difficult to think of two other relevant factors. Political leaders in the Third World were clearly as much affected as anyone else in the 1960s and early 1970s by the glamour of large-scale enterprises and by the value of size for its own sake. They may also have sensed correctly that successful co-op enterprises are easier to prescribe than to achieve.

The curious upshot of all this is that the great bulk of the 'Workers Productive and Artisanal Co-ops' affiliated to the ICA from the Third World in the mid-1970s were children, not of the post-colonial period of co-operative values, but of the colonial period itself. More than 80 per cent of the affiliations came from four countries in the Indian Ocean area: from India, Pakistan, Bangladesh and Sri Lanka. The breakdown of Third World workers' productive and artisan co-ops affiliated to the ICA in 1974 is given in their statistics: Asia, 29,746; Latin America, 358; Africa, 1,298; (total: 31,420); India, Bangladesh, Pakistan and Sri Lanka, 26,031.

A UN report* of the late 1960s points to the fact that the great bulk of these Indian Ocean area workers' co-ops date from the colonial period. It records a set of comparative figures from the same countries at the time

---

* *Nature and Role of Industrial Co-operatives in Industrial Development*, United Nations Industrial Development Organisation, Vienna, 1969.

it was written. There were then roughly half as many enterprises again of this type – just over 39,000 against just over 26,000 in 1974. Moreover the report makes clear that a large proportion were co-ops of hand-loom weavers, and it traces these back to an initiative taken by the government of Madras (possibly as a result of prodding from Ghandi) in 1923. True, it also reports the existence of workers' co-ops other than those of hand-loom weavers: of brickmakers, shoe makers, carpenters, tanners, potters, basket makers and so on. It seems clear, nevertheless, that the co-ops of hand-loom weavers were by far the most important – at least by any measurement of turnover – and that the bulk of these enterprises were born in the period of British rule. It seems most probable that the numbers have been gradually running down from a peak which occurred some time during the colonial period. The run down may indeed have been faster than the 1974 ICA figures suggest, for it is widely believed that its affiliation totals may well include large numbers of dormant enterprises. The key point, in any event, is that this is basically a set of enterprises born from the mixed loins of British colonial paternalism and Ghandi's enthusiasm for the spinning-wheel. They may well be of considerable academic and historical interest, but their potential for impact in the late 1970s and beyond seems likely to be small.

The Latin American contribution to Third World experience of workers' co-ops is much smaller than that of Asia – if the ICA figures and if the same 1960s UN report, are to be believed. The relative Latin American contribution is indeed even more lop-sidedly small if we confine ourselves to ICA affiliations; this suggests that 349 of the continent's 358 workers' co-ops in 1974 were concentrated in Argentina. When the UN report was written, the transport industry accounted for the largest number of those Argentinian enterprises. At the same date there were even larger numbers of transport co-ops – for river, sea, overland traffic – in Mexico. It is not clear whether these latter had succumbed by the mid-1970s or whether they simply chose not to affiliate to the ICA.

The same and other sources report the existence of a handful of Latin American enterprises which started capitalist undertakings and were transformed into workers' co-ops after running into difficulties of one kind and another: two cement plants and a newspaper in Mexico, and an aircraft repair works in Costa Rica, for example. Given the political and economic climate in which all these Latin American enterprises have been operating what may be most surprising is that any have existed at all. Moreover, from a British standpoint, it would be quite wrong to be dismissive about the record – there were apparently many more co-operative enterprises in Argentina than in the UK in the mid-1970s, and in the prevailing conditions really heroic efforts may perhaps have been required even to survive. On the other hand, it seems improbable that we should learn any major new lessons if it were possible to study them in detail.

In Africa, my own experience of two African countries suggests that the ICA's figures should be treated with more than usual caution. For what it is worth, of the ICA's 1974 continental total of 1,298, more than 1,000 affiliated enterprises were Nigerian – with the balance split between Zambia, Tanzania, Mauritius, Uganda and Kenya. Due to President Julius Nyerere's evident commitment to radical policies, it may perhaps be that the enterprises affiliated from Tanzania are serious undertakings and more or less genuine examples of workers' co-ops. However, in the other cases, and particularly perhaps that of Zambia (which registered the second largest number of such affiliated enterprises), and of Nigeria itself, I would be sceptical about both the numbers and the genuineness of the co-operative structures involved. There may well be real examples, as that UN report suggests, of tiny groups of woodcarvers, potters and the like, which are organized formally or informally on a co-operative type basis. But I would doubt whether the reality goes very much further.

On the other hand, whether my scepticism about these African workers' co-ops is well or ill founded the common-sense point for this book concerns not so much their reality as their relevance; to a greater or less extent, it applies to enterprises of this kind throughout the Third World. The point is that, particularly in Africa and Asia, the material and technical conditions – and the availability of capital – are such that the experience of any contemporary workers' co-ops is almost bound to be very different from the experience of their counterparts in more developed areas. Perhaps above all, the case for workers *industrial* co-ops is certain to be very different in countries where the majority of the population still works on the land and where the main priority is to devise arrangements which will increase *agricultural* production. My conclusion is, therefore, that while there are certainly some isolated examples of successful workers' co-ops in the Third World, and while a study of their history may well be of considerable academic interest, they do not in the late 1970s have much to tell us about how these enterprises may develop either over the next decade or so or in the economically more advanced parts of the world.

For the student of workers' co-ops and similarly structured enterprises, to cross the Atlantic and to switch attention to the relevant US experience, whether of the late 1970s or of earlier generations, is to move into an environment which is in one respect strikingly different. Compared with the situation in Western Europe the strength and authority of US private capitalism seemed in the late 1970s to be unshaken and only marginally challenged. And so it must have seemed, with only minor qualifications in particular industries and at particular times, for most of the 150 odd years since the serious start of US industrialization. For US private capitalism has simply not had to face the sustained hostility of a strong working-class movement and of powerful trade unions ideologically committed to its replacement. Expressed in a different way, an acceptance of the basic legitimacy of the capitalist system has extended much further down the social and income scales in the US than it has in Western Europe.

This legitimacy appears to be reflected in American experience of workers' co-op type enterprises in the late 1970s, which thus differs from the experience in Europe. Most of these enterprises seem to come much closer to models of workers, capitalism – or to the ideas of the 'Working Class Ltd' current in the UK in the 1860s and 1870s – than do their contemporary counterparts in Western Europe. The differences must not be exaggerated. I am also far from clear whether we could trace them back to a similar set of differences in the last century even if the data were available. But in the situation of the 1970s it is impossible for the fair-minded student not to be struck by them. Characteristically the American workers' co-ops of the 1970s are based – in contrast to many in Europe – on fully individuated worker–ownership and on individual shares in enterprise asset growth. It is as if working people in America have felt much less inhibited than their European brothers and sisters about acknowledging the little capitalist inside them – and that may be true. It is obviously tempting too, to relate this acknowledgment to that very much more extended US acceptance of the legitimacy of private capitalism – and to the absence of any really sustained working-class challenge to it. Unlike the situation in Europe, it seems implausible to suppose that social and political forces in America will eventually result in collectively owned, but worker controlled and democratic enterprises; on the other hand they just might result in some form of capitalism-for-the-workers or *granulated* capitalism.

However, after giving due emphasis to this apparent ideological difference, the fair-minded student will find that the actual record of these enterprises on the two sides of the Atlantic is, on the face of it, remarkably similar. Both records can be traced back at least as far as Owenite and other millennialist ventures with world-amending goals in the first third of the nineteenth century; again, both have gone through phases when the great bulk of new initiatives have been of the 'cloth cap' co-op or artisan enterprise type; in both we find examples of enterprises given away to their workforces by 'high-minded' or otherwise motivated private capitalists; in both again we find examples of private capitalists being bought out by their workforce. On the American as well as the European side of the Atlantic, the number of such enterprises began to grow in the 1970s as efforts were made to save jobs following capitalist disinvestment or failure. Comparing the records in the UK and the US, it also seemed in the late 1970s as if both the cumulative historical total of such enterprises and the number of still operational survivors was remarkably similar – roughly 500 in the case of the cumulative totals and somewhere between thirty and fifty survivors.

For reasons of space and of inaccessibility of data, the pre-1970s US record can be sketched but briefly. However, Derek Jones* has pulled together most of the best available statistics dealing with the period to 1939 and these were published in a Yugoslav journal in 1977. His tables include a figure of 421 for the cumulative total of such US enterprises, for which there is reasonably reliable evidence, over the period covered. They indicate various phases of apparent mushrooming in the numbers of new initiatives, particularly in the 1880s and then again in the generation from 1910 to the outbreak of the Second World War. Jones also draws attention to a number of clusters of US workers' co-ops concentrated in particular industries and in particular areas over the long period which he covers down to 1939: co-operative cooperages in Minneapolis, co-operative foundries in New York, boot and shoe co-ops in Massachusetts and shingle weaving co-ops in Washington. Of course, there have been similar clusters in the UK record – of boot and shoe, and clothing co-ops in the East Midlands, for example. Evidently a successful workers' co-op on either side of the Atlantic has been capable of producing some kind of demonstration effect and thus of stimulating parallel initiatives in the same area.

Of the various clusters which Jones identifies the survivors of two almost certainly accounted for more than half of the US 'workers' co-op sector' in the mid-1970s. These are a group of plywood co-ops concentrated in the region of the Pacific North West and a group of refuse-collecting enterprises in the San Francisco area. The earliest enterprise in each of the two clusters was started between the wars, and each seems to be more or less closely linked with particular immigrant communities: with Scandinavians in the case of the plywood co-ops and with Italians in the case of the refuse-collecting ones. Some approximate

---

* *Economic Analysis and Workers' Management* vol. 11, 1977, pp. 3–4.

data for the two clusters in the mid 1970s is set out in Table 11.2.

TABLE 11.2   The refuse collecting and plywood co-ops of San Francisco and the Pacific North West

	Refuse collection	Plywood
No. of enterprises surviving	18	12
Total since first was founded	26	12 +
Size range by workforce	80–450	15–400
Size range by turnover	$3m–$15m	$250,000–$10m

Sources: 'Plywood Co-operatives', Paul Bernstein in *Working Papers for a New Society* vol. 2, no. 2, pp. 24–34. Raymond Russell *et al.*, 'Refuse Collecting Co-operatives', in *Working Papers for a New Society* vol. 5, no. 2, pp. 30–6, supplemented by author's estimates.

The enterprise structures which have been adopted in these two clusters of workers' co-ops are very similar and seem at least in part, to reflect an ideology of workers' capitalism. Enterprise membership is defined by shareholdings and in both these must be paid for by the individuals concerned. The majority, though by no means all workers, are shareholders and thus full members. In both it is not normal, though in neither is it unknown, for non-workers (e.g. those retired or those temporarily working away from the co-op) to retain their shareholding and thus their membership and the rights which go with it. On the other hand, they include important and essentially egalitarian provisions governing the inter relationships of the members: no member's shareholding may be larger than any others; the income of members will normally be the same, except to the extent that some have chosen to work longer hours than others.

Enterprise control rests clearly with the General Meeting of all members. In each case the General Meeting is the body which elects the board of directors, but in the plywood enterprises the board is essentially a policy-making one which appoints a non-member general manager – and sometimes supporting executives – to handle day-to-day business management. In the refuse collecting co-ops, on the other hand, the elected board itself appears to undertake all or most of the main management tasks.

There have, it is true, been failures and liquidations among both sets of enterprises, hence it would be quite wrong to claim that when a shareholding has been purchased there has been no associated risk. There is also strong anecdotal evidence that members of successful enterprises have been in a position to enjoy substantial capital gains. For example it has been reported that a member's shareholding in the Sunset Scavenger Co. of San Francisco was redeemed for $12,000 in 1959 and that the corresponding figure in 1975 was $50,000. In another case, among the plywood enterprises, workers' shareholdings are reported to have sold for $200,000.

More information about relative performance and productivity is available relating to the plywood co-ops than to the refuse-collecting group. Paul Bernstein, the compiler of data on the plywood enterprises, quotes a study in the 1950s which found that output in the co-ops averaged 115-20 sq. ft of plywood per man hour compared with 80-95 sq. ft in conventional capitalist companies; and the same article claims that the corresponding figures in the 1960s were 170 sq. ft and 130 sq. ft respectively. Even more strikingly it refers to an acknowledgment by the US Internal Revenue Service and by the relevant tax court judges that overall productivity was 25 to 60 per cent higher in these plywood co-ops than in their conventional counterparts. It is probable that similar structures resulted in similar productivity benefits in the case of the refuse-collecting co-ops. The only relevant evidence which I have been able to find for them – in the article cited earlier – is that their worker–members (though not their worker non-members) normally received substantially higher incomes than would be expected for the going rate for the job outside. In the Sunset Scavenger Co. and in the Golden Gate Disposal Co. worker-members are reported to have enjoyed minimum annual incomes of between $19,000 and $21,000 in 1976 compared with a pre-overtime minimum rate of $14,000 outside.

These plywood and refuse collecting co-ops, however, would have provoked the wrath of the Webbs. Notwithstanding both their measure of success and the real elements of inter-membership egalitarianism in their structures, they offer examples of precisely those two kinds of 'degeneration' which the Webbs saw as the inescapable doom of democratic enterprises. They offer examples of enterprises which have 'degenerated' by selling themselves out to capitalists, and all or nearly all these enterprises have also 'degenerated' in the second sense identified by the Webbs: they have recruited non-member workers. Although these non-members have normally remained in a minority, it is clear from all the published accounts that, both in terms of income and of other conditions, they have tended to be treated as second-class citizens.

Professor Vanek, based at Cornell in the US and knowledgeable about these enterprises, would reformulate these criticisms in more technical language, and add to them: he would see the recruitment of non-member workers as due to the mistake of vesting enterprise control in shares rather than in work; he would also argue that the fully individuated ownership structures adopted by these co-ops is a further mistake; he would go some way towards agreeing with the Webbs in that line of criticism and argue that such structures are bound to expose the isolated workers' co-op to the possibility – even the probability if they are successful – of capitalist take-over. He would further argue that such structures amount to inefficient mini capital markets and produce 'sub-optimal' investment decisions. Finally, he would argue that long-term solutions for ensuring the stability of workers' co-ops cannot be found in an individual enterprise basis but must be sought in federated groups. As to that, it is important to make clear that while these plywood and refuse collecting co-ops may be seen as genuine clusters, concentrated in one area and in one industry, the individual enterprises have always remained fully independent and have made no attempt to form themselves into federal groupings.

In so far as I am qualified to express an opinion, I would endorse all these criticisms of Professor Vanek. On the other hand it would, I think, be perverse if these criticisms were allowed to obscure the very real achievements of these enterprises or the evidence they offer of greatly improved work motivation. After all, a majority in both cases have survived – and a majority in both cases had survived by the late 1970s for more than twenty years. They also appear to demonstrate substantial comparative advantages in both productivity and annual incomes, and at the same time to offer the prospect of quite handsome capital gains. Of course, it is true that their results have been achieved partly at the expense of those second-class citizens in the non-member worker category, but the available evidence suggests that that has been a fairly minor part and that real comparative advantages would still have been demonstrated even if no non-member had ever been recruited. I would conclude that, while these refuse collecting and plywood co-ops may not tell us anything new, and while they should doubtless be encouraged to modify their structures in line with the criticisms of Professor Vanek, their record on balance is highly positive and encouraging. Certainly, were I ever to switch to full-time refuse collection, I would much sooner join one of those San Francisco co-ops – provided I could avoid non-member worker status – than I would enroll in a similar operation run by a private capitalist or the local authority. And one cannot help wanting to know whether Mr Wedgwood Benn (or rank and file members of the Tribune Group) would make the same choice or not!

If we exclude a growing number of democratically structured mini-enterprises in the wholefood and similar lines of business, the second main component of the North American workers' co-op sector in the late 1970s was accounted for by a group of essentially job-saving enterprises. They had emerged in their new forms not earlier than around the mid-1970s. All had previous 'incarnations' as straight capitalist undertakings and had been re-established as workers' co-ops following voluntary or forced decisions by former owners to wind them up. A total of five were being actively studied by the New Systems of Work and Participation Program at Cornell University when I visited there in 1977, but no one knows what the total figure around the US and Canada may be. Some of those to whom I spoke at Cornell suspected that it was not less than a dozen. To illustrate the point the following three are job-saving co-ops in the US and Canada (1977): Byers Transport, Alberta, providing road transport; the Saratoga Knitting Mill, Saratoga (NY), making knitwear; the Vermont Asbestos Group, Lowell (Vt) producing asbestos fibre.

No single or uniform enterprise structure was adopted by these enterprises when they took on their new form. In line with the plywood and refuse collecting co-ops, all vested final control in the ownership of shares and not in the mere fact of working – and all allowed for individual ownership. Unlike the plywood or refuse collecting co-ops on the other hand, they did not insist that all shareholdings be equal. Moreover, in at least one case, that of the Vermont Asbestos Group (VAG), members of the local community were permitted to subscribe for a minority of the shares.

Because of a spectacular increase in the price of its shares, the Vermont Asbestos Group attracted most attention of these various enterprises up to the end of 1977. The workforce and others who had purchased shares in the new venture in March 1976 had paid just $50 for each of them. In August 1977 a formal offer of $2,500 was put to stockholders by a local group of Vermont businessmen. For various reasons this offer did not prove generally acceptable. A few months later a sale was reported to be under discussion at $3,000 per share.*

It would indeed be encouraging for advocates of workers' co-ops if it could be realistically claimed that this spectacular rise in VAG's share price was attributable mainly to improved work motivation and consequent upward adjustments of productivity. In fact, very different factors seem to have been involved. The original selling price agreed with the former conglomerate owners, General Analene and Film, had been low, and the shares had been very highly geared in relation to much larger amounts of bank borrowing – which had been guaranteed by the Vermont Industrial Development Corporation. Then again asbestos fibre prices had shown a sharp increase between March 1975 and the end of 1976. Finally, the new workers' co-op at Lowell in upper state Vermont, succeeded in renegotiating with the US Environmental

---

* For fate of Vermont Asbestos Group, see 'Asbestos Farm', *The Economist*, 22 April 1978, p. 59.

Protection Agency a series of very tough and expensive remedial measures which had previously been imposed on General Analene.

In fact there was at best, no more than anecdotal evidence of improved worker productivity when I was at Lowell in mid-1977. The level of conflict at the mine was such that it seemed doubtful whether there were any net productivity gains at all. The sources of conflict were not hard to identify. Differential share ownership had not been prohibited – as it is in the plywood and refuse collecting co-ops – and on average, the staff and management members held substantially more shares per head than ordinary shop-floor workers. These two groups, blue-collar and white-collar, shop floor and management, had come to control roughly equal blocks of shares in the mine when I was there in 1977. The result, by all accounts, was that normal antagonisms between shop floor and management had become, if anything, more exacerbated at Lowell after two years of worker ownership than they had been before.

It would be unfair to judge these North American job-saving co-ops by the very abnormal record of the Vermont Asbestos Group. It would be absurd to judge them a success because of a spectacular rise in the VAG share price. It would be equally absurd to judge them a failure because the change of structure at the Lowell asbestos mine seems to have increased rather than diminished conflict. In general it was, of course, far too early to say with any confidence at the end of 1977 how these enterprises would develop.

However, the point is that even if they should all fail, it will almost certainly be legitimate to argue that their record should not be taken as condemning workers' co-ops of the right kind. For such evidence as there is suggests that their structures are at fault and, because they allow differential share ownership and vest control with shares, even more faulty than those of the refuse collecting and plywood co-ops. But the more likely upshot seems to be that they will produce both positive and negative evidence. It will then be possible to see the North American experience of workers' co-ops – despite its emphasis on individual ownership – as very similar to that in the main countries of Western Europe though not, of course, to that of the industrial co-ops in the Basque provinces of Spain.

With one main exception, which I shall come on to at the end, workers' co-ops and similar enterprises in areas of Western Europe other than France, Italy and the Basque provinces of Spain, seemed in the late 1970s to present a picture very similar to that in the UK. In other words they were small groups of predominantly small enterprises. Characteristically too these were co-ops of two main generations and types. There were a few surviving artisan enterprises with their roots and inspiration in the European co-operative movement of the late nineteenth century. Alongside these venerable survivors there were examples of workers' co-op type enterprises which went back no further than the post-war period, and which in many cases were the creations of the 1970s. This latter category included some co-operative enterprises which started life as conventional capitalist undertakings. In total these other Western European co-ops probably employed fewer than 20,000 people. On the other hand, despite their marginal character, these enterprises were beginning to attract a disproportionate degree of attention in the second half of the 1970s.

The situation in Holland, for example, in late 1977 exhibited many of the characteristics which I have argued are typical. There was no doubt about the level of interest: two high powered research studies, one trade union and the other government funded, were under way. A year before, a comprehensive academic study had been published covering all the known workers' co-ops in Holland between 1901 and 1958. (It showed, not surprisingly, that few had survived; the record was one of courage and effort but also very largely of failure.) Evidence of a less theoretical revival of interest was provided by the astonishing flow of enquiries reported by Holland's federation of workers' co-ops − the Associatie van Bedrijven of Co-operatieve Grodslag (or the ABC for short). Enquiries, both from companies interested in transforming themselves into co-ops and from people with ideas about starting new co-operative type ventures from scratch, had been reaching the federation's Utrecht office at a rate of about one per week from the beginning of 1975.

As against this evidence of undoubted interest, the best informed guess about the number of actual workers' co-ops in Holland at the end of 1977 put the figure between fifty and sixty. With one main exception, all of these were thought to be in the category of small or very small enterprises. One reason for the uncertainty, and the consequent need for guess-work, was that only a minority of Holland's workers' co-ops chose to affiliate to the ABC in 1977 − no more than a dozen, with a combined workforce of about 1,400 and a turnover of some £34m.

Yet even these modest total figures may give a misleading picture of the typical Dutch workers' co-op. For three building enterprises together accounted for about 1,200 of this total workforce and a co-operative of consulting engineers accounted for a further 100. It follows that a majority (eight) of the co-ops affiliated to the ABC in 1977 employed together not much more than 100 people. Two of these were, in fact, little co-operative architectural ventures involving not more than ten people together; under English law, neither architects nor engineering consultants would normally be eligible to adopt a co-operative enterprise form.

It was the largest of the Dutch workers' co-ops which seemed in 1977 to be the most interesting and the most appropriate for comparative attention. This is a building enterprise, Co-op Bouwbedrijf H. Moes b.v. based at Zwolle in north central Holland with a total workforce of roughly 900. It had been founded, in conventional capitalist form, by Mr H. Moes in 1932 and became a co-operative on the founder's retirement in March 1976. Both by turnover (roughly £20m) and by workforce size it was then, almost certainly, among the twenty-five largest building enterprises in Holland, with the bulk of its work accounted for by local authority housing and the balance from a combination of industrial and commercial projects.

Essentially this Dutch building enterprise was transformed into a co-op because no member of the family's younger generation wished to take over the business when its founder, Mr Moes, came up for retirement. Various alternative futures were, however, very much discussed before the final decision to restructure the enterprise on co-op lines was actually taken. There seems to be no doubt that a straightforward sale to outside financial interests could have been negotiated without too much difficulty. On the other hand, senior management was opposed to that course. It was argued strongly, among other things, that a new set of conventional owners might well not be in sympathy with the active policies of fostering good industrial relations which the company had evolved.

More important, perhaps, than this rejection of a straightforward sale to a fresh set of capitalists, was the very thorough preparatory work which was done before the new co-op structure was approved. An industrial sociologist was commissioned, with the full support of the local trade unions, to enquire into the reactions of the workforce. His researches were launched in March 1974, two years before the actual conversion took place. His findings seem to have been genuinely unambiguous: a majority of the workforce, both blue- and white-collar, was in favour of a co-operative form.

The particular form chosen has at its centre the concept of a completely collectivized ownership. The co-op's membership — and membership is open to the entire workforce subject only to a probationary period — owns the assets of the business as a collective owner. The main arguments which determined this choice of form were that in this way the co-op would be protected against decapitalization and against any capital transfer taxes in the future. These arguments were held to outweigh the main consideration which points in the opposite direction: the lower motivation which may be expected when co-operative ownership is completely collectivized.

For his part Mr Moes agreed to sell the business to the new co-op for a price of Flrs 4.25m (or roughly £1m). He further agreed that he would advance Flrs 1m of this sum to the co-op, interest free, for five years. The balance of the purchase price was put up by the banks, and the transaction was generally seen as favourable to the co-op: Mr Moes could well have settled for significantly more in a straightforward sale to a capitalist buyer.

Of course, the co-op's experience was really too short by the end of 1977 to permit any confident judgments about its long-term future. However, profit levels in the first year of trading as a co-op were considered satisfactory by management and judged to be very much in line with, if not slightly better than, the average for similar sized Dutch building enterprises. Yet perhaps the main point emphasized by the co-op's management at the end of 1977 was the excellence of its relations with the trade unions. It emphasized also in that context that union support for the whole conversion exercise had been of crucial importance.

It was perhaps the much more positive attitude of the trade unions towards the idea of workers' co-ops which distinguished the late-1970s situation in Holland from that in, say, the UK. It is not only that the relevant unions were supportive and helpful about the conversion exercise in Zwolle. Evidence of trade union open mindedness is provided by their sponsorship of that research project into workers' co-ops mentioned earlier. Most strikingly of all, through an agreement with the ABC federation, the Dutch trade unions, via the union-controlled Koopmans bank, are prepared to participate in the financing of co-operative ventures.

A rather similarly positive set of trade union attitudes is to be found in Denmark which offers another parallel with the situation in Holland. The question of how many workers' co-ops and similar enterprises there are – and of how many people they employ – is at least as hard to answer with regard to Denmark. The latest statistics published by the ICA in London offer the surprising figure of 70,000 Danish members of Workers' Productive and Artisan Co-ops in 1974. It is freely admitted that that is wrong and may overstate the true position by a factor of ten. (The explanation seems to be that customers of the fairly large number of Danish 'canteen co-ops' are classified as members of these enterprises.) There is also considerable doubt about the actual number of Danish enterprises, with estimates ranging from under 100 to about 150.

Like the corresponding groups in Holland and the UK these Danish co-ops* include survivors from the age of comparative co-operative flowering at the end of the last century as well as much more recent creations. As elsewhere, too, they include conversions from capitalist beginnings as well as enterprises which started as co-ops. Like the position in France, a large proportion of these Danish co-ops – more than half according to one estimate, slightly less than half according to another – is accounted for by enterprises engaged in building and civil engineering. More unusually, at least compared with other European experiences, the bulk of the balance is made up by enterprises in just two other areas: bakeries and commercial canteens.

I suspect that for a number of reasons – German influence being one, the dominant position of agriculture in the country's co-operative tradition another – the environment in Denmark is probably less conducive than in Holland for any substantial development of workers' co-ops. There is an added similarity with West Germany in that since the war both countries have been much more successful than, say, France and the UK in seeing to it that small and medium-sized enterprises are able to compete in the market. Since medium and small-sized firms are the most obvious candidates, there are likely to be proportionately fewer conversions in West Germany and Denmark than in the UK or in France.

In West Germany itself there were workers' co-ops in the second half of the nineteenth century, as there were elsewhere in Western Europe. A request on their behalf, that they should be granted financial aid from the state was even put to Bismark. But these early German versions of 'cloth cap' and artisan co-ops seem, if anything, to have been even less successful than they were elsewhere. Bismarck's early social welfare legislation may partly explain the difference. German acceptance of authority and the absence (anyway before 1945) of any strong traditions of democratic freedom and personal independence may well be other relevant factors.

In any event, and if anything more so than in the UK, the German co-operative movement turned away from production and strongly into consumer co-ops and credit unions before the end of the nineteenth century; what has characterized subsequent German history has not been a sector of workers' co-ops but more a sector of 'commonweal' (Gemeinwirtschaft) enterprises. The latter have the legal form of joint stock companies but are owned and controlled by the trade unions or the

---

* I am indebted to Paul Derrick for help on the Danish co-ops.

consumer co-ops or by a combination of the two. After a forced interruption during the Hitler period, they were revived after the Second World War and have developed strongly since, particularly in the areas of banking, insurance and housing.

The upshot in the late 1970s was that as a result of these and other factors, anything which could properly be called a workers' co-op sector was even more diminutive in West Germany than elsewhere in Western Europe. It is true that one medium-sized glassworks was transferred into the control of its workforce in the 1960s, and there are very likely to be at least a handful of similar cases. There are also bakery co-ops, but these latter are apparently more like co-operative groupings of very small enterprises than workers' co-ops in the strict sense. Very little else in the way of actual co-operative enterprises appeared to exist in West Germany in the late 1970s. Given the country's rather different traditions, its relative success in maintaining a vigorous sector of small and medium-sized firms — and, of course, the much more general popular acceptance of the legitimacy of capitalism — it seemed unlikely in early 1978 that the position in West Germany would change very much over the next decade.

The only other Western European country for which the latest (1974) ICA statistics showed affiliations in the category 'Workers' Productive and Artisan Co-ops' was Switzerland. A total of forty-two such enterprises were recorded. No doubt such affiliations have to be treated with caution. On the other hand there is an obvious congruence between the values of sturdy Swiss independence — and those implicit in the country's cantonal political arrangements — and the values underlying one particular tradition of independent workers' co-ops. More specifically too, the historic anarchism of the Swiss mountain watch-makers of the last century will have tended to dispose them favourably towards co-operative values. Conversely, the very success of Swiss capitalism suggests that these values and traditions may well be losing their influence and that, at the least, there is unlikely to be any very vigorous search in Switzerland for alternative enterprise forms. However in the meantime, and rather surprisingly, a small number of workers' co-ops in Switzerland apparently survive.

Though the ICA statistics show no affiliations of workers' co-ops from either Norway or Sweden, evidence of the existence of some Swedish enterprises of this kind became available in 1976. The results of a private survey which then appeared suggested that there were forty-five such enterprises in Sweden, employing about 2,400 people. According to Col Campbell (to whom I am indebted for this information), these were all of fairly recent origin and had all formerly been capitalist undertakings. Following the survey's publication, a government committee has, again according to Campbell, started to examine the possibility of promoting a workers' co-op sector in the Swedish economy. On the other hand, so centralized is the Swedish labour movement and its traditions that it seems improbable that anything much will come from this initiative.

The final enterprise of this type which I want to include in this study is SALTUV in Valencia. It was glanced at among those thumb-nail sketches of a handful of workers' co-ops on pp 16 ff. Here I wish to look at it in slightly more detail, partly because aside from those San Francisco refuse collection co-ops it is the only example, so far as I know, of a municipal-type enterprise structured as a workers' co-op. On the other hand, there seems to be no logical reason why municipal services – assuming that people are prepared to pay for them – should not be sold to the public by enterprises structured in that way.

In the post war years, Valencia's urban transport was still the concession of a private capitalist concern. However, the concession was due to expire in 1964 and the company did not take the sort of anticipatory steps which would have evidenced a serious interest in getting it renewed. Plant and equipment were allowed to run down and no effort was made to replace what was essentially a tramway system with more modern arrangements. A small group of employees – three tram drivers, a maintenance mechanic and a clerk – did however start to express concern about their own and the system's future well before the concession ran out. As the result of a skilful lobbying exercise it was finally agreed that from mid-1964 a concession should be granted to a new workers' enterprise, SALTUV, which should receive Pesetas 60m (£500,000) as a once and for all capital grant from official funds.

In modernization terms SALTUV's record in the years which followed was impressive enough. All the old trams had been replaced by the end of 1971, and though trolley buses had been initially included as an important element in the programme they, in turn, had been all but phased out when I visited Valencia in early 1977. Moreover, these modernization exercises were carried through against the difficult background of ever-increasing traffic in the Valencia area in the 1960s and 1970s.

It was not only that increased private traffic made modernization and efficient urban public transport more difficult. After a peak in 1961 to close on 117m passenger journeys, the demand for SALTUV's services began to fall sharply. Apart from the competition of the private motor car, the enterprise was having to adjust to changes in the rhythms of the

Spanish working day. Increasingly, the long mid-day break and with it
the return home for an afternoon siesta was being abandoned in favour
of what the French call la journée continue. The demand for SALTUV's
services was being sharply cut back as a result.

These adverse market factors partly explain why SALTUV,
consistently profitable until 1972, moved from profit to loss in 1973, and
was not expected to become profitable again in the near future when I
made my visit. As well as declining demand it had had to cope with the
oil price increases of 1973 and 1974 and with official control of its fares.
The situation seemed far from easy or promising when I was there. On
the other hand, and except to the problematical extent that forced
redundancies might have been easier in a conventional enterprise, it was
difficult to attribute the company's 1977 problems to its workers' co-op
structure. Indeed, it was tempting to accept its claims that because of
better morale and higher productivity its losses were significantly lower,
on a comparative basis, than those of any comparable urban transport
undertaking elsewhere in Spain.

Some support for these claims is indicated by evidence presented to
the 39th International Urban Transport Congress held in Rome in 1971.
The statistical data presented there included comparative tables designed
to measure the 'real' productivity of urban transport undertakings. In
terms of two key measures – numbers of passengers carried and
numbers of kilometres covered per employee – the tables show Valencia
significantly ahead of both Barcelona and Madrid, the only two other
Spanish cities which appear. Of course, such comparisons are always
liable to conceal special factors and should be treated with great caution.
There are also a number of unsatisfactory features about these particular
statistics. All the same, when taken together with the consistent record of
profitability down to 1972, they seem to suggest that workers' co-op
arrangements need not prove disastrous when applied to urban public
transport and may well prove no more unsuccessful than any other.

However, it would be wrong to allow any implication – because they
both fall within the boundaries of the Spanish state – that there is really
anything much in common between SALTUV in Valencia and the
Mondragon co-ops in the Basque provinces. The structures which have
been evolved at Mondragon are far more sophisticated, and their
dynamism is of a different order compared with anything which can be
found in the Valencia enterprise. Moreover, as you would expect from
the fact that its founding fathers were junior employees who remain its
leaders in the late 1970s, the atmosphere at SALTUV when I visited the
company was essentially artisan. Given the character of the work done it
could hardly, I suppose, have been otherwise.

Perhaps the most positive reflection which SALTUV provokes is that a strong and highly motivated workers' co-op in urban public transport might well be more effective than either management or unions in a conventional enterprise in ensuring that the authorities give adequate priority to the needs of public transport. I cannot forget that not long before my visit a contingent of SALTUV buses, together with their 'single operators', had demonstrated outside the Valencia town hall. Their purpose had been to persuade the local authority to introduce bus lanes and so allow for the more efficient use of buses in the city centre. Both their understanding and their interest were sufficient to motivate them in that unusual demand. A set of arrangements which similarly motivated their London counterparts might well prove beneficial not only in terms of their own interests but in those of public transport users as well.

12
Conclusions

A first, modest aim of this book has been to bring together in reasonably accessible and digestible form some objective account of the experience primarily in Britain, France, Italy and the Basque provinces of Spain – but also more sketchily elsewhere – of industrial enterprises which are owned and controlled not by outside shareholders or the state, but by people working in them. There has been, or so I thought, a gap here which needed to be filled; I am fully aware that I am not the person best qualified to fill it. I am equally aware that my account is inadequate and incomplete. However, since my aim has been to reach the general reader rather than the academic specialist it has seemed best to get the record, say, 90 per cent right rather than spend excessive extra time and effort attending to matters of secondary detail.

That has seemed the correct approach on another ground as well. The unsatisfied interest in enterprises of this kind is essentially of a practical rather than an academic nature. Especially in Britain, but to a real extent throughout Western Europe, the conventional structures of private and public capitalism are being questioned in the late 1970s as they have not been for at least a generation. And so the interest in alternative models is increasing. Whether because existing conventional enterprises run into difficulties, or because bolder spirits seek to promote new enterprises in new forms, the demand for information about the experience of more or less genuinely democratic enterprises must surely grow. For these reasons to fill the gap is also to offer some practical guidance; at the very least there is no sense in repeating the errors of the past, and it is for example doubtful whether Sunderlandia would have been set up in the way that it was if information about relevant experience elsewhere had been readily available.

As we have seen, the history of democratic and co-operative enterprises is at least as full of lessons about how *not* to proceed as it is of more positive ones. In particular we have seen that from the days of the London Christian Socialists onwards, there has been a very poor success rate among enterprises set up, from the top downwards, by middle-class people with a generalized interest in reform. Equally, and in a sense on the other side, we have seen that the majority of democratic enterprises, established on working-class initiatives from the bottom up – what I have called the 'cloth cap' co-ops – have remained dwarfish and undynamic despite their surprising survival record. Further, we have seen that structural faults, inadequate access to capital and a hostile environment apart, the relative lack of success of the 'cloth cap' co-ops has been due mainly to weak management: they have not been looking for the thrusting young executives – and the thrusting young executives have not been looking for them. To compare their performance with that of capitalist enterprises is thus, as Marshall suggested more than 100 years ago, absurd. We are not comparing like with like.

However, though the record provides valuable guidance on how to fail it also offers – particularly from the Mondragon experience but to some extent from elsewhere as well – more positive lessons. We have found that a series of necessary conditions need to be satisfied if new democratic enterprises are to have any real chance of long-term success. Of course, there are some necessary conditions – thorough and systematic preparation and planning for example – common to all enterprises democratic or not. I am talking here, however, about a special set of necessary conditions which democratic enterprises must satisfy. The Mondragon co-operatives have found at least four which are crucial: first, the main thrust to get the enterprises off the ground must come from the potential workforce itself; second, the commitment of the workforce needs to be further secured by the requirement of a meaningful capital stake; third, the prospective enterprise must be equipped with a manager or a management team which is at least not inferior to that which a conventional enterprise would enjoy; fourth, these enterprises must work together in materially supportive groupings, for in isolation they are hopelessly vulnerable.

My aim of providing some guide to the experience of democratic enterprises will have been very much satisfied if, as a result, fewer mistakes are made in the future. For, whatever else happens, there are certain to be *some* more cases of would-be 'Wedgwood Benn' co-ops and at least a handful of would-be Sunderlandias and would-be 'Little Women'. If this book helps to highlight pitfalls and to indicate the least unpromising kinds of arrangements to go for, then I shall not feel that the work has been wasted.

However, the evidence of the Mondragon experience, coupled with that of changed and much more positive shop-floor attitudes in these kinds of enterprises elsewhere, suggests that more optimistic conclusions may be in order – and thus that much more ambitious aims may be legitimate. The Mondragon success *can* be taken to indicate that a large scale switchover to Mondragon-type structures in this country might make excellent sense. We must look at the arguments for and against, and we must attempt some assessment of the practical prospects.

The most apparently compelling case against the restructuring of enterprises on the lines of democratic control and worker ownership, as at Mondragon, has always been empirical: the record has not been good enough to justify the risks. Those who argue in this way may be prepared to concede that the sweepingly dismissive assessments by the Webbs and others should now be revised. Yet they will cling to their belief that the record has been, at best, very unexciting and that the great majority of these enterprises have been outperformed by their conventional competitors.

There is no point in examining the evidence all over again. There have been many more failures than successes. But the point is that once Mondragon has been included in the record an altogether more positive assessment becomes arguable. For Mondragon not only provides evidence that an extraordinary success is at least possible. Much more than that, Mondragon provided a convincing explanation for failure elsewhere. The reason is that, unlike the vast majority of similar enterprises, the Mondragon co-ops have enjoyed access to capital and a quality of management not inferior to their conventional competitors. They have also, it may be said, evolved a far more sophisticated and finely balanced set of structural arrangements than any other co-operative ventures elsewhere – and they have found a coherent and mutually supporting group. Still the main point is that, at Mondragon for the first time in history, Marshall's conditions for a fair test between capitalist enterprises and 'associations of labourers' have been met. The Mondragon co-ops have been in a position to compete on even terms – almost without qualification no other similar enterprises have been. Thus, at least until further evidence becomes available, that is the best explanation for the widespread failure in the record.

Although the main case against co-operative enterprises has been empirical there have historically been (as we saw earlier), and there still are in the late 1970s, a whole array of theoretical arguments mustered against them. The strength of these modern theoretical arguments is concentrated on the Left, or rather in the organized labour and trade union movements, but from some quarters on the Right voices can also be heard raising theoretical objections.

There is nothing to be gained by trying to gloss over the fact that trade union objections to any large-scale Mondragon building are likely to prove a very hard nut to crack. For in addition to the ideological opposition of the 'Leninist-Stalinist Left' – which may well be the least of problems – the trade union movement still harbours strong tactical objections. Most important of all, from the shop floor to the union head office, those whose main working lives have been devoted to traditional union activity would clearly feel themselves threatened.

It is difficult to argue or sympathize with the ideological opposition to Mondragon-style enterprises or a Mondragon-style economy as voiced by the unbending Marxist 'Left': they seem to reject all forms of pluralism, socialist or otherwise; they seem to reject the retention of any market mechanisms; and they seem to reject all forms of 'working-class leadership' except those embodied in bureaucratic central planning and single-party politics. Evidently they still believe that a centrally planned economy, organized by bureaucrats in the name of working-class interests and directed by a political party with unchallengeable authority, is a sensible goal for Britain. It is hard to know how to argue with people committed to such goals – beyond making it clear that they are not shared.

But it is worth pointing out that these extreme positions are not now widely held. The weight of working-class hostility to Mondragon-style arrangements springs much more from tactical and personal worries – and from their middle-class overtones – than from ideology. The preferred ideological position is now less extreme, less hardline and less theoretically hostile to Mondragon. Particularly if a Mondragon economy is presented – as indeed it should be – as a type of Yugoslav system with the communist party removed, with some personal capital ownership added – and with narrower income differentials – then it is hard to believe that a majority of British Labour voters would object to it on ideological grounds. If anything they might be inclined to reject it as 'too socialist'.

The tactical objections of the Labour and trade union movements are very much stronger, being both more persuasive and more widely held. Various different elements can be disentangled here. First, there is the feeling that almost any collaboration between shop floor and management is tactically unsound – at least while capitalism survives. A Labour Party Study Group Report* of the early 1970s clearly has this sort of thinking behind it. Making a general case against worker participation in profit sharing schemes, the authors proclaim that

profit sharing can all too easily encourage workers to accept the

---

* 'Capital and Equality: Report of a Labour Party Study Group', Labour Party, London, 1973, quoted by John Elliot in *Conflict or Co-operation? The Growth of Industrial Democracy*, Kogan Page, London, 1978, p. 188.

ideology of management that they are somehow part of a company team ... [and] it can also encourage the belief that the interests of managers, and those of workers, are 'when you come down to it', really 'identical'.

There is something more here than just the traditional and wholly understandable trade union hostility to profit-sharing schemes. There is almost the implication that it is in the workers' tactical interest to make the capitalist system work as badly as possible. Moreover, there is clearly the thought that any reform designed to improve its efficiency – however the benefits may be distributed – must be against the interests of working people. It is as if capitalism must be overthrown first and only then can experiments in improved production arrangements be allowed to get under way. Of course, as I argued earlier, it is precisely because under capitalism the interests of the workforce and the enterprise are distinct, that such tactical arguments make obvious sense.

Yet the most deep-seated objections to reforms in the Mondragon direction will surely come from those with the most direct vested interest in the *status quo*: the full-time trade union officials and that much larger body of men – the shop stewards and other union activists – who get their main satisfactions through 'defending the conditions of working people' or through 'fighting for working-class interests'. For if structural conflict were to be removed from the factory, what would there be for them to do? It is not cynical, but simply a statement of fact, to say that because their functions are to oppose capitalism these people would be lost without it; if there was nothing to oppose, the traditional trade union functions would simply fall away. That surely explains to a large extent why those most directly involved in the trade union movement are determined to maintain the situation which allows them to sustain their familiar adversary role. Ultimately no one likes to be faced with a sharp change in their programmes and roles, and the shop steward's role would – at the very least – have to be radically adjusted in a Mondragon-type economy. There is, it is true, some evidence that shop-floor activists in the Italian 'Lega' co-ops are prepared, as we have seen, to accept some adjustment. But it is easy to be pessimistic about whether their UK counterparts would show similar flexibility.

To the extent that those committed to traditional trade union adversary roles (to something like permanent class conflict) also tend to speak most strongly in favour of public ownership, the trade union establishment has something of a dilemma on its hands. For is it really conceivable that under a system of total public ownership the British trade union movement could continue to confront management as it does today? It would certainly be unprecedented. The state capitalist economies have all in practice eliminated traditional trade union freedoms. Even if in that situation, there were no political or ideological objections to allowing those freedoms to continue, there would surely be economic objections; for it is hard to believe that a less efficient productive system than one based on total public ownership and totally free trade unions could conceivably be devised.

That is a dilemma which trade unionists will have to face if their present policies of squeezing private capitalism and extending public ownership can be successfully continued for another decade or so. It certainly suggests that the attitudes of people like the Tribune Group may not lead to a very coherent economic future for Britain. Indeed, it seems legitimate at this stage to ask trade unionists whether their professional–functional objections to Mondragon-type enterprises can be justified in terms of the real interests of working people. Doubtless nannies feel professionally threatened by children growing up, and colonial governors feel professionally threatened by the movement of 'native peoples' to independence. Might it not be right to see 'professional' trade union objections to genuinely democratic enterprises rather in this light? Or, to take another possible parallel, are their 'professional' objections rather like those of Civil Servants in the housing department of the town hall when programmes for mass owner occupation by working people are being considered?

In the end, reasonable people are bound to agree that the professional and functional interests of trade union officials should not be allowed to stand in the way of Mondragon-style reforms if it can be shown that working people would be better off in such an economy than they are at present. Moreover, to be fair the General Secretary of the TUC, Mr Len Murray, has been reported as saying that he would settle for an alternative to trade unions if a better way of protecting and improving working people's conditions could be found. So we must assume that if the case for Mondragon-style experiments can be made out on material and empirical grounds Mr Murray would not oppose initiatives in that direction.

I think we will have to assume, finally, that some way could be found of meeting the 'tactical' trade union objections to reforms in a Mondragon direction. The point is that the switch to a Mondragon-style worker–ownership cannot convincingly be represented as a form of 'collaboration' with capitalism. The capitalist sector as we know it, and as the trade unions have fought it, is reduced by such a switch – just as it is by a switch into public ownership. The main difference is that ordinary working people and not just bureaucrats will be the beneficiaries.

A longer perspective may enable us to see these tactical 'Left' objections to Mondragon-style arrangements more clearly. Underlying them is, I think, the fear that a 'Mondragon sector' in the economy might in some way help to give capitalism a new lease of life. It would, of course, stand in the way of bureaucratic socialism, but more important, if I am correct about the feelings of these objectors, the existence of a Mondragon sector might save capitalism from 'getting its just deserts'. It might be the 'thin end of the wedge' for breaking working-class objections to capitalism and even for calling 'No side' in the class war.

As we shall see later there is the mirror image of this Left objection from the Right. The point to make here is that a Mondragon sector, though it might well take some of the sting out of the class war, would be working for its own interests and not for either traditional capitalism or for the state sector; it would be a genuine third alternative. Assuming it was anything like as successful as it is in the Basque country there would be a queue of workers – from both capitalist and nationalized undertakings – applying to join. Perhaps some trade unionists might even start demanding that the enterprises in which they worked be converted on Mondragon lines.

It is essentially as a genuine third alternative, and as perhaps the key ingredient in a genuine economic pluralism, that the opponents of private capitalism must be persuaded to see the case for a Mondragon sector. It is hard not to sympathize with their rooted objections to anything which would serve to sustain the prerogatives of traditional private capitalism. However, they must also acknowledge the different, but not less compelling objections to bureaucratic socialist structures and to public ownership as it was historically conceived and as it has evolved. Like the Italian communists they must be persuaded to endorse pluralism. No doubt, as we have seen, there are ambiguities in the PCI's endorsement, but the endorsement of pluralism as an ideological acceptable goal is at least a first step.

Before turning to the objections from the Right, there is one argument against the kind of worker–ownership practised by the Mondragon co-ops which can be heard from both ends of the spectrum. It is usually expressed by saying that this kind of ownership puts the worker's savings as well as his job at risk simultaneously; he has 'all his eggs in one basket' and that is not a risk to which he should ever be exposed.

If we ignore for a moment the initial capital stake which the Mondragon worker–owner must put up, then it is clear that this argument rests on faulty logic. For the savings which the member of a Mondragon co-op then has at risk are in no way equivalent to the ordinary savings of workers in conventional enterprises. They are an extra, his share of profits as a worker-member of his co-op, which his counterpart in a conventional business simply does not enjoy. Moreover, it is not as if, at Mondragon, these profit shares are credited to a worker's account at the expense of either his wages or his pension rights. For, as we saw earlier, both his wages and his pension benefits are superior to 'going' rates in the region. Thus the Mondragon worker–owner enjoys everything enjoyed by other workers *plus* a share of profits on top; that this extra asset is at risk is surely, therefore, of very minor account. For everyone would choose to own a risky asset if the alternative was not owning that asset at all.

Of course, those who object to putting workers' savings at risk may still use their argument against the initial £1,000 or £2,000 which those joining the Mondragon co-ops must contribute. One answer to that objection is to point out that those sums, though important enough to ensure commitment and positive motivation, are really quite small – not more than 1 per cent or 2 per cent in relation to prospective life-time earnings in the money of the late 1970s. Another argument would be that at least in the Basque country these capital contributions have not proved a barrier to recruitment; up to mid-1977 there had always been more people wishing to join on these terms than available places. If ordinary people choose to risk their savings in this way there is something quite unacceptably 'governessy' about telling them not to. After all, as with other self-employed people, it is their own savings – not, for example taxpayers' money – which they are putting at risk. Seen in this light, these arguments appear simply as a special case of wider paternalistic objections to giving workers ultimate responsibility and to genuinely democratic industrial arrangements.

These wider paternalistic objections are most commonly voiced from the Right. ('What, old Sid sharing in ultimate responsibility for policy at Mill? Whatever next? Anyway he's far too busy thinking about much more important things, like his spring onions or his Saturday game o' bowls'.) But a similar paternalism underlies bureaucratic socialism and indeed the attitudes of those full-time trade union officials who insist on negotiating 'on behalf of' the shop floor.

Can this kind of paternalism be accepted as a convincing argument against the introduction of Mondragon-type arrangements? Only, I suppose, if it can be shown that 'old Sid' and his like suffer from some kind of built-in tendency to reach irresponsible decisions. But that gets us back to the empirical record. Of course, there are examples there on both sides: of highly responsible decision making and behaviour by the Albi glassworkers, and at Mondragon and elsewhere; and of much less responsible behaviour by the people employed in those artisan co-ops of the Christian Socialists and by many others. Each must interpret the record on his own judgment of the evidence, but it seems at least plausible to suppose that when ordinary people have been well prepared for their responsibilities as workers–owners, and when their interests are clearly committed to long-term as well as short-term goals, they will confound the paternalists by the decisions they make. After all, when working people become owner–occupiers, do they not normally confound the bureaucrats and the paternalists in the housing departments of the town hall?

There is one other rather specific argument against Mondragon-type arrangements which is frequently heard from the Right. Its usual form is an assertion to the effect that democratic decision making is necessarily slow and inefficient. One answer is simply again to point to the Mondragon record; whatever else is true that record seems quite exceptionally dynamic. However, the argument itself rests partly on a misunderstanding of the scope of democratic decision making in a Mondragon-type set-up. As we saw earlier, the democracy of the Mondragon workforce is involved with basic policy decisions rather than with day-to-day management. Because broad policy, and management itself, enjoy the acceptance of the workforce, ordinary management decisions can be taken, if anything, more effectively and as rapidly at Mondragon as elsewhere.

It is, of course, true that there are certain kinds of decision which the sovereign democracy of a Mondragon co-operative workforce might well be most reluctant to take. In particular, a Mondragon management could not hope to use the weapon of redundancy which Sir Arnold Weinstock has wielded with such vigour at GEC. At Mondragon a 'no redundancy' rule is simply accepted as one of the constraints of the game. It would also be argued that it is a rule which both encourages far-sighted management − and stimulates genuine manpower planning − and is a sort of condition for winning shop-floor acceptance for a basically market system. Further, it would be claimed that even if profits have been slightly lower as a result of this constraint, overall human welfare has unquestionably been increased.

The final argument from the Right against Mondragon-style arrangements is, of course, that they constitute a creeping form of socialism and/or of workers' power. Attitudes of this kind certainly explain part of the hostility in the Right-wing Press to the 'Wedgwood Benn' co-ops. Indeed that kind of hostility to working-class enterprises has a long history stretching back to Rochdale and even before − it was very much alive and well when Sunderlandia was being established in 1973. Nor is it surprising. For just as full-time trade unionism feels threatened by Mondragon-type enterprises, so does traditional capitalism. On the other hand, and to be fair, contemporary intellectuals of the Right tend to respond favourably to the idea of Mondragon co-operatives.

These hostile attitudes on the Right are, of course, the mirror image of those on the Left: to the Left a Mondragon sector is the thin end of the wedge for a capitalist revival; to the Right it is the precursor of socialism and workers' power. Of course, in that matter of power for ordinary working people (as opposed perhaps to 'class power'), hostile capitalists are correct in this perception. Yet the kind of socialism which a Mondragon sector would encourage is very different from the bureaucratic variety of the Webbs. It is a socialism which consists of a self-reliant solidarity between groups of workers of all kinds – white-collar as well as blue-collar, management as well as shop floor – who share a direct and very real interest in the success of their enterprise.

None of these arguments, neither those from the Left nor those from the Right, seem to carry much weight against the establishment of a Mondragon-type co-operative sector in the economy. Of course, they do suggest that it may be difficult to recruit much support from those, on either side of the great class divide, with a vested interest in the *status quo*. But that is clearly something else. Perhaps support will have to be sought mainly from the Liberals. Next we consider the arguments in favour of establishing such a sector.

The first arguments for the establishment of a Mondragon-type sector in the British economy are that it should reduce class warfare, both inside and outside the factory gates, and improve shop-floor motivation. These are not simply old middle-class arguments for greater shop-floor productivity in a new guise. For what is needed apart from anything else is a major reduction in the feelings of aggression with which management and labour face each other in British industry. Even without any direct productivity gains, enormous quantities of psychological wear and tear could be saved – many who refuse, as things are, to consider working in industry would be inclined to think again.

The potential material gains through high productivity are considerable as well. I quoted earlier the celebrated report of the Central Policy Review staff which described how with all other conditions held the same – identical models, identical plant, identical layout and so on – the British motor industry worker was achieving roughly half the output produced by his continental opposite number. No doubt the motor industry is a special case – though there are specific comparisons where

Britain's relative performance is even worse, as well as others in which it is less bad. I also quoted a more comprehensive study,* of productivity differentials in the subsidiaries of multi-national companies. It showed, for example, that US productivity was more than 50 per cent ahead of the British while average productivity in Germany and France was respectively 35 per cent and 28 per cent better. In the opinion of the author roughly half of these differences should be accounted for by lower labour productivity as opposed to other factors. The author also emphasized that the 'British Disease' was as widespread among the white-collar workforce as on the shop floor.

The point about this sort of study is not the particular numbers. We do not want to get bogged down in arguments about whether the productivity of the French paper bag industry is 25 per cent or 30 per cent higher than the same industry in Britain. At least after that most comprehensive NEDO study (also referred to earlier) we know that the productivity of British manufacturing industry is substantially inferior to its West German counterpart in virtually all sectors. The precise figures are much less important than the fact of the substantial gap.

Improved individual worker motivation and the beginnings of genuine vertical team-work between shop floor and management could obviously hoist the productivity performance of British manufacturing industry very quickly indeed. The point is that, in a Mondragon sector, these would not be the sort of productivity improvements which working people could reject — as simply greater degrees of worker exploitation. For the workers and no one else would be the greatest beneficiaries.

However, improved motivation and team-work, in a Mondragon sector of the economy, would produce great benefits outside as well as inside the factory gates. Since the workforce would be the owners of profits, we should see the first beginnings of a real distribution of individual wealth which is long overdue. Under traditional private and state capitalism alike no substantial spread of productive wealth is really possible. For the few in the first case, the state in the second, are the owners both of the productive assets and of profits. Mondragon-type enterprises are the only ones which can really spread productive wealth around in any substantial degree.

One further prospective external benefit deserves to be mentioned. Adjustments between wages and profits such as those brought about by changes in government price-fixing policies would not be nearly so socially divisive as they are today. There should be a marked reduction

---

* C. F. Patten, 'The Efficiency of British Industry', *Lloyds Bank Review*, January 1977.

in workers' denunciations of greedy, money-hungry bankers – and in the denunciation by bankers (and others) of lazy and bone-idle workers. The quality of life would surely be improved.

But the prospect of specific benefits of this kind are only part of the case for urging the establishment – somehow – of a Mondragon-style co-operative sector in the British economy. The other part of the case is that there is no promising alternative, so far as I know, which might lead to substantial improvements in Britain's industrial performance.

There are, it is true, two apparent alternatives to just plain soldiering on which will have supporters at opposite ends of the political spectrum. At one extreme there is the Tribunite alternative which would extend the public sector to cover the whole of the national economy except perhaps for corner shops and other really small-scale enterprises. At the other extreme there is the alternative of rolling public ownership backwards and of seeking to make a kind of knight's move into a world of tough minded capitalism on US or West German lines. Are either of these two alternatives at all realistic or desirable?

Advocates of the Tribunite alternative face formidable difficulties. They have to persuade a sceptical public against all the evidence that state-owned industries can be operated efficiently. They also have to persuade us that their economic goals are compatible with the kind of individual freedoms and civil liberties which still seem to be valued by a majority of the electorate. But the fundamental difficulty which faces the Tribunites is, I think, rather different. It may be expressed by saying that it has so far proved impossible to translate their own 'class power' values into institutions which can inspire the imagination and loyalty of ordinary working people. For there is no more love among the mass of Labour Party voters than there is elsewhere in the community for the nationalized industries, for local authority housing, for the National Health Service and the rest. That is what makes the Tribunite programme so unrealistic in electoral terms, whether we see it as desirable or not.

Yet none of this means that the opposite alternative looks at all realistic either. For, despite the fact that they have not been translated into successful and attractive institutions, those 'class power' values of the Tribunites can still be used to mobilize organized labour against any policies which can be perceived as a threat to working class interests. Surely that is what Mr Wilson (as he then was) discovered in 1969; and what Mr Heath discovered later at the hands of the miners. It is surely a forlorn hope for the Right that Mrs Thatcher and Sir Keith Joseph will do any better. For 'Tory unemployment' resulting from the pursuit of tough monetarist policies is unlikely to be perceived as less of a threat to working-class interests than Mr Heath's incomes policy or Mr Wilson's attempt to impose token fines on wildcat strikers. If anything it must be expected to provoke far greater resentment. Thus if Mrs Thatcher and Sir Keith are aiming to use monetary policy to bulldoze a way through to the tough-minded capitalism of West Germany or the US, they are surely going to be thwarted.

If the Tribunites will not succeed in transforming the economy on total public ownership (Eastern European) lines, and if Mrs Thatcher and Sir Keith Joseph will not get away with forcing a knight's move towards the tough-minded capitalism of West Germany and the US, we seem to be left with no alternative but to struggle on. Is it sensible to be more or less optimistic or more or less pessimistic about that prospect?

Faced with the prospect of soldiering on, one group of optimists argue that there is nothing to worry about anyway. They are like the family doctor who feels that his main task is to persuade the patient to 'adjust' to his illness and to believe that, despite all appearances, his condition is not really too bad. The British, so this fashionable argument runs, may well be becoming the world's worst industrial performers – but that is because they've decided that they simply do not like the strain and the dirt and the noise of factory production. In short they have *chosen* to be afflicted by the 'British Disease'; and how right, how civilized their choice is.

Optimists of this rather special kind do not normally bother to ask themselves how a country of Britain's size and population can expect to maintain even its present levels of material living if factory production is going to decline still further. Coming as they almost invariably do from the professional and middle class, they have also generally failed to notice that there is an enormous unsatisfied demand for higher material living standards among those below them on the income scale.

This first group of optimists shades imperceptibly into a second who share the belief that Britain's career as a manufacturing country is more or less over, but who recognize that there is thus a problem of maintaining living standards. Their general answer to that problem is to say that the production and export of '*services*' will have to be stepped up to fill the gap left by the decline in manufacturing. They talk at length about the success of the British banking and insurance industries as earners of foreign exchange through invisible exports. They talk about the output and export of cultural products – books, newspapers, television programmes. They argue that given such very special attractions as the Royal Family, a hereditary peerage and Stonehenge, the country's potential for attracting overseas tourists has not really begun to be exploited. They mention quite new export possibilities – like packaged degree kits from the Open University and even the Public Schools. When pressed to explain how living standards could be maintained during a switch from industrial to service production, they talk first about North Sea oil; and they go on to remind you that the contents of only one Mentmore have so far been offered to overseas buyers.

Without denying that there is considerable scope for further increasing Britain's production and export of services, it seems unrealistic to believe that that would be enough to maintain present material living standards. For one thing no population of similar size and accepted minimum material standards has ever managed to pay for its imports in that way. Second, it is far from clear how many of the present shop-floor workforce in British industry, particularly in the North of England, would be willing or able to switch to the service sector. It is the kind of vista which may look plausible from the vantage point of an office in Fleet Street or next to the British Museum – but it looks very much less so from Oldham or South Shields.

Occupying a position at the opposite end from the optimists is Mr Peter Jay. His 'hypothesis',* is that the combination of democratic government and of collective bargaining directed by a strong trade union movement cannot be indefinitely sustained. He has expressed this hypothesis in respect of all the Western democracy type countries. But he has argued that it applies particularly to the UK. The essence of the argument is that the monopoly bargaining power of the trade unions causes wages to be fixed above their correct market level – which in turn reduces the demand for labour and thus increases unemployment above its 'natural' rate. But since high unemployment is electorally unpopular, democratic governments are then forced to stimulate job creation by expanding the money supply. While this remedy may temporarily reduce the dole queues, he argues, even that short term advantage is achieved only at the cost of giving an accelerating push to inflation. In the end, he concludes, these processes can only lead to quite intolerable levels of unemployment or of inflation or both. Either the two together, or one by itself, must then cause political and social breakdown and the collapse of democracy.

Mr Jay claims that, after adjusting for business cycles, both unemployment levels and inflation rates have progressively increased in all the Western democracy type countries since the early 1950s, but especially so in Britain. It is to this he points as the evidence on which his hypothesis is based. He is careful to avoid forecasting how long it is

---

* In his Harold Wincott lecture published by the Institute of Economic Affairs and entitled *A General Hypothesis of Employment, Inflation and Politics*, 1975.

likely to be, either in Britain or elsewhere, before the breakdown point is reached; but he seems in no doubt at all that it must eventually come unless the monopoly wage bargaining power of the unions can somehow be finished or outflanked. There is the clear implication that if nothing is done Britain may be expected to reach breakdown point first.

The only way out, as Mr Jay sees it, is a virtually total transformation which gives us 'The Workers' Co-operative Economy'* in the place of the one we have. It is interesting that, with the important qualification that it would not include individual worker–ownership stakes, Mr Jay's 'workers co-operative economy' is very like a Mondragon sector extended across the economy as a whole. Yet that is not the relevant point here. The Jay 'hypothesis' is what is important in this context, and it is important because it suggests that the alternative of plodding on as we are is not really available. If we think we can simply stay in the same place we are wrong; because the inner workings of the *status quo* will inexorably make things worse – with ever higher inflation and ever higher unemployment and no prospect of the kind of production increases which might help us to live less uncomfortably with these two problems.

As an economist of the barely amateur category I am not in any position to vouch for Mr Jay's hypothesis, but the point is that we can share his pessimism without necessarily accepting either all the sequential steps in the hypothesis or his almost determinist attitude towards it. Adequate grounds for this pessimism are provided by the continuing relative decline of British manufacturing industry and the absence of any new factor in prospect which looks capable of reversing the trend.

In fact 'undramatic pessimism' seems to me to be the correct attitude to adopt towards the prospect that the British economy will simply soldier on, without major structural change, for as far ahead as we can now see. In some ways it is an Argentinian prospect – with industrial production likely to remain more or less stationary; with the trade unions being reasonably successful about defending the living standards of their members and with the country's industrial equipment, at least relative to its competitors, continuing to run gently down hill. However, partly because of North Sea oil, partly because of the British character, I would guess that however bleak these prospects, we could manage to survive without major breakdown for at least another couple of decades.

It is a far from invigorating outlook. For, if I am right, the position looks like this: we rule out major structural changes in the direction

* Lecture to the Manchester Statistical Society, on 17 March 1977.

which the Tribunites favour; we rule out the kind of knight's move to a tough-minded capitalism which Mrs Thatcher and Sir Keith Joseph would like to engineer; we do not really believe that our economic future can be secured by an enormous switch of resources into the service sector. On the other hand, and unlike those curious and complacent optimists, we do not really enjoy the 'British Disease' and feel reluctant to 'adjust' to it. Although we do not foresee dramatic disasters round the corner we cannot pretend to be at all enthusiastic about the prospect.

The case for bringing, or trying to bring, a Mondragon-type co-operative sector of the economy into existence rests, it seems to me, as much on this review of alternative prospects as on the specific advantages which might flow from it. Each of the two parts of the case are important. Taken together they must, I think, compel attention from all except those dogmatically committed to the conventional solutions of Left and Right.

It would be premature, and out of place in a book of this kind, to attempt a detailed discussion either of the scope of any possible Mondragon-type co-operative sector or of how it might be brought into existence. However, a few very general (and almost self-evident) points may be in order. They are quite closely in line with the conclusions of a short study report* on the Mondragon Bank and the Mondragon co-operatives which was financed by the Anglo German Foundation for the Study of Industrial Society and was published by them in 1977; and of which I was one of the co-authors. On the other hand neither my co-authors, nor the Anglo German Foundation can be held responsible for anything said here.

Medium-sized enterprises (employing up to say 500 people) in what I earlier called 'good Second Division' industries seem to me at once the most eligible and most promising candidates for inclusion in a first experimental Mondragon co-operative sector. To aim higher at the start (either in terms of scale or technology) would be sharply to increase the risks of failure; to aim lower would be to run the opposite risk of achieving no significant impact even after a real success.

Enterprises could be recruited to the new sector as a result either of having been set up in Mondragon form from scratch or of having been converted from pre-existing capitalist or private sector firms. But, of course, as well as these productive enterprises themselves, the sector would require at least a minimum of secondary institutions on

---

* *Worker Ownership: The Mondragon Achievement*, Anglo-German Federation for the Study of Industrial Society, 1977.

Mondragon lines. Eventually – assuming the sector prospered – it might well be right for it to have a full array of these secondary Mondragon institutions: its own bank, contracting agency and management support institution; its own educational and training establishment; and its own social service organization. However to begin with the contracting agency and management support institution might perhaps be enough. Funds from outside the sector itself would probably be needed to support such secondary institutions at the start.

Since a system of mainly individual ownership is plausibly seen by the Mondragon co-ops as one of the key factors in their success, finance would have to be available to enable the workforce to purchase their individual capital stakes. Personal bank loans would be the obvious solution at the outset. It might be necessary in the early stages for these to be covered at least in part by official guarantees from central or local government – but the individuals concerned should almost certainly be required to offer counter indemnities to the guarantors.

Should any formal procedures be laid down for enabling or facilitating the conversion into Mondragon-type co-ops of existing enterprises in the private capitalist or public sectors? Various necessary conditions would clearly have to be fulfilled. The most important of these would be a vote by a substantial majority of the weekly and monthly paid workforce for conversion to the new arrangements. Once that condition had been satisfied, the public could well be persuaded to be generous – both in terms of the asking price for public sector enterprises and in terms of exempting former private owners from any capital gains tax liability which would otherwise result from the conversion. After all, no extra bureaucrats, or members of strong Civil Service unions, would be created by such decisions, and in the case of former public sector enterprises it might even be possible to reduce official bureaucracy.

Two other obvious questions arise. The first is whether it would make sense for the new sector to be initially concentrated in one region. The Mondragon co-ops have clearly derived great additional strength from Basque loyalties, and regional support is a source of strength which should not lightly be foregone. Regions like South Wales or the West Midlands have obvious attractions as areas in which the new sector might initially be concentrated. This is an issue, however, which verges on detail and thus can sensibly be left unsettled. So too can the question of what relationship, if any, the new sector should have either with the surviving 'cloth cap' co-ops in Britain or with the ICOM companies. As we saw earlier, their structures differ quite sharply from the Mondragon model.

It is easy to see that if we could divest ourselves of the baggage of history and start again, the model of the Mondragon co-ops would be a much more compelling blueprint for production enterprises than either the private or state capitalist models that we use. No one in their senses would choose a model which sets the two key elements in the enterprise, the shop floor and management, effectively at each other's throats. No reasonable and freedom-loving member of a prospective enterprise team would wish to hand over final control to far-away capitalists – still less, to far-away Civil Service bureaucrats in some industrial ministry who, on the rare occasions when they do visit the enterprise, travel first class at the taxpayer's expense.

Yet each of the two main political parties either blind themselves to this perception or are prevented by their vested interests in the *status quo* from acting upon them. Of course, it is true that the Tories are fond of commending the values of self-reliance, responsibility and hard work which are clearly among the essential ingredients of the Mondragon set-up. What they fail to perceive is that by making the shop-floor worker into a dependent wage earner, the system of private capitalism which they defend is directly inimical to the development of those virtues. In their courting of the working-class Tory they are rather like white South Africa courting the coloured and black populations in that country. Both invite support for their beliefs and values, but the Tories are unwilling to 'open up' ownership and 'open up' decision making through a radical reform of capitalism – when those are the pre-conditions of any widespread practice of the virtues they commend. Just as the white South Africans are unwilling to open up *their* institutions to blacks and coloured – who are invited to adopt white values but stay outside the club.

However, if the Tories have their hands tied by their links with private capitalism, so do Labour politicians by their links with the trade unions. Of course, it is true that the Labour Party is fond of commending the values of group solidarity and mutually supportive arrangements, which are the other main ingredient in the Mondragon set-up. But the Labour Party is too committed to bureaucratic solutions and too much concerned with class power values and the class struggle to favour the kind of enterprise-level solidarity which grows up from the bottom – and is not simply evoked by class leaders – in the Mondragon co-operative.

In any case, or so it seems to me, the leaders of the Labour movement only really understand one element – their hostility to private capitalism – in the make-up of working people. They correctly recognize anti-capitalist feelings as strong, but then they go on drawing the same false conclusions of which the Webbs were guilty. Because working people are anti-capitalist it is believed wrongly that they favour bureaucratic and woodenly collectivist solutions. My own experience is that when their anti-capitalist (and anti-middle class) feelings are not in play, ordinary working people favour 'owner–occupier' type solutions rather than bureaucratic and collectivist ones.

What is needed, surely, is a political voice which is prepared to see virtues at both ends of the individualist collectivist spectrum – prepared to endorse both group solidarity and self-reliance. It is an absurd and destructive politics which presents the two ends of that spectrum as alternatives between which a community has to choose. For to survive at all a community must encourage both solidarity and self-reliance. The old controversy between Darwin and Kropotkin about animal behaviour provides a kind of parallel. They both looked at the same evidence, but Darwin emphasized the individual strengths needed in the struggle to survive. Kropotkin, who loved to report that he had once observed a pelican feeding a blind fellow, argued that social cohension was the key. It must be clear at once that both are required in any successful community, human or animal.

The structures evolved by the Mondragon co-ops and the values they reflect seem to me to come closer than anything else I know to striking the correct balance. But then who is for balance in a polarized political society? At the political party level it looks as if only the Liberals are free to be; for they are not tied either to big capitalism or organized labour. However, in industry itself, as opposed to politics, the prospect just might be marginally brighter. For management and the shop floor, were they to join forces in the enterprise, could presumably say good-bye both to outside capitalists and outside unionism. Together management and the shop floor could build a worker-owned democratic economy on Mondragon lines. The organized bureaucracy of .capital and the organized bureaucracy of the labour unions could simply be told 'A plague on both your houses. We don't need either of you. And both of you are parasitic to the real business of production.'

Appendix
The co-operatives of Mondragon

Foundry and forging products

Name	Place	Main products	Started	empl't
Amat	Mondragon	Pipe fittings	1963	368
Ampo	Idiazabel	Moulded steel	1964	212
Ederlan	Escoriaza	Iron smelting	1963	614
Enara	Onate	Forgings	1962	177
Funcor	Elorrio	Iron smelting	1956	306
Tolsan	Amorebieta	Forgings	1957	132
Enterprise total 6		Employment total 1,809		

Capital goods

Name	Place	Main products	Started	empl't
Arrasate	Mondragon	Machine tools	1957	469
Batz	Yurre	Injection moulds	1963	52
Danobat	Elgoibar	Machine tools	1966	597
Egurko	Zumaya	Wood working machinery	1969	98
Electricidad Gaztelu	San Sebastian	Electrical plant	1967	48
Fagor Industriel	Onate	Catering plant	1973	266
Goiti	Elgoibar	Machine tools	1962	118
Guria	Irun	Excavating plant	1961	282
Irizar	Ormaiztegui	Coach bodies	1963	251
Lealde	Lequeitio	Machine tools	1974	19
Matrici	Zamudio	Die moulds	1963	175
Ortza	Pamplona	Die moulds	1974	21
Soraluce	Vergara	Machine tools	1961	176
Zubiola	Azpeitia	Wood-working machinery	1967	112
Enterprise total 14		Employment total 2,684		

To complete the industrial picture there are five more industrial co-ops for which complete data is not available: Aurrenak; Ederfil; Kide; Kendu; Poyam.

262   *Appendix*

Building materials, etc.

Name	Place	Main products	Started	empl't
Covimar	Amorebieta	Marble materials	1965	95
Orona	Hernani	Lifts	1964	314
Ulma	Onate	Scaffolding	1962	497
Urssa	Vitoria	Metal frames	1961	251
Vivendas y Contratas	San Sebastian	House building	1960	80
Enterprise total 5		Employment total 1,237		

Consumer durables and furniture

Citamare	S s'v'Del Valle	Furniture	1966	82
Coinma	Vitoria	Furniture	1964	53
Construcciones San Jose	Hernani	Waste grinding plant	1958	37
Danona	Azpeitia	Furniture	1962	338
Dormicoop	Elgueta	Furniture	1959	44
Eredu	Icaztegueta	Camping gear	1963	41
Gurola	Azcoitia	Furniture	1968	75
Orbea	Eibar	Bicycles	1969	192
Ulgor	Mondragon	Domestic appliances	1956	3,462
Enterprise total 9		Employment total 4,324		

Intermediate goods and components

Alecoop	Mondragon	Testing equipment	1966	587
Alkargo	Gatica	Transformers	1965	141
Bertako	Pamplona	Components	1969	32
Biurrarena	Renteria	Machine parts	1967	54
Cikautxo	Berriatua	Rubber products	1971	116
Coinalde	Vitoria	Nails	1965	26
Copreci	Arechavaleta	Domestic appliance components	1963	831
Doiki	Ermua	Precision parts	1972	37
Eika	Marquina	Electronics	1973	36
Ekain	Usurbil	Electronics	1974	21
Elkar	Bilbao	Graphic arts	1967	30
Embega	Estella	Metal printing	1971	82
Fagor Electrotecnica	Mondragon	Domestic appliance components	1966	615
Gaiko	Alsasua	Components	1974	36
Goizper	Anzuola	Clutch gear	1961	112

Name	Place	Main products	Started	empl't
Impreci Litografia	Vergara	Car parts	1962	180
Danona	Lezo	Graphics	1965	61
Maier	Guernica	Electronics	1973	43
Matz-Erreka	Anzuola	Nuts and bolts	1973	85
RPK	Vitoria	Components	1974	71
Santalaitz	Vergara	Die moulds	1962	25
Tajo	Oyarzun	Plastic injection moulding	1963	210
Talleres Ochandiano	Ochandiano	Food handling plant	1958	52

Enterprise total 23		Employment total 3,483		

Index